1st Workshop on Perspectivist Approaches to NLP (NLPerspectives 2022)

Held at LREC 2022

Marseille, France
20 June 2022

Editors:

Gavin Abercrombie
Valerio Basile
Sara Tonelli
Verena Rieser
Alexandra Uma

ISBN: 978-1-7138-6130-0

Printed from e-media with permission by:

Curran Associates, Inc.
57 Morehouse Lane
Red Hook, NY 12571

Some format issues inherent in the e-media version may also appear in this print version.

Association for Computational Linguistics
209 N. Eighth Street
Stroudsburg, Pennsylvania 18360

Phone: 1-570-476-8006
Fax: 1-570-476-0860

acl@aclweb.org

Additional copies of this publication are available from:

Curran Associates, Inc.
57 Morehouse Lane
Red Hook, NY 12571 USA
Phone: 845-758-0400
Fax: 845-758-2633
Email: curran@proceedings.com
Web: www.proceedings.com

LREC 2022 Workshop
Language Resources and Evaluation Conference
20th June 2022

1st Workshop on Perspectivist Approaches to NLP (NLPerspectives)

PROCEEDINGS

Editors:
Gavin Abercrombie
Valerio Basile
Sara Tonelli
Verena Rieser
Alexandra Uma

Proceedings of the LREC 2022 workshop on Perspectivist Approaches to Disagreement in NLP (NLPerspectives)

Edited by:
Gavin Abercrombie, Valerio Basile, Sara Tonelli, Verena Rieser, Alexandra Uma

For more information:
European Language Resources Association (ELRA)
9 rue des Cordelières
75013, Paris
France
http://www.elra.info
Email: lrec@elda.org

Message from the organisers

This volume documents the Proceedings of the 1st Workshop on Perspectivist Approaches to Disagreement in NLP, held on June 20th as part of the LREC 2022 conference (International Conference on Language Resources and Evaluation).

Until recently, the dominant paradigm in natural language processing (and other areas of artificial intelligence) has been to resolve observed label disagreement into a single "ground truth" or "gold standard" via aggregation, adjudication, or statistical means. However, in recent years, the field has increasingly focused on subjective tasks, such as abuse detection or quality estimation, in which multiple points of view may be equally valid, and a unique 'ground truth' label may not exist. At the same time, as concerns have been raised about bias and fairness in AI, it has become increasingly apparent that an approach which assumes a single "ground truth" can erase minority voices.

Strong perspectivism in NLP (Basile et al., 2021a) pursues the spirit of recent initiatives such as Data Statements (Bender and Friedman, 2018), extending their scope to the full NLP pipeline, including the aspects related to modelling, evaluation and explanation.

The workshop explores current and ongoing work on the collection and labelling of non-aggregated datasets, and approaches to modelling and including these perspectives, as well as evaluation and applications of multi-perspective Machine Learning models.

A key outcome of the workshop will be to build on the work begun at `https://pdai.info/` to create a repository of perspectivist datasets with non-aggregated labels for use by researchers in perspectivist NLP modelling.

We would like to thank our sponsors for helping to make this workshop possible.

Google

Organizers:

Gavin Abercrombie – Heriot-Watt University
Valerio Basile – University of Turin
Sara Tonelli – Fondazione Bruno Kessler
Verena Rieser – Heriot-Watt University
Alexandra Uma – Heriot-Watt University

Programme Committee:

Riza Batista-Navarro – University of Manchester
Federico Cabitza – University of Milan-Bicocca
Amanda Cercas Curry – Bocconi University
Shiran Dudy – University of Colorado Boulder
Marco Guerini – Fondazione Bruno Kessler
Lucy Havens – University of Edinburgh
Ali Hürriyetoğlu – Radboud University Nijmegen
Elisa Leonardelli – Fondazione Bruno Kessler
Marta Marchiori Manerba – University of Pisa
Federico Nanni – Turing Institute
Inna Novalija – Jozef Stefan Institute
Viviana Patti – University of Turin
Masimo Poesio – Queen Mary University of London
Manuela Sanguinetti – University of Cagliari
Zeerak Talat – Digital Democracies Institute

Table of Contents

Workshop Program
Monday 20 June 2022

14:00 Introduction

14:05 Invited talk: Su Lin Blodgett (Microsoft Research)

15:00 Lightning talks

16:00 Break

16:30 Posters

17:30 Panel discussion

Proceedings of the 1st Workshop on Perspectivist Approaches to NLP @LREC2022, pages 1–9
Marseille, 20 June 2022

Disagreement space in argument analysis

Annette Hautli-Janisz[1], Ella Schad[2], Chris Reed[2]
[1]Department of Computer Science and Mathematics, University of Passau
[2]Centre for Argument Technology, University of Dundee, UK
firstname.lastname@uni-passau.de
{ella, chris}@arg.tech

Abstract

For a highly subjective task such as recognising speaker intention and argumentation, the traditional way of generating gold standards is to aggregate a number of labels into a single one. However, this seriously neglects the underlying richness that characterises discourse and argumentation and is also, in some cases, straightforwardly impossible. In this paper, we present QT30nonaggr, the first corpus of non-aggregated argument annotation. QT30nonaggr encompasses 10% of QT30, the largest corpus of dialogical argumentation and analysed broadcast political debate currently available with 30 episodes of BBC's 'Question Time' from 2020 and 2021. Based on a systematic and detailed investigation of annotation judgements across all steps of the annotation process, we structure the disagreement space with a taxonomy of the types of label disagreements in argument annotation, identifying the categories of *annotation errors, fuzziness* and *ambiguity*.

Keywords: broadcast political debate, argumentation and conflict, Question Time, Inference Anchoring Theory

1. Introduction

State-of-the-art research in Natural Language Processing, in particular in areas like discourse parsing and argument mining, crucially relies on manually labelled data in order to be able to derive well-motivated computational models. However, labeling arguments and speaker intentions in natural language dialogue are tasks that are highly subjective: judgements are based on the knowledge of the topic under discussion, the speakers involved in the debate and their background. But even more so, it is the language of argumentation and debate that sets the challenge, independently of the underlying theory of argumentation, the annotation granularity and experience levels of the annotators.

Stab and Gurevych (2014) are the first ones to explicitly state that it is "hard or even impossible to identify one correct interpretation" of a particular argument structure, an issue confirmed by Lauscher et al. (2018) and Lindahl et al. (2019). Example 1 illustrates the issue based on an excerpt from our own data: Chika Russell, in a BBC's 'Question Time' on 8 July 2021, makes a comment in the context of UK local elections in 2021. The underlined part is argumentative and has been analysed with significantly different argument structure, provided in Figure 1: On the left-hand side, we find a serial structure including a rephrase ('Default Rephrase') and an inference ('Default Inference'), the right-hand side uses different segmentation and only has the propositional relation of 'Default Rephrase'.

(1) Chika Russel: *I have a view on how the election has gone. Call me Mystic Meg, if you will, people feel really forgotten, they feel let down. They feel the opportunities are not what they were.*

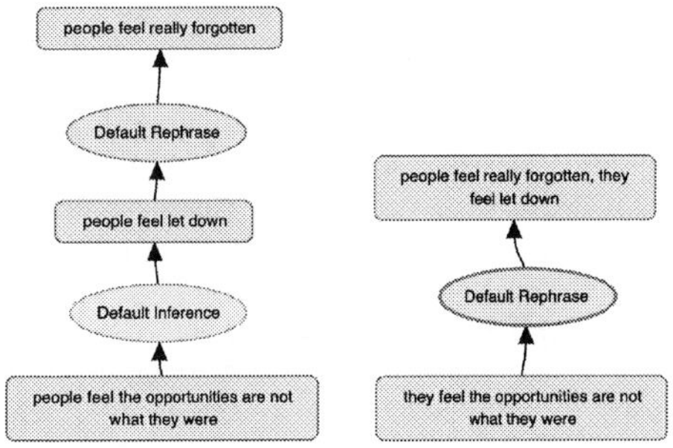

Figure 1: Two analyses for Example (1)

Although there is a clear understanding in the community that the analysis of argumentation is challenging due to a variety of factors, corpus development in this area is done in the "traditional" way: judgements are first collected based on guidelines for annotation, disagreements between labels are then resolved based on a (variety of) heuristics and eventually gold labels are assigned to argumentative units and the relations between them. These resolved labels then serve as the training base for a variety of machine learning techniques, with the significant drawback that they do not pass on the richness of information that is in fact encapsulated in the language.

In this paper, we present QT30nonaggr, the first corpus of non-aggregated argument annotation. QT30nonaggr encompasses 10% of QT30, the largest corpus of dialogical argumentation and analysed broadcast political debate to date with 30 episodes of BBC's 'Question Time' from 2020 and 2021 (Hautli Janisz et al., 2022). Based on a systematic and detailed investigation of annotation judgements across all steps of the annotation process, we structure the disagreement space with a taxonomy of the types of label disagreements in argument annotation, identifying the categories of *annotation errors, fuzzy language* and *ambiguity*. We therefore contribute a resource to the current and more general discussion of how computational models can be evaluated if more than one annotation label is available for an item, set out by (Uma et al., 2021). QT30nonaggr will also be the first non-aggregated corpus of argumentative data included in the Perspectivist Data Manifesto (`https://pdai.info/`).

2. Background

The core step in creating gold standards for supervised discourse parsing and argument mining is the resolution of multiple labels into a single "gold" label. This is done across all steps of manual argument analysis as defined by Lawrence and Reed (2020): text segmentation, argument/non-argument classification, simple argument structure and refined argument structure. The overwhelming number of approaches use the majority vote for deciding on a specific label (Rosenthal and McKeown, 2012; Stab and Gurevych, 2014; Wachsmuth et al., 2014; Hidey et al., 2017; Egawa et al., 2020). Habernal and Gurevych (2017) use majority voting, but employ adjudication in cases where majority is not possible (disagreement in segmentation leading to a different argument relation identification). Walker et al. (2012) use the mean rating across annotators for their labeling decision, Mochales and Moens (2011), Peldszus and Stede (2015) and Alliheedi et al. (2019) employ adjudication with an expert annotator to resolve label disagreements. Bar-Haim et al. (2020) use a threshold of 60% to judge whether an individual label is reliably annotated, judgements below that level are inconclusive which is claimed to be due to ambiguity. Toledo et al. (2019) and Gretz et al. (2020) take a number of annotator performance measures to discard what are presumed to be low-quality judgments. For cleansing argument data, (Dorsch and Wachsmuth, 2020) assume that in the case of indecisive annotations, the instance is kept in the dataset.

A more thorough investigation of the disagreement space for argument labeling is done to a significantly lesser extent: Stab and Gurevych (2014) investigate the disagreements encountered by way of confusion probability matrices for argument components and argumentative relations. They show that the major disagreement is between claims and premises and support/attack relations. Hidey et al. (2017) use an agreement matrix to show that disagreements are mostly between semantic types of claims, but they also note that ambiguity can lead to disagreements in segmentation and consequently argument structure. Habernal and Gurevych (2017) find that implicitness or topic relevance are relevant factors, Torsi and Morante (2018) show that segmentation, topic relatedness and commitment are crucial and Egawa et al. (2020) conclude that the majority of disagreement stems from semantic similarity.

The work presented in this paper deviates significantly from previous work: First, our annotation is not restricted to finding potentially isolated, but topic-relevant claims and relations. Instead, we label the complete debate with speaker intention and argumentation, including segments in which there is no argumentation, allowing us to derive how the debate unfolds. Secondly, we characterize the disagreement space along three dimensions which are implicitly (and sometimes explicitly) stated in related work: judgements go against the annotation guidelines (*Annotation Errors*), structures can be semantically and pragmatically fuzzy, i.e., judgements vary because the language is underspecified and leads to different interpretations (*Fuzziness*), and structure can be outright ambiguous, i.e., annotators pick up clearly separate interpretations based on syntactic, (lexical) semantic or pragmatic ambiguity (*Ambiguity*). Thirdly, we provide a non-aggregated resource for argumentative debate, QT30nonaggr, which serves as the basis for a large-scale investigation of the disagreement space in speaker intention recognition and argument analysis.

3. Inference Anchoring Theory (IAT)

Budzynska et al. (2014) and Budzynska et al. (2016) provide a theoretical scaffolding to handle *dialogue and argument structures, and the relations between them*, named Inference Anchoring Theory (IAT). The framework has been applied to over 2.5 million words in fifteen languages (available freely online at `corpora.aifdb.org`) and postulates three types of relations: (i) relations between content (propositional content of locutions); (ii) illocutionary connections that link locutions with their content and (iii) relations between locutions in a dialogue, called transitions. Given the scope of this paper, we only focus on the latter: relations between propositions, i.e., argumentative relations that hold between propositional content of speaker utterances.

3.1. Propositions

Propositions are derived from locutions and have the following properties: They are grammatical instantiations of the content of the locution. They have to be interpretable without context, i.e., they are standalone propositions that need to be intelligible without knowledge of surrounding propositional content. As a consequence, propositions may have to be reconstructed, so for instance elliptical or anaphoric expressions contained in the locution are resolved in the proposition. An example of this is the proposition of the third locution in Figure 2: 'they feel let down' (right-hand side) is resolved to 'people feel let down' in the proposition (left-hand side). The guideline for the annotators is to do minimal reconstruction in creating the proposition.

3.2. Propositional relations

Argumentative structures are relations between propositions; core IAT assumes three different relations that

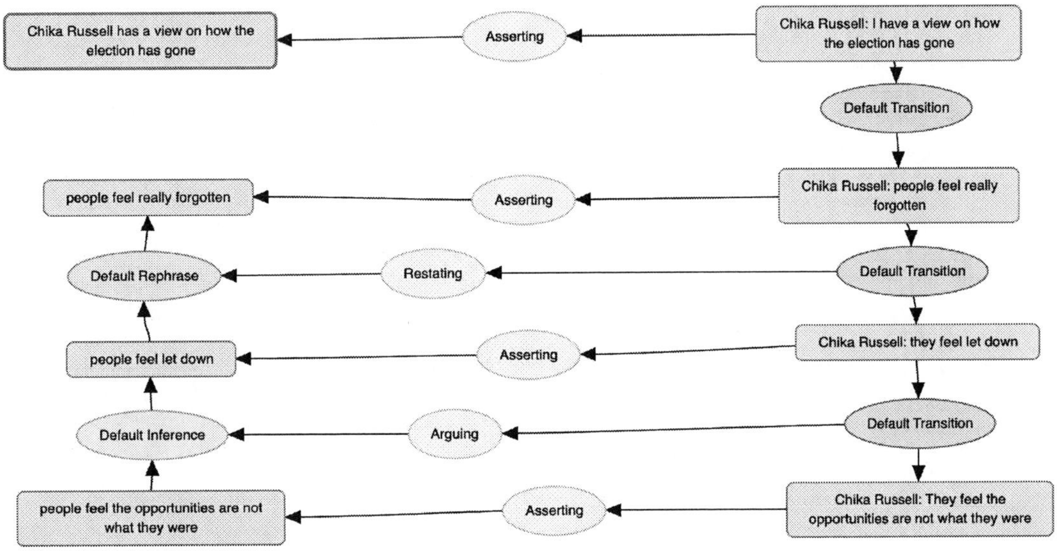

Figure 2: IAT diagram of Example (1), featuring locations (blue nodes on the right-hand side), propositions (blue nodes on the left-hand side), illocutionary relations (yellow nodes in the middle), dialogical relations (purple nodes on the right) and propositional relations – 'Default Inference' (green), 'Default Rephrase' (orange) and 'Default Conflict' (red).

are designed to capture argumentative structure in dialogue:

Inference (Support, 'Default Inference', RA, green node) Holds between propositions when one (or more) proposition is used to provide a reason to accept another proposition.

Conflict (Attack, 'Default Conflict', CA, red node) Holds between two propositions when one proposition is used to provide an incompatible alternative to another proposition.

Rephrase (Rephrase, 'Default Rephrase', MA, green node) Holds between two propositions when one proposition is used to rephrase, restate or reformulate another proposition. Rephrases also hold between questions and answers.

These relations are 'Default' in the sense that they can be instantiated with more specific relation types, for instance with presumptive argument scheme types (Walton et al., 2008).
Figure 2 provides the full IAT structure for one of the two analyses of Example (1), taken from the QT episode on 22 July 2021. Given the multiple layers of analysis needed for modeling dialogical argumentation, IAT graphs are divided into three different parts:

- The 'right-hand side' of nodes in the graph in Figure 2 is equivalent to a series of argumentative discourse units (Peldszus and Stede, 2013), i.e., the minimal unit into which the transcribed text is segmented. Each ADU has discrete argumentative function and records the name of the speaker in the form of 'firstname lastname : *locution content*'.
- The left-hand side encodes the propositional content of locutions, and the relationships of inference, conflict and rephrase between those propositional contents (as presented by the interlocutors).
- Those propositions are anchored in the dialogue via illocutionary connections (the 'middle', relations between locutions and propositions). These illocutionary acts capture speaker intention and are drawn from speech act theory (Searle, 1969; Searle and Vanderveken, 1985). There is a set of 10 relations that are used in IAT, namely *Asserting, Agreeing, Arguing, Assertive Questioning, Challenging, Disagreeing, Pure Questioning, Restating, Rhetorical Questioning* and *Default Illocuting*. For the scope of the current paper, however, we only focus on the left-hand side of the diagram: propositions and the argumentative relations between them.

3.3. Argument analysis

IAT analyses are produced with OVA+ (Online Visualisation of Argument – `http://ova.arg.tech/`), an open-source online interface for the analysis of argumentation in dialogues (Janier et al., 2014). OVA+ allows for a representation of the argumentative structure of a text as a directed graph. However, OVA+ does not allow for an encoding of ambiguity or fuzziness, i.e., an annotator cannot indicate that she has identified a structure that licenses more than one solution. The guideline here is to pick the structure that is most likely given the speaker and the context. For compiling QT30nonaggr, we therefore use IAT graphs that are created by different annotators and compare their analyses.

These graphs are created in several steps which mostly correspond to those based on the steps for manual argument analysis set up by (Lawrence and Reed, 2020) and briefly described here:

Chunking The starting point for analysis is a text of around 10,000 words (+/- 20%) that is first chunked into (40-80) excerpts each comprising around 150-250 words – passages that are small enough to be considered in total by an analyst, but large enough to include substantial dialogical exchange. We exploit natural topical, thematic and turn-based breaks to guide this chunking process. This chunk is then passed to different annotators for analysis.

Segmentation In the first step, an analyst segments the text into (argumentative) discourse units (or 'locutions' in IAT), producing between five and thirty locutions per excerpt. Going back to Example 1, the analyst decides whether to split the excerpt in two or three locutions. In the same step, the analyst reconstructs information to be recorded in the proposition, for instance anaphora and ellipses (see §3.1).

Classification of units The analyst then identifies whether a locution has indeed argumentative function or not. A crucial decision factor here is speaker intention: was the speaker intending to make an argument here, also given the larger societal or political context. This decision can go hand in hand with the previous step of segmentation: an analyst might have different solutions to capturing the argumentative structure and makes a first decision by segmenting the text in a particular way, shown in Figure 1.

Structure identification After classification an analyst immediately adds the type of propositional relation and the illocutionary connection between locutions (right-hand side) and propositions (left-hand side). The result is a map containing between a dozen to a hundred nodes in total, depending on the length and the content of the excerpt.

Review Each analysis map then undergoes peer review by which a randomly chosen second analyst who reviews and discusses annotation choices with the first.

4. Data

As the basis of our investigation we use QT30, the largest corpus of analysed dialogical argumentation ever created (19,842 utterances, 280,000 words) and also the largest corpus of analysed broadcast political debate to date, using 30 episodes of BBC's 'Question Time' from 2020 and 2021 (Hautli Janisz et al., 2022). Question Time is the prime institution in UK broadcast political debate and features questions from the public on current political issues, which are responded to by a weekly panel of five figures of UK politics and society. QT30 is highly argumentative and combines language of well-versed political rhetoric with direct, often combative, justification-seeking of the general public. In total, the corpus features 10,818 propositional relations, i.e., argumentative structures. Inference ('supports') and Rephrase have the highest frequency, 48% and 42.6%, respectively. Conflicts are significantly less frequent, making up only 9.4% of all relations between propositions. The resource is freely available at `http://corpora.aifdb.org/qt30nonaggr`.

The annotation was conducted by 38 students of linguistics, philosophy, literature and computer science in Scotland, England, Germany and Poland. More than 60 students took part in one of three rounds of training in 2020 and 2021. Topic of the 15 hour course (taught in person once in 2020 and then virtually three times in 2020 and 2021) was a general introduction to argumentation theory and detailed instructions on applying Inference Anchoring Theory to dialogical argumentation across genres. Due to the strict quality restrictions for QT30, only the top 38 annotators were selected to contribute.

The Combined Argument Similarity Score (CASS) (Duthie et al., 2016), which calculates separate scores for segmentation, argumentative structures and illocutionary forces and aggregates them into a single score for annotator agreement, for all of QT30 is 0.56, signaling moderate agreement. Despite the fact that other papers report slightly higher CASS scores – 0.752 in Visser et al. (2019) and κ = 0.75 in Budzynska et al. (2014)) – inter-annotator agreement for QT30 is based on a very heterogeneous but realistic dataset for quantifying annotation reliability: it features annotations by all 38 annotators which are based on a variety of experience levels due to the incremental formation of the annotation team.

Given the significant expertise level of the annotators, we hypothesize that the CASS score hints at more systematic annotation differences that go beyond simple annotation errors. Instead, we hypothesise that it hints at the deeper issue of subjectivity in discourse-level tasks such as argument analysis, manifested by the fuzziness and ambiguity of language and discourse in general. The different dimensions of labeling disagreements are elaborated on in the following.

5. A taxonomy of label disagreements

As the basis for our empirical investigation of label disagreements in argument analysis, we randomly select four excerpts of each episode (about 8-10% of QT30) and request a second annotation by a random other member of the annotation team. This second annotation is conducted in the standard procedure described in §3.3, review is done by another randomly assigned annotator. The annotators are not aware that they contribute their analysis for the purpose of identifying labeling disagreements instead of regular corpus analysis.

For the empirical analysis of the disagreed-upon labels, one of the most senior analysts is manually investigating the two different graphs per excerpt in parallel. There were several loops in identifying an appropriate partitioning of the disagreement space, based on previous work and informed by the special patterns that dialogical argumentation is delivering. In the following we present the three dimensions that allow us to characterise the disagreement space for dialogical argument analysis, distinguishing the categories of *annotation errors*, structures of *fuzziness* and *ambiguity*.

5.1. Annotation errors

The first dimension of label disagreements are simple annotation errors that violate annotation criteria which are clearly stated in the annotation manual.[1] We illustrate those categories with clear-cut examples from the corpus.

Discourse-structuring material is retained (ERR-DISC) This category captures any discourse material that is wrongly retained in the proposition. A typical example is a discourse marker such as 'because', which is kept in the proposition despite the fact that its meaning is captured by the relation between propositions, e.g. 'Default Inference'.

Another example is the recording of epistemic markers like 'I think' in the proposition. Such material is again not a part of the asserted content proper, as it signals the knowledge or belief – the epistemic attitude – of the speaker towards the proposition at issue. (Occasionally the epistemically qualified proposition is precisely what is at stake – *No, no he'd didn't* ***think it*** *he* ***knew it*** – but this is an extreme exception.) A clear example (node #657575) is offered by (2) and its alternate (3) :

(2) I think the handling of the pandemic has shown there will be divides after it's over.

(3) the handling of the pandemic has shown there will be divides after it's over.

Grammar errors (ERR-GRAM) The annotation guidelines require every proposition to be grammatically well-formed. This particularly holds for syntactic structure, which is not always standard in natural occurring dialogue and needs to be corrected by the annotator. This may include extraneous punctuation, such as ellipses or periods, as well as wrongly capitalised letters or wrong conjugation.

Reconstruction errors (ERR-REC) Another key requirement of IAT analysis is that every proposition is intelligible without additional context. This means that for instance anaphora and elliptical constructions are resolved where possible. The guideline is to stay as close to the original text and only add minimal extra material to facilitate understanding. With ERR-REC we mark any proposition that is wrongly reconstructed, i.e., using a wrong referent. An interesting example is provided by the two reconstructions of (4) (node #838276) in (5) and (6). Here, the context does not license the reconstruction with the structure in (5), instead 'it' is resolved with full clause ('letting footballers and VIPS in without quarantine while lockdown is still in place').

(4) It is deep hypocrisy

(5) Robert Buckland is hypocritical

(6) letting footballers and VIPs in without quarantine while lockdown is still in place is deep hypocrisy

Erroneous relations (ERR-REL) This category captures annotation of propositional relations that violate the guidelines, for instance if the connection between a premise and a conclusion is pointing in the wrong direction, or – given that IAT is tracking the dialogical unfolding of argumentation – where a conflict is analysed from earlier to later discourse material (whereas only material that has already been introduced into the discourse can be the target of a conflict). Another common pattern of ERR-REL is erroneously marking question-answering – particularly because in political discussion, question-answering and question-avoiding is so common. An incorrect analysis of a response as an answer is shown in Fig. 3; the correct analysis is in Fig. 4, that highlights the fact that the response in fact provides no answer at all.

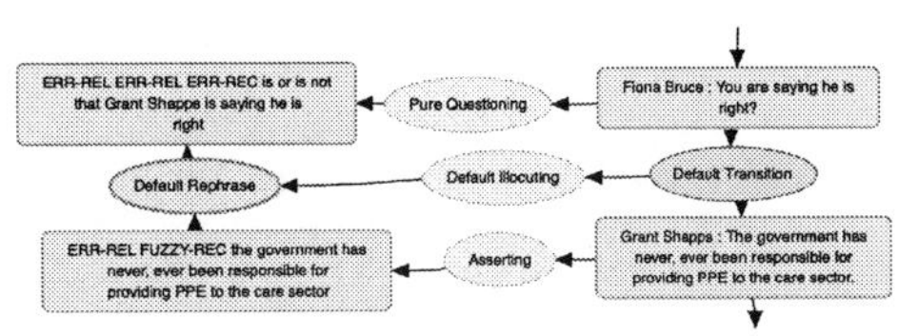

Figure 3: Incorrect annotation of question-answering in AIFdb map #23446

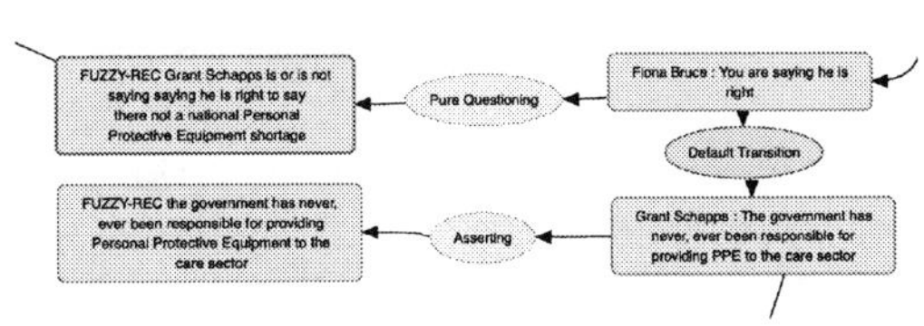

Figure 4: Correct annotation of non-question-answering in AIFdb map #23125

Erroneous splitting (ERR-SPLIT) The guideline for splitting text into segments clearly states that segments do not go beyond the sentence boundary. They

[1] `http://www.arg.tech/f/IATannotationguidelines.pdf`

also specify that any unit with discrete argumentative function has to be kept separately. For instance, the 'if...then' construction in Fig. 6 is an instance of a clear-cut inferential relation between the 'if'-clause and the 'then-clause' (despite them being inverted). The alternate analysis in Fig. 5 one misses the split and therefore the argumentative relation. In this case, we also mark ERR-REL on the wrongly-split proposition.

5.2. Fuzziness

This dimension of the disagreement space originates to some extent in the genre under investigation: natural, spontaneous argumentation features language patterns that are vague, fuzzy and therefore result in different analyses which themselves are valid, but illustrate the uncertainty in representing partially underspecified or vague language.

Fuzzy content (FUZZY-DISC) With this category we label all instances where the content of the locution is fuzzy in terms of whether parts of the locution serve as discourse-structuring material (which is not captured in the proposition) or contribute content that is (potentially) argumentatively relevant and therefore kept in the proposition. Fig. 7 shows a good example, in which the *winding me up* material has been analysed as a proposition (allowing it thereby to be referenced argumentatively later – "*yeah, it really winds me up too*" for example).

Fuzzy reconstruction (FUZZY-REC) This disagreement label is used in cases where the reconstruction of anaphoric or elliptical content varies across annotations. This is particularly the case for the reconstruction of 'that', where annotators judge the scope of the antecedent to be of varying length such as the different between the analyses in maps #22924 and #22930, (7) and (8), respectively. In some cases, annotators vary in their exact spell-out of the antecedent (though they mean the same entity), e.g., 'David Unknown' in node #843333 versus 'David Davies' in node #720703.

(7) leaving the European Union has or has not helped in speeding up the process of vaccine creation

(8) leaving the European Union has or hasn't helped in speeding up the vaccination delivery process

Fuzzy relation (FUZZY-REL) In this category we subsume all instances where the relation between the propositions ('Default Inference', 'Default Conflict' and 'Default Rephrase') is the same between two maps, however the splitting of argumentative units is slightly different. This can, for instance, mean that one analyst has chosen a linked argument structure (more than one premise leading to the conclusion, the premises are dependent on each other) versus a convergent argument (more than one premise to the conclusion, but the premises are independent of each other).

Fuzzy transcript input (FUZZY-TRANS) This category of disagreement is due to the data source under analysis: IAT analysis is conducted based on transcripts of natural dialogues and we do see cases in which the stenographer is not able to provide a clear recount of the conversation, for instance due to crosstalk or interruptions between interlocutors. This can lead to fragmented text which annotators treat differently in their analyses.

5.3. Ambiguity

The third dimension of disagreement captures ambiguous structures in the dialogue. In contrast to fuzzy language, we treat ambiguity as those instances where a string yields two fully discrete discourse or argumentative structures. In the following we briefly illustrate the different types of ambiguity that arise in the data:

Ambiguous anaphoric expressions (AMB-ANAPH) Given that annotators have to create propositions that are understandable without context, one core step of analysis is anaphora resolution. Similarly to (Poesio and Artstein, 2005), we also note the key challenge that the demonstrative 'that' poses for reconstruction. But it is also structures as in example 5.3, taken from a discussion on the Omicron wave in the episode on 1 July 2021:

(9) Andy Burnham: *I think I'm right in saying cases were highest day than they were in January. That's a worry. But you are right to say, Fiona, it isn't translating into hospitalisation. I was discussing the figures just before the show with David. So creeping up.*

The last sentence sentence contains an elliptical construction, which was resolved to 'deaths are creeping up' (map #23384) by one annotator, whereas the other analysis captures it as 'cases are creeping up' (map #23385). Both structures are discrete and correct and are therefore marked for ambiguity.

Ambiguous argument structure (AMB-REL) This category encompasses all analyses that exhibit two discrete argumentative structures. An example of this is given in Figure 1: Based on a different splitting decision, different argument structures arise: a serial argument with three propositions, connected by a 'Default Rephrase' and a 'Default Inference' (left-hand side) versus two propositions related by a single 'Default Rephrase'. Both analyses are valid given the context and are therefore labeled as ambiguous.

Ambigous splitting (AMB-SPLIT) Central to the analyses in Figure 1 and directly related to the previous category of AMB-REL is the category of ambiguous splitting, i.e., argumentative units have different length, but both segmentation decisions are well-motivated and adhere to the annotation guidelines.

In what follows, we briefly describe QT30nonaggr, the resource that is generated based on the analysis of the disagreement labels.

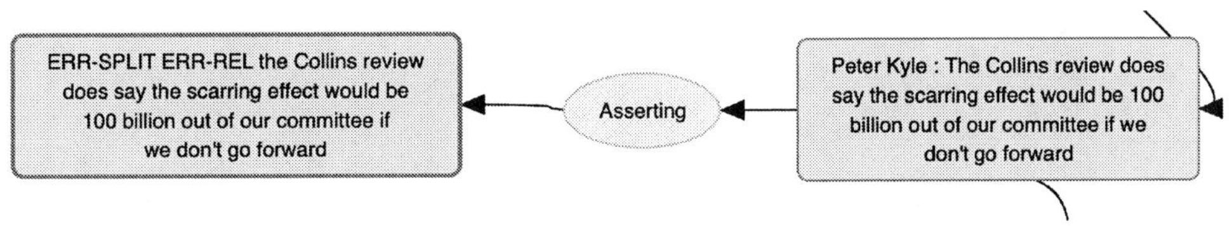

Figure 5: Incorrect splitting of if-then in AIFdb map #23298

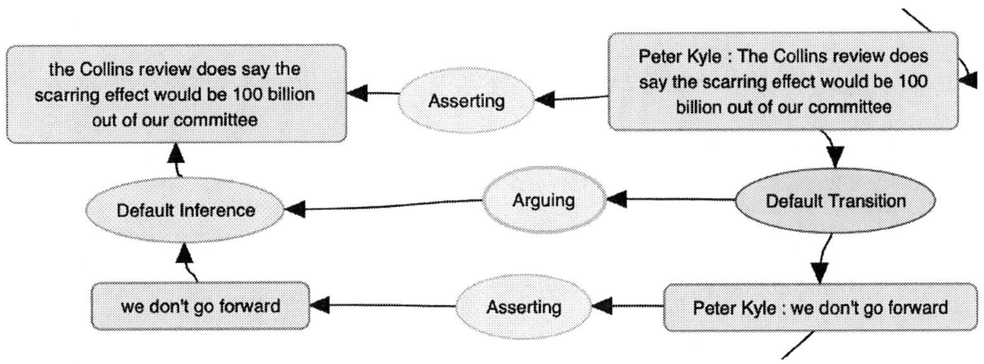

Figure 6: Correct splitting of if-then in AIFdb map #23290

6. QT30nonaggr

QT30nonaggr contains 67 excerpts which are annotated independently by two annotators (134 graphs in total). The length of excerpts ranges between 150-250 words. Overall, the resource contains 1817 propositions with an average length of 14.19 words per proposition. 'Default Inference' is the most frequent propositional relation (546), followed by 'Default Rephrase' (485) and 'Default Conflict' (106).

QT30nonaggr contains the full IAT graphs (as illustrated in Figure 2) plus the disagreement labels specified in §5. Identifying disagreements in illocutionary labels (the yellow connections in the middle of Figure 2), we leave for further work, however we tend to see significantly fewer disagreements there than in actual argument analysis.

Table 1 gives the detailed numbers for the disagreement space in QT30nonaggr: The category of annotation errors makes up the largest share of label disagreements by far – 907 out of 1402 (65%). Disagreements based on fuzzy language are second-most frequent (288/1402 – 20%), instances of ambiguity make up 207 out of 1402 disagreements (15%). Some disagreement labels appear in a vast majority of maps, the top ones being ERR-REL (92%), AMB-REL (85%) and FUZZY-REC and ERR-REC (both 82%). This confirms findings of previous work, e.g., (Stab and Gurevych, 2014), which shows that it is particularly the identification of relations that presents a challenge.

Label	% of graphs	# of labels
Errors		**907**
ERR-DISC	83%	130
ERR-GRAM	44%	46
ERR-REC	82%	258
ERR-REL	92%	355
ERR-SPLIT	71%	118
Fuzzy		**288**
FUZZY-DISC	41%	40
FUZZY-REC	82%	176
FUZZY-REL	49%	47
FUZZY-TRANS	27%	25
Ambiguity		**207**
AMB-ANAPH	21%	14
AMB-REL	85%	146
AMB-SPLIT	48%	47
Total		**1402**

Table 1: The detailed number for characterising the disagreement space of QT30nonaggr.

7. Summary

The analysis and reconstruction of argument is a challenging task. When taught as part of a critical thinking undergraduate programme, or in the context of study skills, or even in formal settings such as intelligence analysis or jurisprudence, it is well recognised that texts will support multiple interpretations. More recently, this has yielded particular challenges for the computational linguistics community, which naturally works from an assumed basis of a single, agreed-upon, gold standard. In our work constructing the largest corpora of annotated argument and debate currently available, we have encountered these challenges

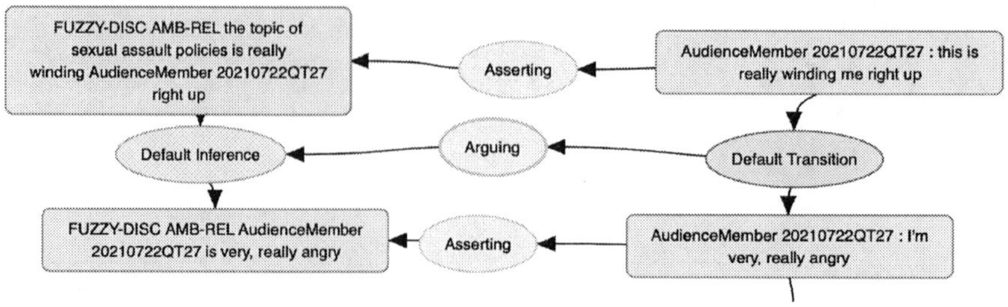

Figure 7: Material that is arguably discourse structuring in AIFdb map #23458

head-on, and have collated our experiences into a new non-aggregated corpus, QT30nonaggr, which not only documents cases of mismatching annotations, but also aims to provide an initial classification of the most prominent ways in which annotation discrepancies occur. Though as De Morgan famously said, "*There is no such thing as a classification of the ways in which men may arrive at an error: it is much to be doubted whether there ever can be,*" our approach here is to provide a starting point for exploring how errors might be arrived at both in annotating argumentation and reasoning structures, and, thereby in the long run, also in how errors are arrived at in general understanding of such structures.

8. Bibliography

Alliheedi, M., Mercer, R. E., and Cohen, R. (2019). Annotation of rhetorical moves in biochemistry articles. In *Proceedings of the 6th Workshop on Argument Mining*, pages 113–123, Florence, Italy, August. Association for Computational Linguistics.

Bar-Haim, R., Eden, L., Friedman, R., Kantor, Y., Lahav, D., and Slonim, N. (2020). From arguments to key points: Towards automatic argument summarization. In *Proceedings of the 58th Annual Meeting of the Association for Computational Linguistics*, pages 4029–4039, Online, July. Association for Computational Linguistics.

Budzynska, K., Janier, M., Kang, J., Reed, C., Saint-Dizier, P., Stede, M., and Yaskorska, O. (2014). Towards argument mining from dialogue. In *Proceedings of the Fifth International Conference on Computational Models of Argument (COMMA 2014)*, pages 185–196. IOS Press.

Budzynska, K., Janier, M., Reed, C., and Saint Dizier, P. (2016). Theoretical foundations for illocutionary structure parsing. *Argument & Computation*, 7(1):91–108.

Dorsch, J. and Wachsmuth, H. (2020). Semi-supervised cleansing of web argument corpora. In *Proceedings of the 7th Workshop on Argument Mining*, pages 19–29, Online, December. Association for Computational Linguistics.

Duthie, R., Lawrence, J., Budzynska, K., and Reed, C. (2016). The CASS technique for evaluating the performance of argument mining. In *Proceedings of the Third Workshop on Argument Mining (ArgMining2016)*, pages 40–49, Berlin, Germany, August. Association for Computational Linguistics.

Egawa, R., Morio, G., and Fujita, K. (2020). Corpus for modeling user interactions in online persuasive discussions. In *Proceedings of the 12th Language Resources and Evaluation Conference*, pages 1135–1141, Marseille, France, May. European Language Resources Association.

Gretz, S., Friedman, R., Cohen-Karlik, E., Toledo, A., Lahav, D., Aharonov, R., and Slonim, N. (2020). A large-scale dataset for argument quality ranking: Construction and analysis. *AAAI 2020*, 34.

Habernal, I. and Gurevych, I. (2017). Argumentation mining in user-generated web discourse. *Computational Linguistics*, 43(1):125–179, April.

Hautli Janisz, A., Kikteva, Z., Siskou, W., Gorska, K., Becker, R., and Reed, C. (2022). Qt30: A corpus of argument and conflict in broadcast debate. In *Proceedings of the 13th Language Resources and Evaluation Conference (LREC2022)*. ACL.

Hidey, C., Musi, E., Hwang, A., Muresan, S., and McKeown, K. (2017). Analyzing the semantic types of claims and premises in an online persuasive forum. In *Proceedings of the 4th Workshop on Argument Mining*, pages 11–21, Copenhagen, Denmark, September. Association for Computational Linguistics.

Janier, M., Lawrence, J., and Reed, C. (2014). Ova+: An argument analysis interface. In *Computational Models of Argument: Proceedings of COMMA*, volume 266, pages 463–464.

Lauscher, A., Glavaš, G., and Ponzetto, S. P. (2018). An argument-annotated corpus of scientific publications. In *Proceedings of the 5th Workshop on Argument Mining*, pages 40–46, Brussels, Belgium, November. Association for Computational Linguistics.

Lawrence, J. and Reed, C. (2020). Argument mining: A survey. *Computational Linguistics*, 45(4):765–818.

Lindahl, A., Borin, L., and Rouces, J. (2019). Towards assessing argumentation annotation - a first step. In

Proceedings of the 6th Workshop on Argument Mining, pages 177–186, Florence, Italy, August. Association for Computational Linguistics.

Mochales, R. and Moens, M.-F. (2011). Argumentation mining. *Artifical Intelligence and Law*, 19:1–22.

Peldszus, A. and Stede, M. (2013). From argument diagrams to argumentation mining in texts: A survey. *Int. J. Cogn. Inform. Nat. Intell.*, 7(1):1–31, jan.

Peldszus, A. and Stede, M. (2015). An annotated corpus of argumentative microtexts. In D. Mohammed et al., editors, *Argumentation and Reasoned Action – Proc. of the 1st European Conference on Argumentation, Lisbon*. College Publications, London.

Poesio, M. and Artstein, R. (2005). Annotating (anaphoric) ambiguity.

Rosenthal, S. and McKeown, K. (2012). Detecting opinionated claims in online discussions. *2012 IEEE Sixth International Conference on Semantic Computing*, pages 30–37.

Searle, J. and Vanderveken, D. (1985). *Foundations of Illocutionary Logic*. Cambridge: Cambridge University Press.

Searle, J. (1969). *Speech acts: An essay in the philosophy of language*. Cambridge: Cambridge University Press.

Stab, C. and Gurevych, I. (2014). Annotating argument components and relations in persuasive essays. In *Proceedings of COLING 2014, the 25th International Conference on Computational Linguistics: Technical Papers*, pages 1501–1510, Dublin, Ireland, August. Dublin City University and Association for Computational Linguistics.

Toledo, A., Gretz, S., Cohen-Karlik, E., Friedman, R., Venezian, E., Lahav, D., Jacovi, M., Aharonov, R., and Slonim, N. (2019). Automatic argument quality assessment - new datasets and methods. In *Proceedings of the 2019 Conference on Empirical Methods in Natural Language Processing and the 9th International Joint Conference on Natural Language Processing (EMNLP-IJCNLP)*, pages 5625–5635, Hong Kong, China, November. Association for Computational Linguistics.

Torsi, B. and Morante, R. (2018). Annotating claims in the vaccination debate. In *Proceedings of the 5th Workshop on Argument Mining*, pages 47–56, Brussels, Belgium, November. Association for Computational Linguistics.

Uma, A. N., Fornaciari, T., Hovy, D., Paun, S., Plank, B., and Poesio, M. (2021). Learning from disagreement: A survey. *Journal of Artificial Intelligence Research*, 72:385–1470.

Visser, J., Konat, B., Duthie, R., Koszowy, M., Budzynska, K., and Reed, C. (2019). Argumentation in the 2016 us presidential elections: annotated corpora of television debates and social media reaction. *Language Resources and Evaluation*, Feb.

Wachsmuth, H., Trenkmann, M., Stein, B., Engels, G., and Palakarska, T. (2014). A Review Corpus for Argumentation Analysis. In Alexander Gelbukh, editor, *15th International Conference on Intelligent Text Processing and Computational Linguistics (CICLing 2014)*, pages 115–127, Berlin Heidelberg New York, April. Springer.

Walker, M., Tree, J. F., Anand, P., Abbott, R., and King, J. (2012). A corpus for research on deliberation and debate. In *Proceedings of the Eighth International Conference on Language Resources and Evaluation (LREC'12)*, pages 812–817, Istanbul, Turkey, May. European Language Resources Association (ELRA).

Walton, D., Reed, C., and Macagno, F. (2008). *Argumentation Schemes*. Cambridge University Press.

Proceedings of the 1st Workshop on Perspectivist Approaches to NLP @LREC2022, pages 10–19
Marseille, 20 June 2022

Analyzing the Effects of Annotator Gender Across NLP Tasks

Laura Biester,[1] Vanita Sharma,[1] Ashkan Kazemi,[1]
Naihao Deng,[1] Steven Wilson,[2] Rada Mihalcea[1]
[1]Computer Science & Engineering, University of Michigan, USA
[2]Computer Science & Engineering, Oakland University, USA
{lbiester,svanita,ashkank,dnaihao}@umich.edu, stevenwilson@oakland.edu, mihalcea@umich.edu

Abstract

Recent studies have shown that for subjective annotation tasks, the demographics, lived experiences, and identity of annotators can have a large impact on how items are labeled. We expand on this work, hypothesizing that gender may correlate with differences in annotations for a number of NLP benchmarks, including those that are fairly subjective (e.g., affect in text) and those that are typically considered to be objective (e.g., natural language inference). We develop a robust framework to test for differences in annotation across genders for four benchmark datasets. While our results largely show a lack of statistically significant differences in annotation by males and females for these tasks, the framework can be used to analyze differences in annotation between various other demographic groups in future work. Finally, we note that most datasets are collected without annotator demographics and released only in aggregate form; we call on the community to consider annotator demographics as data is collected, and to release dis-aggregated data to allow for further work analyzing variability among annotators.

Keywords: annotator demographics, dataset construction, crowdsourcing

1. Introduction

Natural Language Processing (NLP) has seen a surge in the number of tasks as well as datasets during the last decade (Storks et al., 2019; Li et al., 2022; Nelson et al., 2022). With the success and requirements of deep learning techniques, large scale datasets have been proposed for various NLP tasks (Bojar et al., 2014; Yang et al., 2015; Zhang et al., 2015; Hendrycks et al., 2021). The mainstream formulation of supervised learning tasks across a range of areas trends towards preserving a single ground truth label for each example. However, such a setting ignores the possibility that different annotators may annotate the same example differently (Al Kuwatly et al., 2020). According to Basile et al. (2021), such disagreements between annotators are widespread. Moreover, Geva et al. (2019) showed that the annotator disagreement might significantly affect the performance of a model, indicating that our community may benefit from paying closer attention to annotator disagreement (Davani et al., 2022). Instead of focusing on high agreement scores for subjective datasets, we can be more cognisant of disagreements and build systems that are accommodating of different perspectives and needs, leading to novel insights and reducing harm (Uma et al., 2021; Davani et al., 2022).

In this work, we study how annotator demographics might relate to disagreements across four NLP tasks. Some examples of anecdotal differences in annotation in the datasets we study are shown in Figure 1. We include tasks that are commonly considered to be highly subjective (e.g., affect in text) and tasks that are considered more objective (e.g., natural language inference). In particular, we are interested in determining whether there are systematic, statistically significant differences in annotation that can be attributed to the gender of the annotators.

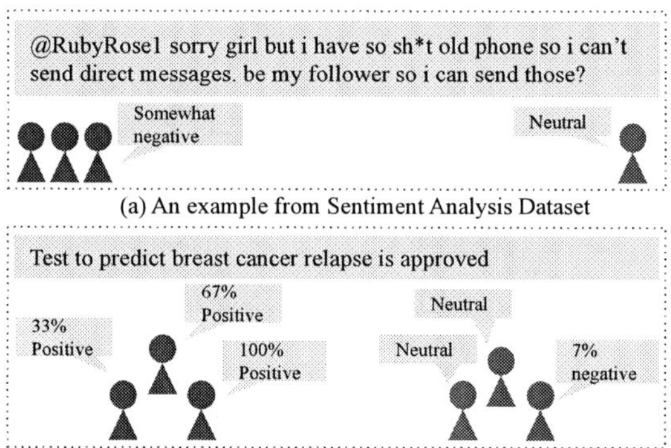

(b) An example from Affective Text Dataset

Figure 1: Examples of annotation difference between female annotators (left, purple) and male annotators (right, green).

First, taking a holistic view of the datasets, we develop a method to test if the overall distributions of annotations differ between male and female annotators. We visualize how the distribution of scores given by male and female annotators differs; for all four tasks (and a number of subtasks), the visualizations appeared to show some differences in the distribution of annotations by male and female annotators. However, after performing permutation testing, we find that for most tasks, we can not reject the null hypothesis that the observed differences could be due to random noise. For one task, sentiment analysis, we found that the male annotators gave more intermediary labels (e.g., somewhat positive/somewhat negative) than female annotators.

Next, we expand on an existing method (Prabhakaran et al., 2021) to study the extent to which male and female annotators agree with aggregate labels. In partic-

Dataset	# Male Annotators	# Female Annotators	# Datapoints	Mean Annotations per Datapoint	Annotation Type	Ratings per Datapoint
Affective Text	3	3	1000	6.00	Interval	7; anger, disgust, fear, joy, sadness, surprise, valence
Word Similarity	196	157	498	38.74	Ordinal	2; similarity, relatedness
Sentiment Analysis	736	744	14071	4.21	Ordinal	1
Natural Language Inference	282	211	1200	9.26	Ordinal	1

Table 1: List of linguistic tasks included in this study.

ular, we ask: (1) Is there a difference in the extent to which males and females agree with aggregate labels across the full dataset? and (2) Do female annotators have a higher agreement score with the aggregate of female annotators than with the aggregate of male annotators (and vice-versa for male annotators). For all pairs of agreement distributions that we study, we find no statistically significant difference.

While the results largely reveal no systematic difference in annotation that can be attributed to the gender of annotators and should thus be considered a negative result, our work contributes a robust framework with which to study differences in annotation between two or more groups from multiple angles. The framework is developed for two demographic categories and either ordinal or interval data, but could easily be applied to categorical or binary labels in a one-vs-all setup to work with multiple groups. We hope that this work can instigate further work on demographic differences in annotation, as our negative result cannot be generalized to all NLP tasks and datasets, nor can it be generalized to all demographic groups.

2. Related Work

Annotator Disagreement. As pointed out by Basile et al. (2021), annotator disagreement is ubiquitous, especially in the AI field (Smyth et al., 1994; Poesio and Artstein, 2005; Aroyo and Welty, 2015). People have long proposed that instead of ignoring such a disagreement and having a single groundtruth, we need to preserve annotations from different annotators (Poesio and Artstein, 2005; Recasens et al., 2012).

Reasons for Disagreement. Prior work has detected differences in data annotation with respect to gender in hate speech detection (Gold and Zesch, 2018), POS tagging and dependency parsing (Garimella et al., 2019). This work is often inspired by findings in linguistics, e.g., gender differences in the use of finite adverbial clauses (Mondorf, 2002). Beyond differences related to gender, researchers have studied difference in data annotation with respect to individual annotators (annotator bias) (Ross et al., 2010; Otterbacher, 2018; Larimore et al., 2021) and annotator disagreements (Pavlick and Kwiatkowski, 2019). Furthermore, Geva et al. (2019) reveals that annotators' individual differences affect model performance on natural language understanding tasks, which can lead to problems in model generalization to new users. Most prior work focuses on a single task or a single benchmark to study the data disagreement (bias) introduced by demographic features. In contrast, our paper considers four different NLP datasets, giving a more comprehensive analysis of potential differences across groups of annotators in a range of NLP tasks.

Disagreement Measurement. In order to systematically investigate the bias or disagreements, Geva et al. (2019; Garimella et al. (2019; Wich et al. (2020; Al Kuwatly et al. (2020) trained classifiers on subset of annotators, and use performance difference to demonstrate the existence of bias. Additionally, Wich et al. (2020) used an unsupervised graph method to group annotators and studied the difference between the groups. To measure the agreement between subgroups of annotators, Larimore et al. (2021) used Krippendorf's alpha score (Krippendorff, 2011), Gold and Zesch (2018) used Best-Worst-Scaling by Louviere et al. (2015), and Wich et al. (2020) reported Cohen's kappa (Cohen, 1960) and Krippendorf's alpha score.

3. Data

We study four NLP tasks using datasets that share the following properties: individual annotations are made available along with gender labels for those individuals, and items in the dataset have multiple annotations. We include datasets with interval and ordinal ratings; a summary of our datasets is presented in Table 1.

In the early stages of this study, we surveyed a number of language resource papers describing benchmark datasets to see if they mentioned the demographics of their annotators. To a large extent, we found that they did not; a few authors explicitly stated that no demographic information was collected, while one author stated that they included exclusively annotators located in the United States and Canada, likely to restrict the varieties of English represented by the annotators (Rajpurkar et al., 2016). With respect to user privacy, it is responsible practice not to collect more user-level information than is needed for data processing, and so it is reasonable that many previous studies chose not to store attributes of annotators like gender. However, not collecting these attributes also precludes the possibility of studying whether certain groups are under or over-represented in the dataset, and what effects representation may have on models.

We then emailed authors of twenty-three papers that did not explicitly state that they did not collect annotator metadata, and we received responses from sixteen authors. Most authors stated that they did not collect or consider collecting annotator demographics alongside their annotations. It is therefore worth noting that the tasks we chose to study were largely chosen due to feasibility (access to data) rather than due to our intuitions about the tasks themselves. However, there are some inherent reasons why these tasks are interesting to study. First, affect and sentiment are subjective, but perhaps less clearly linked to identity than hate speech detection, a task for which annotator identity has been shown to correlate with differences in annotation (Gold and Zesch, 2018). Moreover, while it is typically considered to be more objective, systematic disagreement has also been found in natural language inference annotation (Pavlick and Kwiatkowski, 2019).

A limitation of the data we use is that there is little representation of people who do not fit in the gender binary; accordingly, we only study differences between male and female annotators in this work. We hope that larger datasets that indicate annotator characteristics will allow for studying gender differences in annotation beyond the gender binary in the future.

Detailed descriptions of each task follow.

Affective Text

The affective text dataset is from the SemEval-2017 Task 14 (Strapparava and Mihalcea, 2007). In particular, we use the test dataset, which consists of one thousand headlines, each annotated by six annotators. The original authors provided the gender of the annotators, three of whom were male and three of whom were female. We note that unlike our other datasets, gender was not self-reported by the annotators; rather, it was ascribed by the dataset collector, who was acquainted with the annotators. We are releasing the individual annotations for the SemEval-2007 Task 14 in conjunction with this paper, along with the gender of each annotator.[1]

The text is annotated for six emotions: anger, disgust, fear, joy, sadness, and surprise. The scale used for rating is 0 (the emotion is absent from the headline) to 100 ("maximum emotional load"). Additionally, each headline is annotated for valence on a -100 (highly negative) to 100 (highly positive) scale; 0 is neutral.

Word Similarity

The word similarity dataset was collected using Amazon Mechanical Turk. The annotators self-report a number of their demographic characteristics, including gender, which was reported in a dropdown listing Male, Female, and Other.

The annotators were given pairs of words, and asked to rate them on two five-point Likert scales. In the similarity task, they were asked how similar words were, on a scale from "completely different" to "very similar". In the relatedness task, they were asked how related words were, on a scale from "unrelated" to "very related". A number of examples were given to guide annotators:

Similar words: alligator/crocodile, love/affection

Related words: car/tire, car/crash

Annotations where the annotator incorrectly answered a qualification question were excluded. Approximately 25% of the annotated word pairs were drawn directly from SimLex-999 (Hill et al., 2015); the remaining pairs were inspired by Garimella et al. (2017). Specifically, they were balanced such that approximately 1/4 of the remaining pairs represented common word associations for four demographic groups: males, females, people located in the United States, and people located in India. This sampling strategy suggests that gender differences in the annotations are more likely than they would be in word pairs selected without considering gender.

Sentiment Analysis

We use a sentiment analysis dataset created with the intention of measuring age-related bias in sentiment analysis (Diaz et al., 2018). The training data text is sourced from samples in the Sentiment140 dataset (Go et al., 2009) containing the strings "young" and "old"; the test data text is scraped from blog posts that discuss aging. In collecting this data, the authors also collected a number of the annotator's self-reported demographic attributes, including but not limited to gender, age, and race. Genders reported in the dataset included Male, Female, and Nonbinary (one annotator). More than 1400 annotators rate sentiment on a five-point Likert scale (very negative, negative, neutral, positive, very positive). There are on average 4.21 annotations per datapoint, but we note that not all datapoints have a variety in annotator gender. The dataset is publicly available (Diaz, 2020).

Natural Language Inference

The natural language inference (NLI) dataset we use is CommitmentBank (De Marneffe et al., 2019). The annotators for the dataset were asked to determine the extent of speaker commitment to complements of clause-embedding predicates under an entailment canceling operator (e.g. question, negation, and so on). The authors provided us with the annotator gender and age, which were collected during the original annotation as part of the survey given to annotators. Gender was reported as free-text; we mapped MALE and MALE+ to the male category and FEMALE, WOMAN, FEMAL, and FEMALLE to the female category. We removed one annotator who reported different demographics in different Amazon Mechanical Turk tasks, and a small number of annotators whose reported gender did not fall into the male/female binary due to lack of data. Each datapoint is ranked on a seven-point Likert scale (-3: the annotator believes that the author of the text is certain that the prompt is false, 0: annotator believes that the author of the text is not certain whether the

[1] https://github.com/MichiganNLP/Affective-Text-Individual-Annotations

prompt is true or false, 3: the annotator believes that the author of the text is certain that the prompt is true). For the NLI task, items were labeled based on whether at least 80% of annotations were within three ranges: $[1,3]$ (entailment), $[0]$ (neutral) or $[-3,-1]$ (contradiction) (Jiang and de Marneffe, 2019). We use the original ratings in the range $[-3,3]$ in our analysis.

4. Methodology

We use two methods to robustly measure whether there are underlying differences in how male and female annotators annotate each of our four datasets. The first method, described in Section 4.1, directly measures the differences in overall scores given by male and female annotators. This type of analysis is likely to capture shifts in the distribution of scores given by different sets of annotators – for instance, it would capture if male annotators are more likely to label positive sentiments than female annotators. Even a simple linear shift in the distribution of annotations could affect models, especially if ordinal labels are converted to binary, which is a common experimental setting, e.g., in sentiment analysis (Socher et al., 2013). The second method, described in Section 4.2, takes into account aggregate scores to determine to what extent male and female annotators differ from various aggregates. If significant differences were found, this type of analysis would signal the need for multi-perspective modelling.

4.1. Distribution Analysis

We split annotations into those provided by male and female annotators, then visualize the scores given by those annotators; for the affective text dataset, we use a kernel density estimation plot because the annotations are on an interval. For ordinal data, we use a barplot. A key advantage of this type of analysis is that it produces clearly interpretable results; the plots allow us to directly see how the male and female annotators differ.

To ensure the significance of our findings, we employ permutation tests; our null hypothesis is that gender does not affect the distributions of annotations. We define two test statistics, which we will refer to as t_{obs}.

For interval data, we begin by computing the cumulative sum of % of annotations for each gender with each possible rating from min (the minimum score in the range) to max (the maximum score in the range), which represents the empirical distribution function. Our test statistic is the area between the curves of the two empirical distribution functions. With cumulative sum vectors M and F, this area can be computed as $t_{obs} = \sum_{i=min}^{max} |M_i - F_i|$.

For ordinal data, we formulate our alternative hypothesis for each task by observation of how the two groups differ in the bar charts. We compute the difference in percentage of annotations with scores that meet the conditions of the alternative hypothesis. Specifically, given the total number of annotations and choices given to the annotators within the relevant condition C for the task, we compute $t_{obs} = \sum_{c \in C} |P(c|f) - P(c|m)|$, which represents the extent to which the distributions across labels differ for the two annotator groups.

We then randomly assign annotators to groups a (size = # of male annotators) and b (size = # of female annotators) and recompute the test statistic 10,000 times[2] with those groups instead of m (all male annotators) and f (all female annotators), creating an array of test statistics T_{perm}. Finally, we compute our p-value as the percentage of values in T_{perm} that are greater than t_{obs} (e.g., have a larger difference in the distribution).

4.2. Agreement Analysis

We expand upon the methodology from (Prabhakaran et al., 2021). They compute agreement using Cohen's kappa between each in-demographic annotator and the *majority vote* of the overall annotator pool. We use the same sentiment analysis dataset they study, but do not condense the labels to a binary scale. This means that we change our agreement metric to Krippendorff's alpha, due to its ability to compute agreement of ordinal and interval data between any number of annotators. We then compute the agreement of each in-demographic annotator with the *aggregate* of the overall annotator pool (labeled F-ALL, M-ALL). We also add two other measurements: the agreement of each in-demographic annotator and other in-demographic annotators (labeled F-ALLF, M-ALLM) and the agreement of each in-demographic annotator with all out-of-demographic annotators (labeled F-ALLM, M-ALLF). In all computations, the in-demographic annotator who is being compared to the aggregate is excluded from the aggregation.

We aggregate labels using the mean for interval data and a median for ordinal data; if the median is not an integer, we take the mean of two agreement scores for each annotator: one with the ceiling of the medians and one with the floor. The algorithm is formalized in Algorithm 1.

To measure the significance of our results, we performed t-tests for three metrics of interest across all of our datasets:

F-ALL vs. M-ALL This two-sided t-test determines if there is a statistical difference between the extent to which male and female annotators agree with the aggregate of all annotators. A difference here would show that the aggregate is more representative of one gender.

F-ALLF vs. F-ALLM This one-sided t-test determines if female annotators agree with other female annotators more than they agree with male annotators.

M-ALLM vs. M-ALLF This one-sided t-test determines if male annotators agree with other male annotators more than they agree with female annotators.

[2] Or fewer, if every possible permutation is covered with fewer tests

Algorithm 1 Agreement Comparison Algorithm

The algorithm takes as input A, a matrix of annotations where annotators are rows and datapoints are columns, G, a list of genders of annotators in A, and i, an individual annotator index.
Our aggregation function, `agg`, is median for interval data and mean for interval data. We use the `krippendorff` function for agreement.
$krip_{ALL}$ is used for F-ALL and M-ALL, $krip_{EQ}$ is used for F-ALLF, M-ALLM, $krip_{OTH}$ is used for F-ALLM, M-ALLF. The scores for each annotator i are used in the visualization.

```
procedure FILTER(A, G, i, all, eq)
    A^G ← []
    for k ← 1, |A| do
        ▷ exclude target annotator from aggregate
        if i != k then
            if all then
                Append A_k to A^G
            else if eq && G_i == G_k then
                Append A_k to A^G
            else if !eq && G_i != G_k then
                Append A_k to A^G
            end if
        end if
    end for
    ▷ Return other annotators depending on all/eq
    return A^G
end procedure

procedure ANN_AGREEMENT(A, G, i)
    ▷ aggregate and filter set of annotators
    agg_ALL ← agg(FILTER(A, G, i, true, true))
    agg_EQ ← agg(FILTER(A, G, i, false, true))
    agg_OTH ← agg(FILTER(A, G, i, false, false))

    ▷ find agreements with krippendorff's alpha
    krip_ALL = krippendorff(A_i, agg_ALL)
    krip_EQ = krippendorff(A_i, agg_EQ)
    krip_OTH = krippendorff(A_i, agg_OTH)

    return krip_ALL, krip_EQ, krip_OTH
end procedure
```

For both types of analysis, we use the Benjamini-Hochberg (Benjamini and Hochberg, 1995) False Discovery Rate correction to account for performing multiple statistical tests.[3]

5. Results

5.1. Distribution Analysis

Our plots of the affective text distributions (Figure 2) revealed an interesting pattern: the male annotators more commonly gave a rating close to zero, indicating the text was absent of an emotion. A similar pattern is observed for the valence task, for which annotations ranged from -100 to 100; the male annotators more frequently used 0, which was the "neutral" label.

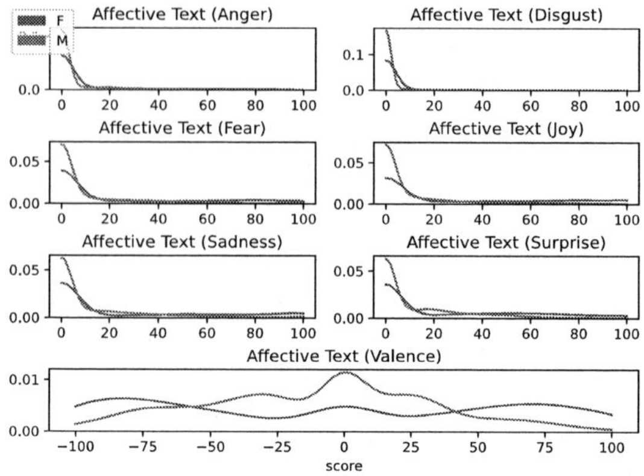

Figure 2: Kernel density estimation plots of affective text annotations.

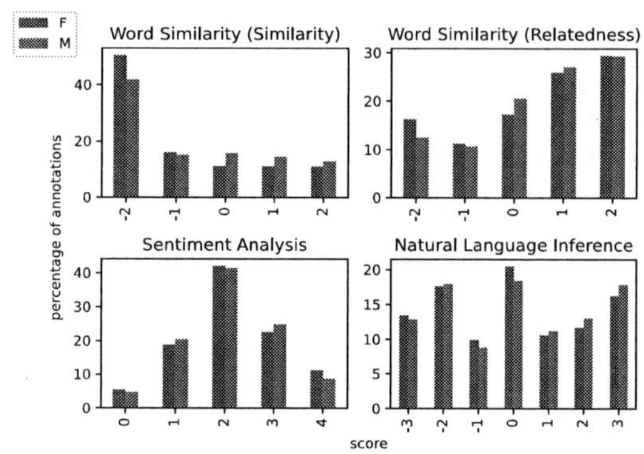

Figure 3: Bar plots of word similarity, sentiment analysis, and NLI annotations.

The plots for word similarity (Figure 3) do not reveal such stark differences; however, we do see that male annotators appear to generally give higher scores, while female annotators more commonly chose -2; while the differences are not as clear, a similar pattern can be observed for word relatedness and NLI. On the sentiment analysis dataset, female annotators appear to more commonly give scores neutral, very positive, or very negative ratings, while male annotators give more intermediary ratings of somewhat positive/somewhat negative.

These observations form the basis for the metrics used in our permutation tests. For the word similarity task, we compute the difference in percentage of scores greater than or equal to 0. For NLI, we compute the difference in percentage of scores greater than or equal

[3] $\alpha = 0.05$.

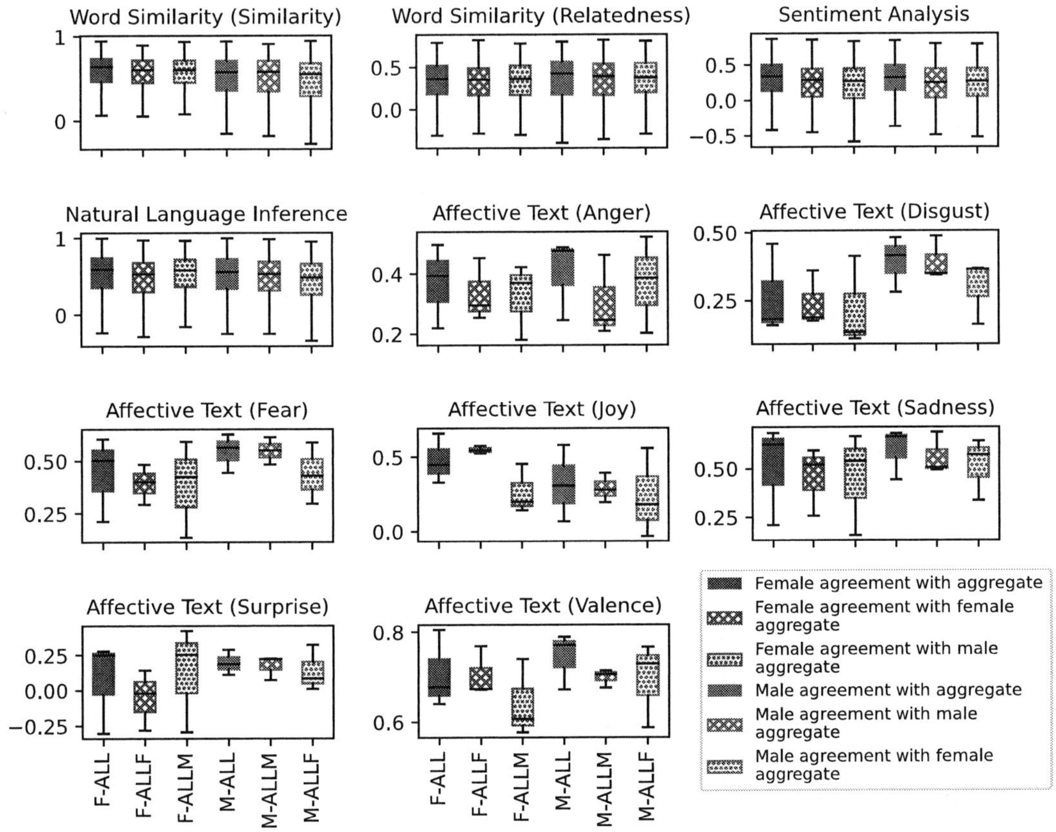

Figure 4: Boxplots representing the results of our agreement analysis.

to 1. For the sentiment task, we compute the difference in percentage of scores of 1 or 3.

The permutation tests (Table 2) reveal a significant difference ($p < 0.05$) in sentiment analysis annotations. While the plots appear to reveal consistent differences in affective text annotations, the permutation tests show that this result may be attributed to only one or two annotators with extreme behavior, and looks meaningful due to the small number of annotators overall. The word similarity and NLI tasks also did not produce significant results; however, the p-value for word similarity was very close to our significance level, indicating that studying gender differences in annotation of other similar datasets with different word pairs may be worthwhile in future work.

Task	p-value
Word Similarity (Similarity)	0.0528
Word Similarity (Relatedness)	0.7910
Sentiment Analysis	**0.0209**
Natural Language Inference	0.7592
Affective Text (Anger)	0.5500
Affective Text (Disgust)	0.3143
Affective Text (Fear)	0.3143
Affective Text (Joy)	0.2750
Affective Text (Sadness)	0.3143
Affective Text (Surprise)	0.6111
Affective Text (Valence)	0.2750

Table 2: Results of permutation tests. Results significant at the level $\alpha = 0.05$ are demarcated in **bold**. The false discovery rate correction is performed for results across the table.

5.2. Agreement Analysis

The plots representing distributions of agreements between different genders and aggregations are presented in Figure 4. Among the four ordinal tasks, we find that male and female annotators tend to have similar levels of agreement with the aggregate scores of all other annotators, as was observed by (Prabhakaran et al., 2021) on the sentiment dataset. Furthermore, we find that for both genders, the agreement with the overall aggregate (*F-ALL, M-ALL*) tends to exceed the agreement for the in-demographic aggregate (*F-ALLM, M-ALLF*). This

	F-ALL vs. M-ALL		F-ALLF vs. F-ALLM		M-ALLM vs. M-ALLF	
	tval	pval	tval	pval	tval	pval
Word Similarity (Similarity)	3.08	0.07	-0.56	0.81	0.96	0.77
Word Similarity (Relatedness)	-0.44	0.81	-0.32	0.81	-0.40	0.81
Sentiment Analysis	-0.11	0.94	0.78	0.77	0.09	0.77
Natural Language Inference	1.10	0.77	-1.83	0.97	1.15	0.77
Affective Text (Anger)	-0.29	0.83	0.11	0.77	-0.52	0.81
Affective Text (Disgust)	-1.11	0.77	0.19	0.77	1.17	0.77
Affective Text (Fear)	-0.81	0.77	0.06	0.77	1.21	0.77
Affective Text (Joy)	0.91	0.77	2.92	0.36	0.30	0.77
Affective Text (Sadness)	-0.54	0.81	0.02	0.77	0.41	0.77
Affective Text (Surprise)	-0.62	0.81	-0.72	0.82	0.34	0.77
Affective Text (Valence)	-0.59	0.81	1.06	0.77	0.08	0.77

Table 3: Results of t-tests. No results are significant at the level $\alpha = 0.05$ after the false discovery rate correction was performed for results across the table.

suggests that the statistical effects of having more annotations in the aggregate has a larger effect on agreement than the demographics of the annotators who are included in that aggregate.

The results are mixed for the affective text tasks. This could be in part due to the small number of annotators, but there are a few notable results. We see that for one emotion (joy), female agreement with other females has very little variance, and is much higher than female agreement with other males. However, after controlling for multiple comparisons, this result is not statistically significant. Furthermore, the results differ across the six emotions and valence; we see that for some, there appears to be more agreement between people of the same gender, or between females with the overall aggregate than males. It would be interesting to do these comparisons on a larger dataset with more annotators to determine whether or not there is a difference in how people of different genders annotate each of these emotions, a hypothesis that was supported by some individual examples in the dataset (see Figure 1).

T-tests detailed in Table 3 reveal that there were no statistically significant differences in the pairs of distributions that we compared (see Section 4.2).

6. Discussion

Our results indicate that there is no strong evidence that there are statistical differences between how male and female annotators annotate the four tasks that we studied. The only statistically significant difference we found was for the sentiment analysis dataset; male annotators gave more "intermediary" scores of 1 (somewhat negative) and 3 (somewhat positive) than females when annotating this task. We had initially hypothesized that demographic characteristics of annotators (including gender) may affect annotations and therefore the models trained on various NLP datasets. We were particularly surprised to not find differences in the word similarity dataset, which intentionally included word pairs that represented differing word associations of demographic groups. These differences in word associations were revealed by Garimella et al. (2017), and differences in word associations based on age have also been observed by psychologists (Tresselt and Mayzner, 1964).

This result conflicts with some previous studies, which found a difference in annotations (Al Kuwatly et al., 2020; Larimore et al., 2021; Shen and Rose, 2021; Excell and Al Moubayed, 2021) based on annotator demographics and identities. While our results differ from prior work, it is worth nothing that much of this work focuses on annotation tasks that are more directly related to the identities that were proven to correspond with differing annotations. These works frequently focus on racism, hate speech, and toxicity, which are often targeted at people with certain identities. Hate speech in particular is commonly defined as offensive or degrading language towards a person based on a specific group identify, such as race, ethnicity, gender, or sexual orientation (Parekh, 2006), increasing the likelihood that it will perceived differently by people depending on whether or not they are part of the targeted group(s). The same is true for the labeling of text as corresponding to political ideologies, where the ideologies of the annotators differ (Shen and Rose, 2021).

It is worthwhile to continue studying this problem, as this paper only shows that there are not differences in annotation that can be attributed to *one demographic attribute* (gender) across *four datasets*. We have not proven that there is no difference across the space of all NLP datasets, and we have not proven that there is no difference for other demographic attributes like race or nationality.

A major contribution of our work, therefore, is robust methodology that can expose statistical differences in annotation across groups. By performing permutation tests, we are able to compare the differences we see between male and female annotators to differences that might appear by chance in our annotation pool. Unlike prior work (Prabhakaran et al., 2021), we take this a step further, formalizing metrics for comparing if annotators agree with the set of annotators who share their gender to a larger extent than they agree with annotators who have a different gender. While these methods are used with interval and ordinal data in our work, they could easily be adapted to use with binary or categorical data.

These methods provide multiple ways in which researchers could study whether annotator demographics result in differences in annotation, and we hope that they will be adopted in future work. In order to ease adoption of our methods, our code is publicly available.[4] To aid this important work, we would recommend that dataset curators consider collecting annotator characteristics and releasing dis-aggregated datasets to the extent possible while preserving the privacy of annotators.

7. Limitations and Future Work

The scope of our study is limited to investigating the effects of annotator gender on NLP benchmark datasets. In collecting data for this project, we learned that nearly all widely used NLP benchmarks have not recorded annotator characteristics their construction process. With the scarcity of annotator demographics associated with NLP benchmarks, several challenges arise. First in such data scarcity, studying annotation differences among non-binary crowdworkers is a challenging but important area of future work. Second, our results do not reveal statistically meaningful discrepancies in data annotation among different genders, but we remain cautious of over-generalization as studying gender effects among a handful of annotators and datasets poses challenges to drawing broader conclusions. Third, while it is helpful to include annotator characteristics in constructing new NLP benchmarks, crowdworker privacy should also be considered. We identify privacy preserving approaches for collection and distribution of annotator demographic data as an important area for future work. Additionally, inclusive practices should be followed when asking crowdworkers to identify their gender (Spiel et al., 2019; Larson, 2017).

The evaluation framework used in this study only considers the discrepancies correlated with a single annotator characteristic. We consider generalized additive models (GAMs) with pairwise interactions (Lou et al., 2013) as a potential avenue for modeling intersectionality of annotator demographics (e.g. gender, race, socioeconomic background) in future work. While language generation tasks are an exciting area in NLP, grounded observations about the discrepancies caused by crowdworker gender are difficult to make, as our methodology is mainly applicable to interval, ordinal and categorical benchmarks.

[4] https://github.com/MichiganNLP/Analyzing-the-Effects-of-Annotator-Gender-Across-NLP-Tasks

8. Conclusion

In this paper we studied the effects of annotator gender on four NLP benchmarks and developed a robust evaluation framework for studying annotator demographic effects on datasets. Our results reveal that there are not statistical differences in how male and female annotators annotated the four benchmark datasets we studied. However, we focused on a small number of datasets and one demographic attribute (gender). We chose the datasets included in our study in large part because they were the ones that were available; most existing NLP benchmarks have been collected without annotator demographics.

We strongly advocate that the community should consider collecting demographics of annotators as part of the data annotation process. This data can be used to perform analyses such as those presented in this paper and to ensure that there is no large demographic imbalance in the annotator pool, relative to the population, as such an imbalance could lead to ineffective models if the annotations differ based on demographics.

9. Acknowledgements

We would like to thank Simin Fan and Andrew Lee for their assistance in early stages of this work.

10. Bibliographical References

Al Kuwatly, H., Wich, M., and Groh, G. (2020). Identifying and measuring annotator bias based on annotators' demographic characteristics. In *Proceedings of the Fourth Workshop on Online Abuse and Harms*, pages 184–190, Online, November. Association for Computational Linguistics.

Aroyo, L. and Welty, C. (2015). Truth is a lie: Crowd truth and the seven myths of human annotation. *AI Magazine*, 36(1):15–24.

Basile, V., Fell, M., Fornaciari, T., Hovy, D., Paun, S., Plank, B., Poesio, M., Uma, A., et al. (2021). We need to consider disagreement in evaluation. In *1st Workshop on Benchmarking: Past, Present and Future*, pages 15–21. Association for Computational Linguistics.

Benjamini, Y. and Hochberg, Y. (1995). Controlling the false discovery rate: a practical and powerful approach to multiple testing. *Journal of the Royal statistical society: series B (Methodological)*, 57(1):289–300.

Bojar, O., Buck, C., Federmann, C., Haddow, B., Koehn, P., Leveling, J., Monz, C., Pecina, P., Post, M., Saint-Amand, H., et al. (2014). Findings of the 2014 workshop on statistical machine translation. In *Proceedings of the ninth workshop on statistical machine translation*, pages 12–58.

Cohen, J. (1960). A coefficient of agreement for nominal scales. *Educational and psychological measurement*, 20(1):37–46.

Davani, A. M., Díaz, M., and Prabhakaran, V. (2022). Dealing with disagreements: Looking beyond the majority vote in subjective annotations. *Transactions of the Association for Computational Linguistics*, 10:92–110.

Diaz, M., Johnson, I., Lazar, A., Piper, A. M., and Gergle, D., (2018). *Addressing Age-Related Bias in Sentiment Analysis*, page 1–14. Association for Computing Machinery, New York, NY, USA.

Excell, E. and Al Moubayed, N. (2021). Towards equal gender representation in the annotations of toxic language detection. In *Proceedings of the 3rd Workshop on Gender Bias in Natural Language Processing*, pages 55–65, Online, August. Association for Computational Linguistics.

Garimella, A., Banea, C., and Mihalcea, R. (2017). Demographic-aware word associations. In *Proceedings of the 2017 Conference on Empirical Methods in Natural Language Processing*, pages 2285–2295, Copenhagen, Denmark, September. Association for Computational Linguistics.

Garimella, A., Banea, C., Hovy, D., and Mihalcea, R. (2019). Women's syntactic resilience and men's grammatical luck: Gender-bias in part-of-speech tagging and dependency parsing. In *Proceedings of the 57th Annual Meeting of the Association for Computational Linguistics*, pages 3493–3498.

Geva, M., Goldberg, Y., and Berant, J. (2019). Are we modeling the task or the annotator? an investigation of annotator bias in natural language understanding datasets. In *Proceedings of the 2019 Conference on Empirical Methods in Natural Language Processing and the 9th International Joint Conference on Natural Language Processing (EMNLP-IJCNLP)*, pages 1161–1166, Hong Kong, China, November. Association for Computational Linguistics.

Go, A., Bhayani, R., and Huang, L. (2009). Twitter sentiment classification using distant supervision. *CS224N project report, Stanford*, 1(12):2009.

Gold, M. W. T. H. D. and Zesch, T. (2018). Do women perceive hate differently: Examining the relationship between hate speech, gender, and agreement judgments. In *Proceedings of the 14th Conference on Natural Language Processing (KONVENS 2018)*, pages 110–120, Vienna, Austria.

Hendrycks, D., Burns, C., Kadavath, S., Arora, A., Basart, S., Tang, E., Song, D., and Steinhardt, J. (2021). Measuring mathematical problem solving with the math dataset. *NeurIPS*.

Hill, F., Reichart, R., and Korhonen, A. (2015). SimLex-999: Evaluating semantic models with (genuine) similarity estimation. *Computational Linguistics*, 41(4):665–695, December.

Jiang, N. and de Marneffe, M.-C. (2019). Evaluating BERT for natural language inference: A case study on the CommitmentBank. In *Proceedings of the 2019 Conference on Empirical Methods in Natural Language Processing and the 9th International Joint Conference on Natural Language Processing (EMNLP-IJCNLP)*, pages 6086–6091, Hong Kong, China, November. Association for Computational Linguistics.

Krippendorff, K. (2011). Computing krippendorff's alpha-reliability.

Larimore, S., Kennedy, I., Haskett, B., and Arseniev-Koehler, A. (2021). Reconsidering annotator disagreement about racist language: Noise or signal? In *Proceedings of the Ninth International Workshop on Natural Language Processing for Social Media*, pages 81–90, Online, June. Association for Computational Linguistics.

Larson, B. (2017). Gender as a variable in natural-language processing: Ethical considerations. In *Proceedings of the First ACL Workshop on Ethics in Natural Language Processing*, pages 1–11, Valencia, Spain, April. Association for Computational Linguistics.

Li, Q., Peng, H., Li, J., Xia, C., Yang, R., Sun, L., Yu, P. S., and He, L. (2022). A survey on text classification: From traditional to deep learning. *ACM Trans. Intell. Syst. Technol.*, 13(2), apr.

Lou, Y., Caruana, R., Gehrke, J., and Hooker, G. (2013). Accurate intelligible models with pairwise interactions. In *Proceedings of the 19th ACM SIGKDD international conference on Knowledge discovery and data mining*, pages 623–631.

Louviere, J. J., Flynn, T. N., and Marley, A. A. J. (2015). *Best-worst scaling: Theory, methods and applications*. Cambridge University Press.

Mondorf, B. (2002). Gender differences in english syntax. *Journal of English Linguistics*, 30(2):158–180.

Nelson, P., Urs, N. V., and Kasicheyanula, T. R. (2022). Progress in natural language processing and language understanding. In *Bridging Human Intelligence and Artificial Intelligence*, pages 83–103. Springer.

Otterbacher, J. (2018). Social cues, social biases: stereotypes in annotations on people images. In *Sixth AAAI Conference on Human Computation and Crowdsourcing*.

Parekh, B. (2006). Hate speech. *Public policy research*, 12(4):213–223.

Pavlick, E. and Kwiatkowski, T. (2019). Inherent disagreements in human textual inferences. *Transactions of the Association for Computational Linguistics*, 7:677–694.

Poesio, M. and Artstein, R. (2005). The reliability of anaphoric annotation, reconsidered: Taking ambiguity into account. In *Proceedings of the workshop on frontiers in corpus annotations ii: Pie in the sky*, pages 76–83.

Prabhakaran, V., Mostafazadeh Davani, A., and Diaz, M. (2021). On releasing annotator-level labels and information in datasets. In *Proceedings of The Joint 15th Linguistic Annotation Workshop (LAW) and 3rd Designing Meaning Representations (DMR) Workshop*, pages 133–138, Punta Cana, Dominican Republic, November. Association for Computational Linguistics.

Rajpurkar, P., Zhang, J., Lopyrev, K., and Liang, P. (2016). SQuAD: 100,000+ questions for machine comprehension of text. In *Proceedings of the 2016 Conference on Empirical Methods in Natural Language Processing*, pages 2383–2392, Austin, Texas, November. Association for Computational Linguistics.

Recasens, M., Martí, M. A., and Orăsan, C. (2012). Annotating near-identity from coreference disagreements. In *Proceedings of the Eighth International Conference on Language Resources and Evaluation (LREC'12)*, pages 165–172.

Ross, J., Irani, L., Silberman, M. S., Zaldivar, A., and Tomlinson, B. (2010). Who are the crowdworkers? shifting demographics in mechanical turk. In *CHI'10 extended abstracts on Human factors in computing systems*, pages 2863–2872.

Shen, Q. and Rose, C. (2021). What sounds "right" to me? experiential factors in the perception of political ideology. In *Proceedings of the 16th Conference of the European Chapter of the Association for Computational Linguistics: Main Volume*, pages 1762–1771, Online, April. Association for Computational Linguistics.

Smyth, P., Fayyad, U., Burl, M., Perona, P., and Baldi, P. (1994). Inferring ground truth from subjective labelling of venus images. *Advances in neural information processing systems*, 7.

Socher, R., Perelygin, A., Wu, J., Chuang, J., Manning, C. D., Ng, A., and Potts, C. (2013). Recursive deep models for semantic compositionality over a sentiment treebank. In *Proceedings of the 2013 Conference on Empirical Methods in Natural Language Processing*, pages 1631–1642, Seattle, Washington, USA, October. Association for Computational Linguistics.

Spiel, K., Haimson, O. L., and Lottridge, D. (2019). How to do better with gender on surveys: a guide for hci researchers. *Interactions*, 26(4):62–65.

Storks, S., Gao, Q., and Chai, J. Y. (2019). Recent advances in natural language inference: A survey of benchmarks, resources, and approaches. *arXiv preprint arXiv:1904.01172*.

Tresselt, M. E. and Mayzner, M. S. (1964). The kent-rosanoff word association: Word association norms as a function of age. *Psychonomic Science*, 1(1):65–66.

Uma, A., Fornaciari, T., Dumitrache, A., Miller, T., Chamberlain, J., Plank, B., Simpson, E., and Poesio, M. (2021). Semeval-2021 task 12: Learning with disagreements. Association for Computational Linguistics.

Wich, M., Al Kuwatly, H., and Groh, G. (2020). Investigating annotator bias with a graph-based approach. In *Proceedings of the Fourth Workshop on Online Abuse and Harms*, pages 191–199.

Yang, Y., Yih, W.-t., and Meek, C. (2015). Wikiqa: A challenge dataset for open-domain question answering. In *Proceedings of the 2015 conference on empirical methods in natural language processing*, pages 2013–2018.

Zhang, X., Zhao, J., and LeCun, Y. (2015). Character-level convolutional networks for text classification. *Advances in neural information processing systems*, 28.

11. Language Resource References

De Marneffe, Marie-Catherine and Simons, Mandy and Tonhauser, Judith. (2019). *The commitmentbank: Investigating projection in naturally occurring discourse*.

Diaz, Mark. (2020). *Age Bias Training and Testing Data*. Harvard Dataverse.

Strapparava, Carlo and Mihalcea, Rada. (2007). *SemEval-2007 Task 14: Affective Text*. Association for Computational Linguistics.

Proceedings of the 1st Workshop on Perspectivist Approaches to NLP @LREC2022, pages 20–25
Marseille, 20 June 2022

Predicting Literary Quality
How Perspectivist Should We Be?

Y. Bizzoni, I.M. Lassen, T. Peura, M.R. Thomsen, K.L. Nielbo
Center for Humanities Computing Aarhus, Aarhus University
yuri.bizzoni@cc.au.dk, idamarie@cas.au.dk, tpeura@cc.au.dk, madsrt@cc.au.dk, kln@cas.au.dk

Abstract

Approaches in literary quality tend to belong to two main grounds: one sees quality as completely subjective, relying on the idiosyncratic nature of individual perspectives on the perception of beauty; the other is ground-truth inspired, and attempts to find one or two values that predict something like an objective quality: the number of copies sold, for example, or the winning of a prestigious prize. While the first school usually does not try to predict quality at all, the second relies on a single majority vote in one form or another. In this article we discuss the advantages and limitations of these schools of thought and describe a different approach to reader's quality judgments, which moves away from raw majority vote, but does try to create intermediate classes or groups of annotators. Drawing on previous works we describe the benefits and drawbacks of building similar annotation classes. Finally we share early results from a large corpus of literary reviews for an insight into which classes of readers might make most sense when dealing with the appreciation of literary quality.

Keywords: Quality assessment, Perspectivism, Literary quality

1. Introduction and Motivation

While literary quality can be considered one of the most subjective fields of evaluation, its perception from large amounts of readers over time does show convergent trends: communities tend to establish and update canons; specific texts and narratives manage to remain popular despite the changing of fashions and political phases; authors' names become eponymous of literary quality in different countries and throughout the social spectrum. This duality has arguably generated two opposed polarities when it comes to the definition of what constitutes literary quality: on one side a highly individualistic, idiosyncratic perspective, that sees quality as a function of either individual or collective, but temporary world views, and as such non-convergent if not for ephemeral artefacts, such as transitory canons (Bloom, 2014). On the other side, a ground-truth inspired perspective, that sees literary value as a sort of universal and underlying quality of texts, that shines through the noise of socio-political or individual differences into broad or long-lasting convergences (Guillory, 2013).

The problem of literary quality's subjective status becomes even more intriguing when we turn to the challenge of its formal or computational assessment. Most works in this direction have, until today, assumed the possibility of one single ground truth by modelling literary quality as a single rating or label assigned to a text. These ratings have been retrieved from various sources: literary critics, book sale numbers, bestseller lists, or crowd-sourced reader opinions. Such approaches have had their limitations. Relying only on experts' judgment (e.g. awards, prestigious reviews) would bias the model to reflect only their preferences, but striving for representativity by crowd-sourcing opinions ends up ignoring important differences in the readers' population, as we will discuss in the next sections.

In this paper, we follow the tracks of recent debates in computational linguistics and machine learning about the advantages and limitations of considering different perspectives, what is called "perspectivism" (Basile et al., 2021; Plank et al., 2014). With this in mind, we address the question of how perspectivist we should be when it comes to literary quality. After drawing a spectrum with total subjectivity on one end and the use of a single gold standard on the other, we suggest approaching a middle way, by dividing readers into meaningful classes, each of which can be treated as a single judgment on a literary work. Finally, we present early results on a new corpus of literary reviews validating the feasibility of this approach.

2. Related Work

Several studies have attempted to formally model traits that capture literary quality. The choice of the candidate features for the definition of literary quality has naturally been very broad: some approaches, conflating quality and fame, have focused only on extra-textual features, such as genre and author visibility to predict success in book sales (Wang et al., 2019), or the number of references to a literary work as a measure of canonicality (Ferrer, 2013), whereas others have focused on stylistic features [1], such as syntactic (van Cranenburgh et al., 2019) and semantic (Ashok et al., 2013) complexity, or the emotional flow of a narrative (Maharjan et al., 2018) to predict, for example, the likelihood of a text to become part of a pre-determined literary canon.

[1]For a review of computational stylistics, see Hermann et al. (2020)

What is often less discussed in many of these studies is the problem of defining a ground truth for literary quality: most of the existing literature in automatic quality prediction of narrative texts relies on a single gold standard, adopting what is still today the mainstream approach to machine learning (Basile et al., 2021). Some works, for example, use the Nobel Prize for Literature as a way to assess the quality of an author (Hu et al., 2021), while others draw the average rating for a book from a large-scale reader platform as a ground truth for a text's appreciation (Bizzoni et al., 2021; Maharjan et al., 2018). The number of copies sold is often adopted as a reliable golden label to rank novels, based on the assumption that there is a distinct, overarching set of signals that has predictive power for whether or not a book ends up on the bestseller list (Archer and Jockers, 2016; Wang et al., 2019). Finally, some works have attempted to use the guide of prestigious literary periodicals or references in academic literature in order to create their ground truth for literary value (Ferrer, 2013; Underwood and Sellers, 2016).

Studies questioning the limitations of one or the other approach have appeared: Porter (2018) questions the conflation of quality and prestige, pointing out that the deviation within a single canon might be broader than between canonical and non-canonical works , while van Cranenburgh et al. (2020) designed a new set of experiments to try and tease contextual from textual factors in readers' evaluation of a literary piece (van Cranenburgh and Koolen, 2020), still in general, the existence of one single average representing a text's quality seems to have been preferred by the community.

A different line of research, with a less prominent predictive vocation, has instead focused on the demographic and individual differences between reading preferences. Touileb et al. (2020) explored Norwegian book reviews and found differences in the literary preferences and the expression of sentiments of female and male reviews, depending on genre (Touileb et al., 2020). A similar analysis of Goodreads reviews pointed to the same direction: there are differences between female and male readers, and it is possible to find evidence for it on a larger scale (Thelwall, 2019). Readers' communities and readers' status also seem to influence the way different groups of people perceive a literary text: Squires (2020) discusses the importance of reviews and reviewers in shaping the book circulation and reading practices, while the increasing availability and popularity of social reading platforms allows for the creation of like-tasted reader groups in a way that has not been possible before (Rebora et al., 2021).

3. Between ground truths and relativism: mild perspectivism?

If quality is absolute, why do readers disagree on the quality of a text? Even an individual reader can change their own idea on the literary value of a text over time. If quality is entirely idiosyncratic, how come there are texts that survive the most drastic historical and cultural changes with an almost unfaltering status? *The Aeneid* remained appreciated as a canonical masterpiece in western Europe from the Roman Empire down to modern times.

A similar question has been discussed in other so-called "subjective annotation" tasks in computational linguistics and machine learning (Davani et al., 2022): the attempt at attaining one single meaningful value in similar contests risks to back-fire, creating an artificial representation of the phenomenon one is trying to model. Some researchers have advocated for a new paradigm, "perspectivism" (Basile et al., 2021), to deal with similar problems by considering a plurality of different points of view on the same data, either by building an average from several individual values (weak perspectivism) or attempting to maintain the inter-annotator differences in the dataset and try to model their diversity (strong perspectivsm) (Checco et al., 2017; Cabitza et al., 2020; Akhtar et al., 2020).

When it comes to literary quality, applying either an non-perspectivist approach (such as having one ground truth or a gold standard), or a strong perspectivist approach gives rise to difficulties, and there seem to be apparent limitations to both approaches when brought to their ultimate consequences.

A non-perspectivist approach suggests assessing the appreciation of literary quality through a single gold standard. Such a gold standard can be approximated by aggregating perspectives of different readers in one value (a rating score, the number of copies sold, an average review sentiment, etc.). A weak perspectivist approach is probably ingrained in any such attempt at modelling and evaluating literary quality: even the works that have tried to reduce it to a single number have relied on majority votes from several readers (average ratings from a crowdsourced annotation task; the number of copies sold; the number of ratings; presence in one or more canons; and so forth). Most literary awards are assigned by a committee composed of several individuals, so even when relying on such institutions to define literary quality, a text's value is approximated by collecting and averaging over several points of view. This form of weak perspectivism essentially treats literary quality as an objective measure to be approximated through many individual measurements (Basile et al., 2021). Taking many imperfect measures of the length of a table will bring us closer to its exact length; taking many personal assessments of the quality of a text will bring us closer to its real value. This take on the stance can help us clarify whether, despite the subjective nature of the task, a common ground of convergence does exist on the topic.

Naturally, this approach is at odds with a subjective view of quality assessment and aesthetic deliberation, and reducing a variety of individual opinions to one score is very helpful in some studies, but is bound to leave out important variation.

The opposite approach is to apply a strong perspectivist angle and to keep all of the different appreciations of a book in their diversity, without trying to reduce them to an average. If we believe in the irreducibility of readers' preferences to a meaningful average, and if the perception of literary quality is entirely idiosyncratic, it makes sense to model each reader independently. However, considering each reader's appreciation as an irreducible perspective to keep independent from the others risks confusing, or at best diluting, the very scope of this kind of research: finding out whether, *beyond individual variations*, there can be features that define something like an underlying, universally perceived quality in a text.

A third approach is to take a middle way between the two extremes. This will be outlined in the following section.

4. Looking at readers' classes

Instead of relying on either one gold standard or treating all reader perspectives independently, one possibility is to model readers in different classes and have a majority approach for each class. In the study of canonization and literary fame, some differences between readers have been discussed: for example, readers' gender and ethnicity have been posited as playing important roles in the perception of texts (Keen, 2013), and the challenges minorities might face to enter mainstream literature (Berkers et al., 2014).

Another relevant difference is to be found between lay-readers and professional critics. In the debate, the former are often highlighted as inclined to be fooled by cheap reads, and the latter as incline to inaccessible literature. But even between the 'critics' and 'laymen', we can disentangle important subgroups: an occasional Goodreads user and the maintainer of a book blog are both not literary critics in the most canonical sense, but the latter is probably more dedicated to the art of reading and reviewing than the former. A professional literary critic who writes for a local newspaper and one who writes for a specialized niche magazine might belong to two quite distinct categories in terms of sensibility and severity. There are middle ground identities as well: the work by De Greve and Martens (2021) studies the emerging role of social media and argues that 'lay critics' also act as cultural transmitters, challenging the traditional gatekeepers role of professional critics (Greve and Martens, 2021). These differences neither mean that one of these groups' judgment is more correct than another nor that there is no variation or outliers within these groups – but they indicate classes of what we call sensitivity convergence that are likely to display a higher degree of inner agreement than outer.

Hence, with the sensitivity toward groupings of different readers, the approach of aggregating reader perspectives can be applied in a more fine-grained manner.

Dataset overview	
Nr of reviews	57 369
Male reviewer	18 958
Female reviewer	28 984
Unknown	9 427
Nr of different titles	14 647
Male author	8 056
Female author	6 591
Nr of reviews by media type	
Newspapers	22 131
Blogs	16 791
Online media	10 635
Blog-like websites	3 456
Regional newspapers	2 622
Weekly magazines	1 566
Professional magazines	168

Table 1: An overview of the dataset presented in this paper. The category Online media includes (literary) sites that fall between online newspapers and personal blogs.

Instead of relying on *one* gold standard for an overall literary appreciation, we suggest letting the aggregation and statistical means depend on these reader classes, allowing for multiple points of view. It has been argued that computational methods allow for capturing readers' preferences (Walsh and Antoniak, 2021), what we will next discuss from a Danish perspective.

5. Exploring the classes of Danish readers

As a preliminary study in this direction, we have analysed a large dataset of book reviews published in Danish media, such as newspapers and blogs, from 2010 to 2021. [2]. The composition of the dataset is presented in Table 1. The grades of the reviews are fitted to a shared 6-point scale through a linear transformation. In addition, the dataset contains metadata of the publications, such as publisher house, year of publication, etc.

This dataset is unprecedented in terms of dimension, annotation quality, and diachronic extension for the contemporary Danish scene over several platforms, and offers a unique viewpoint to determine in which classes readers - at least those readers who write reviews - most clearly tend to cluster. Since newspapers, blogs, and other online media are the dominant platforms in the dataset, we focus on these to gain a more informed insight into reading preferences within

[2]The dataset is retrieved from the web page bog.nu, a platform that collects book reviews published in Danish media. Reviews without a numeric rating were attributed a rating by the site administrator. We see the same trends in the data with the ratings retrieved from the original reviews ($> 75\%$) as in the data relying on the estimated rating.

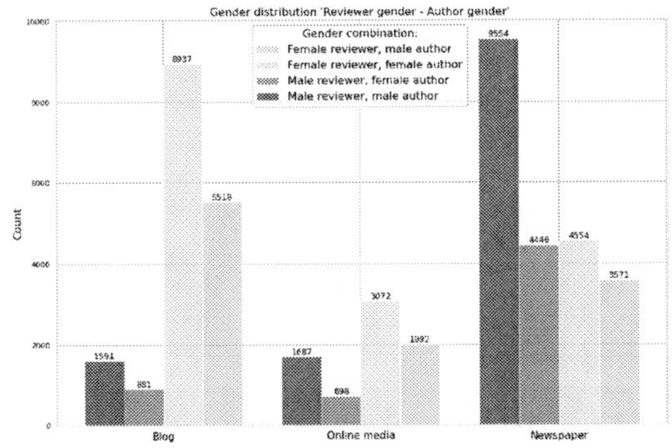

Figure 1: A histogram of the number of reviews shows that male and female reviewers are not equally distributed among the different media types. Blogs and blog-like websites are added together and so are newspaper and regional newspapers.

these media types. Figure 1 shows the gender distribution across three media types - newspaper reviews, online literary reviews and personal blogs - and we see a sharp distinction of reviewer's gender as well as author's gender: male reviewers are more likely to review male authors in newspapers whereas the blogosphere is dominated by female reviewers reviewing female authors.

In this analysis, we are working with a binary understanding of gender and have used a gendered name list to retrieve the gender feature [3]. This method is not an ideal way of approaching gender variables, and we are aware of the problems with this method and how it rules out other gender identities (Dev et al., 2021). However, we find it useful to apply this method in this preliminary study.

Between newspapers and blogs, we can furthermore show a difference in grading. The grades given in newspapers are significantly lower, with an average of 4.1/6, compared to those given in blogs which have an average of 4.5/6. This indicates a difference in review culture, which may be due to blogs being a medium where the emphasis is placed on positive experiences, rather than being professional critics that do not choose the reviewed works according to their preferences. In addition, the social nature of blogs makes it a place to discuss leisure readings with like-minded readers, whereas newspaper reviews tend to be more one-directional. These divided reader profiles also support our argument for modeling reader appreciation in subclasses instead of working with one single gold standard that would apply to all readers.

Figure 2 shows the polarization of the book reviewing scene in Denmark. The ratios on the axes show how books are read between the two genders and across the

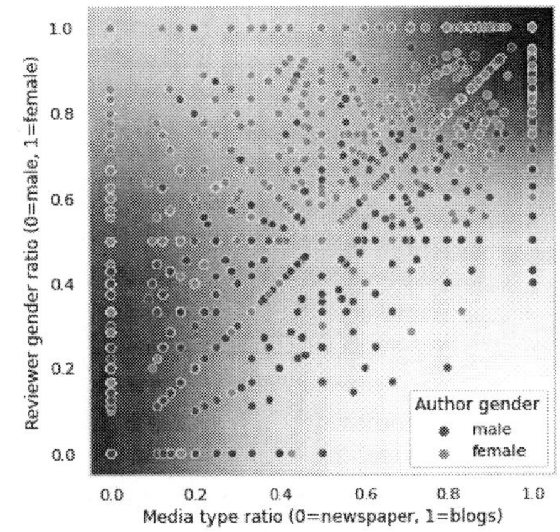

Figure 2: A scatter plot of books reviewed at least 5 times, showing the relative proportion of blog (1) and newspaper (0) reviews on the x axis plotted against the relative proportion of reviewer gender (0 = male, 1 = female) for each title, colored by author gender. As many of the points overlap, the heatmap in the background illustrates where the highest density areas fall.

two media types, the middle point (0.5,0.5) corresponding to works reviewed equally by both genders and on both media platforms. Only titles with five or more reviews were included in this analysis. The heatmap indicates that most titles fall near the two extremes: men seem to dominate the newspaper venues, and the dominance of women in the blogosphere is even stronger. Moreover, the coloring of the plot by author gender reveals that the polarization applies to author gender, too. Along the y axis, we see a clear split at 0.5, showing that books read mostly by female reviewers are also mostly written by female authors, and vice versa. These observations imply that female and male readers read different books, and each groups seems to prefer books written by their own gender.

To obtain a deeper understanding of this polarization, we examined which books had received the highest ratings in each category. When looking at books reviewed by both genders and on both media platforms, the titles that received the best average rating fell in diverse categories. This overarching top includes, among others, Nordic classics, Stoner by John William[4], more modern international bestsellers such as The Goldfinch by Donna Tartt and a graphic novel by Karoline Stjernfelt.

The titles rated the highest by either gender, shows another division: men preferred more canonical books - Herman Melville, Roberto Bolaño, and Victor Hugo being in the top 5 - whereas women preferred reading genre literature, their top-rated books including romance, crime/thriller, and fantasy novels. A similar

[3]We have used the API genderize.io that gives the probability of a name being either male or female, based on a dataset of 250.000 names

[4]Stoner was translated into Danish in 2014, which might explain its sudden occurrence in the dataset.

division was found between the best-rated books in newspaper and blog reviews, although blog reviews were even more dominated by romance books compared to the books most appreciated by female reviewers overall. These observations imply that newspapers, a more established venue dominated by men, focus on canonical works, whereas the constantly evolving blogosphere, dominated by women, seems to seek more leisurable or genre-specific reading.

From these early results it seems that the motivation behind reading, reader status and the gender distribution of authors and readers are valid candidate classes to cluster individual literary perspectives. Thus, as a mild perspectivist approach, we propose taking the degree of professional expertise and the effect of gender into account when assessing literary quality.

6. Discussion

In this article, we have addressed the question of how perspectivist we should be in measuring literary quality. While it has become clear that one literary canon or one gold standard based on e.g., sales numbers cannot capture the variety of aspects readers appreciate in literature, the relevance of a traditional literary canon is reflected in our observations; some works seem to have reached a status that cannot be ignored. However, this literary canon is not a ground truth for quality, and non-canonical popular works might have other features that make them beloved by readers.

Therefore, the problem of literary quality can - and should - be explored from different angles within the same project. Applying strong perspectivism in the future can still be a relevant and viable option to contrast the classes we have divided the Danish readers into.

Furthermore, the division proposed here is not perfect. The division of gender was binary, excluding other gender identities from the current analysis, that need to be considered in the future. Similarly, the contrast of professional and amateur readers is not as absolute as the division into two categories here might suggest. Indeed, some bloggers can be seen as tastemakers that have gained what Driscoll (2019) calls 'readerly capital', and form a lively environments for readers to interact, contributing to a diverse literary space (Driscoll, 2019; Rebora et al., 2021).

In light of the investigated review venues, we can only infer what readers voluntarily reveal about their literary preferences, while they also might have hidden preferences not shown in this data. That could be approximated through a different kind of dataset, such as library loans. With the current method, we are still not capturing all types of readers. Nevertheless, the current findings support the claim that it is not trivial what kind of reader profiles we consider and value when studying literary quality.

7. Conclusion and Future Works

Literary quality is a complex topic, and it remains a challenge for both strong and weak perspectivist stances. In this paper we have tried to consider the pros and cons of both approaches and what adopting them implies. We have, then, suggested a middle way between the two extremes, by dividing readers into meaningful classes that would represent different perspectives on the same text, without holding each individual rating as a independent judgment. Through the analysis of over 57.000 book reviews in Danish media we have shown that some features of the reviewers – especially gender and whether they write for a blog or a newspaper – appear to significantly predict a shift in the assessment of a text, and thus allow for a meaningful clustering of readers into perspective classes.

Naturally, we have much left to do to further explore the relevance of this approach for literary quality modeling. In future we intend to use the existing classes as labels for quality prediction to see whether they can yield a more informative picture of the judgments a literary text is likely to elicit. We would also like to look for subtler differences between the reviewers and compare these findings with other existing resources for literary quality. Another important question we would like to address in the future is whether and when a preference becomes a bias: for example, in what situations controlling for gender preferences should be used to "correct" a system's output rather than just inform it.

Overall, the complexity of the problem and its midway status between objectivity and subjectivity remains a topic for debate both within and beyond computational linguistics, and leaves large room for future developments.

8. References

Akhtar, S., Basile, V., and Patti, V. (2020). Modeling annotator perspective and polarized opinions to improve hate speech detection. In *Proceedings of the AAAI Conference on Human Computation and Crowdsourcing*, volume 8, pages 151–154.

Archer, J. and Jockers, M. L. (2016). *The bestseller code: Anatomy of the blockbuster novel.* St. Martin's Press.

Ashok, V. G., Feng, S., and Choi, Y. (2013). Success with style: Using writing style to predict the success of novels. In *Proceedings of the 2013 conference on empirical methods in natural language processing*, pages 1753–1764.

Basile, V., Cabitza, F., Campagner, A., and Fell, M. (2021). Toward a perspectivist turn in ground truthing for predictive computing. *Conference of the Italian Chapter of the Association for Intelligent Systems (ItAIS 2021).*

Berkers, P., Janssen, S., and Verboord, M. (2014). Assimilation into the literary mainstream? the classification of ethnic minority authors in newspaper reviews in the united states, the netherlands and germany. *Cultural Sociology*, 8(1):25–44.

Bizzoni, Y., Peura, T., Thomsen, M. R., and Nielbo,

K. (2021). Sentiment dynamics of success: Fractal scaling of story arcs predicts reader preferences.

Bloom, H. (2014). *The western canon: The books and school of the ages*. Houghton Mifflin Harcourt.

Cabitza, F., Campagner, A., and Sconfienza, L. M. (2020). As if sand were stone. new concepts and metrics to probe the ground on which to build trustable ai. *BMC Medical Informatics and Decision Making*, 20(1):1–21.

Checco, A., Roitero, K., Maddalena, E., Mizzaro, S., and Demartini, G. (2017). Let's agree to disagree: Fixing agreement measures for crowdsourcing. In *Fifth AAAI Conference on Human Computation and Crowdsourcing*.

Davani, A. M., Díaz, M., and Prabhakaran, V. (2022). Dealing with disagreements: Looking beyond the majority vote in subjective annotations. *Transactions of the Association for Computational Linguistics*, 10:92–110.

Dev, S., Monajatipoor, M., Ovalle, A., Subramonian, A., Phillips, J. M., and Chang, K. (2021). Harms of gender exclusivity and challenges in non-binary representation in language technologies. *CoRR*, abs/2108.12084.

Driscoll, E. (2019). Book blogs as tastemakers. *Participations. Journal of Audience & Reception Studies*, 16:280–305.

Ferrer, C. (2013). Canonical values vs. the law of large numbers: The canadian literary canon in the age of big data. *Rupkatha Journal on Interdisciplinary Studies in Humanities*, 5(3):81–90.

Greve, L. D. and Martens, G., (2021). *The Audience (Dis)Agrees: Studying the Impact of Award-Winning Books on Lay Literary Value Judgements Using Social Media Data*, volume 9, pages 85–130. Barkhuis.

Guillory, J. (2013). *Cultural Capital: The Problem of Literary Canon Formation*. University of Chicago Press.

Herrmann, J. B., Jacobs, A. M., and Piper, A. (2021). Computational stylistics. *Handbook of Empirical Literary Studies*, page 451.

Hu, Q., Liu, B., Thomsen, M. R., Gao, J., and Nielbo, K. L. (2021). Dynamic evolution of sentiments in never let me go: Insights from multifractal theory and its implications for literary analysis. *Digital Scholarship in the Humanities*, 36(2):322–332.

Keen, S. (2013). Empathy in reading. *Anglistik*, 24(2).

Maharjan, S., Kar, S., Montes, M., González, F. A., and Solorio, T. (2018). Letting emotions flow: Success prediction by modeling the flow of emotions in books. In *Proceedings of the 2018 Conference of the North American Chapter of the Association for Computational Linguistics: Human Language Technologies, Volume 2 (Short Papers)*, pages 259–265, New Orleans, Louisiana, June. Association for Computational Linguistics.

Plank, B., Hovy, D., and Søgaard, A. (2014). Linguistically debatable or just plain wrong? In *Proceedings of the 52nd Annual Meeting of the Association for Computational Linguistics (Volume 2: Short Papers)*, pages 507–511.

Porter, J. D. (2018). *Popularity/Prestige*. Literary Lab.

Rebora, S., Boot, P., Pianzola, F., Gasser, B., Herrmann, J. B., Kraxenberger, M., Kuijpers, M. M., Lauer, G., Lendvai, P., Messerli, T. C., and Sorrentino, P. (2021). Digital humanities and digital social reading. *Digital Scholarship in the Humanities*, 36(Supplement 2):230–250, 11.

Squires, C., (2020). *The Review and the Reviewer*, pages 117–132. Routledge. Num Pages: 16.

Thelwall, M. (2019). Reader and author gender and genre in goodreads. *Journal of Librarianship and Information Science*, 51(2):403–430.

Touileb, S., Øvrelid, L., and Velldal, E. (2020). Gender and sentiment, critics and authors: a dataset of Norwegian book reviews. In *Proceedings of the Second Workshop on Gender Bias in Natural Language Processing*, pages 125–138, Barcelona, Spain (Online), December. Association for Computational Linguistics.

Underwood, T. and Sellers, J. (2016). The longue durée of literary prestige. *Modern Language Quarterly*, 77(3):321–344.

van Cranenburgh, A. and Koolen, C. (2020). Results of a single blind literary taste test with short anonymized novel fragments. *arXiv preprint arXiv:2011.01624*.

van Cranenburgh, A., van Dalen-Oskam, K., and van Zundert, J. (2019). Vector space explorations of literary language. *Language Resources and Evaluation*, 53(4):625–650.

Walsh, M. and Antoniak, M. (2021). The goodreads 'classics': A computational study of readers, amazon, and crowdsourced amateur criticism. *Journal of Cultural Analytics*, 4:243–287.

Wang, X., Yucesoy, B., Varol, O., Eliassi-Rad, T., and Barabási, A.-L. (2019). Success in books: predicting book sales before publication. *EPJ Data Science*, 8(1):1–20.

Proceedings of the 1st Workshop on Perspectivist Approaches to NLP @LREC2022, pages 26–31
Marseille, 20 June 2022

Bias Discovery Within Human Raters: A Case Study of the Jigsaw Dataset

Marta Marchiori Manerba, Riccardo Guidotti, Lucia Passaro, Salvatore Ruggieri
University of Pisa
{marta.marchiori@phd., riccardo.guidotti@, lucia.passaro@, salvatore.ruggieri@}unipi.it

Abstract

Understanding and quantifying the bias introduced by human annotation of data is a crucial problem for trustworthy supervised learning. Recently, a perspectivist trend has emerged in the NLP community, focusing on the inadequacy of previous aggregation schemes, which suppose the existence of a single ground truth. This assumption is particularly problematic for sensitive tasks involving subjective human judgments, such as toxicity detection. To address these issues, we propose a preliminary approach for bias discovery within human raters by exploring individual ratings for specific sensitive topics annotated in the texts. Our analysis's object focuses on the Jigsaw dataset, a collection of comments aiming at challenging online toxicity identification.

Keywords: NLP Perspectivism, Human Raters, Individual Annotations, Fairness, Bias, Toxicity Detection

1. Introduction

At every stage of a supervised learning process, biases can arise and be introduced in the pipeline, ultimately leading to possible harm (Suresh and Guttag, 2019; Dixon et al., 2018). The role of the datasets used to train these supervised models is crucial, as they may reinforce such biases and propagate them. There might be multiple reasons why a dataset is biased, e.g., due to skewed sampling strategies or to the prevalence of a particular demographic group disproportionately associated with a class outcome (Ntoutsi et al., 2020), ultimately establishing conditions of privilege and discrimination. (Sap et al., 2019; Davidson et al., 2019; Ball-Burack et al., 2021), for example, show that annotators tend to label as toxic messages in Afro-American English more frequently than when annotating other messages, which could lead to the training of a system reproducing the same kind of racial dialect bias. The phenomenon's complexity is not limited to algorithms but is deeply rooted and bound in historical, cultural, and social perceptions. Therefore, it is very relevant to investigate the impact of annotators' social and cultural backgrounds on the produced labelled data. It is clear that when the labelling is performed on subjective tasks, such as the online toxicity detection, it becomes even more relevant to explore agreement reports and preserve individual and divergent opinions. Having access to the disaggregated data annotations and being aware of the dataset's intended use can inform both models' outcome assessment and comprehension, including facilitating bias detection (Suresh and Guttag, 2019).

Given these evident socio-technical challenges, significant trust problems emerge, mainly regarding the robustness and quality of datasets and the related trustworthiness of models trained on these collections and their automated decisions. Recently, a perspectivist trend has emerged in the NLP community, focusing on datasets collecting human judgments, especially for sensitive tasks involving subjective decisions such as toxicity detection. The main issue concerns the inadequacy of previous aggregation schemes, which assume the existence of a single ground truth and reduce the final label through the standard approaches of disagreement resolution, primarily through majority voting. (Basile, 2020) propose a new paradigm to maintain multiple perspectives naturally arising from raters having different cultural backgrounds. The authors pursue the goal of granting significance to divergent opinions, equally important and correct, according to individual sensitivities. They stress the importance of publishing disaggregated dataset versions and the positive impact of these collections for developing more inclusive yet accurate, fairness-aware measures and automated decisions. (Röttger et al., 2021) critically discuss two annotation approaches: the descriptive-perspectivist paradigm versus the prescriptive-reductionist one. Among other recommendations, the authors suggest that dataset collectors should intentionally choose and pursue one of the two paradigms according to the intended usage for that particular collection.

In line with the perspectivist approach, this work aims to value disagreement and investigate a different way to weight annotations. Specifically, we propose a preliminary approach for bias discovery within human raters[1] by exploring individual ratings for specific sensitive topics annotated in the texts. Although investigating biases within human annotators was already explored in (Sap et al., 2019; Davidson et al., 2019; Ball-Burack

[1] In this contribution, we use the terms *rater* and *annotator* interchangeably.

et al., 2021; Sap et al., 2021), our proposed method, compared to these previous works, is not limited to a single bias ground (e.g., race or gender). Indeed, thanks to the nature of the dataset under examination, the sensitive identities taken into account are more diverse, embracing, for example, sexual orientations, disabilities, religions, etc. Finally, to preserve the role of different perspectives, as performed in the work of (Wich et al., 2020), our assessment focuses on the disaggregated dataset, hence on individual annotations, and not only on the harmonized ground truth. Our analysis focuses on the Jigsaw dataset (Jigsaw, 2018), a collection of comments aiming at challenging online toxicity identification. The dataset is manually annotated to investigate unintended model bias for a broad spectrum of sensitive demographic identities.

Starting from the description of the Jigsaw dataset in Section 2, we report in Section 3 the fairness approach adopted and the preliminary analysis results in Section 4. Finally, in Section 5, we present the takeaways.

2. Dataset Description

This section briefly describes the object of our analysis, i.e., the *Jigsaw Unintended Bias in Toxicity Classification*[2] dataset, published within a Kaggle competition[3] which took place in 2018 (Jigsaw, 2018). Aiming to explore unintended model bias through a broad spectrum of online dialogues, the dataset collects contents from the *Civil Comments* platform that allowed to start conversations and post comments on news sites. Curated by Jigsaw[4], a Google unit dealing with disinformation, toxicity, censorship, and extremisms, the collection gathers posts ranging from 2015 to 2017 annotated by a degree of toxicity by human raters through the crowd rating platform *Figure Eight*.[5] The structure of the dataset, including its cascade annotation, allows for sheding some light on the impact of the sociocultural characteristics of the raters, especially when dealing with sensitive tasks involving subjective decisions such as toxicity detection.

Annotation Process and Labeling Schema. Comments in the dataset were annotated to identify toxicity. Specifically, by toxicity, the curators mean extremely rude, offensive, humiliating, or/and harmful content. The dataset presents several levels of annotation, which we will describe in detail in the next paragraphs. The toxicity is registered across a range of other labels: VERY TOXIC, TOXIC, HARD TO SAY and NOT TOXIC. A comment is considered toxic if the toxicity value assigned by the aggregations of individual raters annotations is greater than or equal to 0.5. Toxic comments were further labelled with the type of abusiveness: TOXICITY, SEVERE TOXICITY, OBSCENE, THREAT, INSULT, IDENTITY ATTACK, SEXUAL EXPLICIT. The dataset was divided by the curators in training $(1,804,874)$, public $(97,320)$ and private test $(97,320)$ sets, for a total of $1,999,514$ instances. To enclose several different perspectives, every comment was annotated by up to 10 raters[6] since the dataset creators acknowledged the subjectivity of the task. Interestingly, some comments were annotated by more than 10 raters, up to even thousands.[7] For a subset of the dataset, annotators were also asked to indicate whether the text mentioned demographic identities, such as specific races or genders. To ensure that the comments in the subset had identity mentions, data were filtered as follows. The curators started with a random sample of around $250,000$ comments. Then, through model predictions and word matching, they found approximately other $250,000$ instances, which most likely contained references to the sensitive identities within the texts. The collection resulting from the union of the two subsets, was then manually labeled by the raters. Identities appearing in more than 500 comments were found relevant, including: *male, female, homosexual (gay or lesbian), christian, jewish, muslim, black, white, psychiatric or mental illness*. Others were detected but occurred less frequently. In addition to the aggregated dataset, the curators also published two additional sheets useful to investigate raters' behaviour (Table 1). The first sheet reports the individual raters annotations of the sensitive identities for a total of $2,597,365$ annotations, collected for $405,159$ unique comments labeled by $4,592$ different raters. The second sheet collects the judgments related to the toxicity degrees, amounting to $15,855,266$ individual annotations for $1,804,874$ unique comments, i.e., the aggregated training set size, labeled by $8,899$ different raters. Both sheets thus contain comments repeated as many times as different annotators were asked to label them (this is why these tables are larger than the dataset for model training).

	Identities	**Toxicity**
Comments	405,159	1,804,874
Raters	4,592	8,899

Table 1: Comments and raters for the individual annotations regarding *(i)* sensitive identities and *(ii)* degrees of toxicity, respectively.

Disaggregated Data. We explore the impact of raters' bias by analysing the dataset of individual judgements related to toxicity. As reported above, the dataset consists of $15,855,266$ individual annotations, often reporting the same, repeated comments labeled by different raters. Specifically, it has $1,804,874$ unique comments, i.e., the aggregated training set size,

[2]Jigsaw Unintended Bias in Toxicity Classification.

[3]Competition overview.

[4]Jigsaw.

[5]The platform was acquired by Appen.

[6]The attributes gathering this information are "toxicity annotator count" and "identity annotator count".

[7]They motivate this choice with very vague reasons: *"due to sampling and strategies used to enforce rater accuracy"*.

labeled by $8,899$ different raters. We add the "target annotator" column. This new attribute has a binary label indicating whether the annotator considered the comment toxic. This information is derived from the individual annotations that collect toxicity grades: specifically, if at least one of the judgments is affirmative, the comment is considered toxic by some annotator. Notably, the value of this attribute may differ from the assigned label in the released training dataset. We also retrieve from the training dataset other important and informative columns, including "target" and all columns reporting the sensitive identities. Henceforth, when we reference the dataset, we address this disaggregated version.

3. Raters Bias Discovery

This section describes the metrics we adopt to detect biases of human raters and the fairness assessment approach we propose.

3.1. Fairness Metrics

To detect potential biases in individual raters, we choose to adopt the *Bias AUCs* evaluation metrics proposed by (Borkan et al., 2019).[8] They are defined as the ROC-AUC computed over specific subsets of the data. The use of these metrics within the competition and the work proposing them (Borkan et al., 2019) focuses on assessing unintended biases of models on the test set. Since our aim is to determine if they can also capture bias in humans, we want to propose their application in a new context, different from the purposes for which they were originally developed. Exploring the comments for which multiple annotations are available in the training dataset, we intend to use the label of the aggregated dataset version as ground truth and the judgment of the individual rater as prediction, thus discovering and evaluating biases within human raters annotations. To compute the ROC-AUC, we sorted the data according to a comment toxicity score, ranging from 0 to 1. Such as score is derived from the individual rater's annotations and computed as the number of toxicities identified (i.e. labelled with 1 by the rater), divided by the number of toxicity types (i.e. 7). According to (Borkan et al., 2019), we formalize the following metrics:

Definition 1 (Bias AUCs) *We define the Bias AUCs measures as:*

$$\begin{aligned} Sub_s &= \mathrm{AUC}\left(D_s^- + D_s^+\right) \\ BPSN_s &= \mathrm{AUC}\left(D^+ + D_s^-\right) \\ BNSP_s &= \mathrm{AUC}\left(D^- + D_s^+\right) \end{aligned}$$

where s is a subgroup, D^+ are the toxic comments, D^- the non-toxic comments, D_s^+ the toxic comments in the identity subgroup, and D_s^- the non-toxic comments in the identity subgroup.

[8]The Kaggle competition proposed the same metrics.

We specify that in the formulas the $+$ symbol operates a concatenation between different subsets of the dataset. The three metrics are calculated separately on these subsets for each sensitive identity. More in detail, in our setting, *Subgroup AUC* (Sub_s) is calculated for toxic and non toxic comments that contain the sensitive identity s. A low score indicates that the annotator deviates from the ground truth of the dataset by differently identifying toxic and non-toxic comments containing that identity. *BPSN (Background Positive, Subgroup Negative) AUC* (BPSN_s) instead is computed for non-toxic comments that contain the sensitive identity s and toxic comments that do not contain it. A low score means that the annotator exchanges non-toxic comments containing the identity for toxic ones that do not (consistently with the ground truth of the dataset). Finally, *BNSP (Background Negative, Subgroup Positive) AUC* (BNSP_s) is calculated for toxic comments that contain the sensitive identity s and non-toxic comments that do not contain it. Obtaining a low score means that the annotator exchanges toxic comments mentioning the identity for non-toxic ones that do not (always according to the ground truth of the dataset).
Since our goal is to analyze the annotators w.r.t. the metrics above, we decided to average them by defining the Average Bias AUC that aggregates the individual *Bias AUCs* scores.

Definition 2 (Average Bias AUC) *We define the Average Bias AUC as*

$$Avg\ Bias\ AUC_s = \frac{Sub_s + BPSN_s + BNSP_s}{3}$$

The intuition is that, given a certain sensitive identity s, we will have a high Avg Bias AUC if the rater is not biased w.r.t. a certain background or subgroup; we will have a low value on the other hand.

3.2. Methodology

This section illustrates the process followed to perform the raters' bias assessment. We applied this methodology for the Jigsaw dataset but it can be easily replicated on other datasets having disaggregated annotations.
To assess biases, we followed the definitions reported in Section 3.1, computing the three metrics, i.e., *Subgroup AUC, BPSN* and *BNSP*. We recall that each measure is computed on different data subsets and for each identity subgroup present in the comments annotated by each rater. Regarding the identities detected in the comments, we adopt the ground truth of the aggregated training dataset because the focus of this analysis is on variation in toxicity judgment. Further investigations on disagreement concerning individual identity annotations will be conducted as future work. As ground truth for the toxicity, we binarize the target score from the aggregated training set. Concerning the predictions, we deploy the individual toxicity judgment of each annotator, as explained in the previous Section 2. After

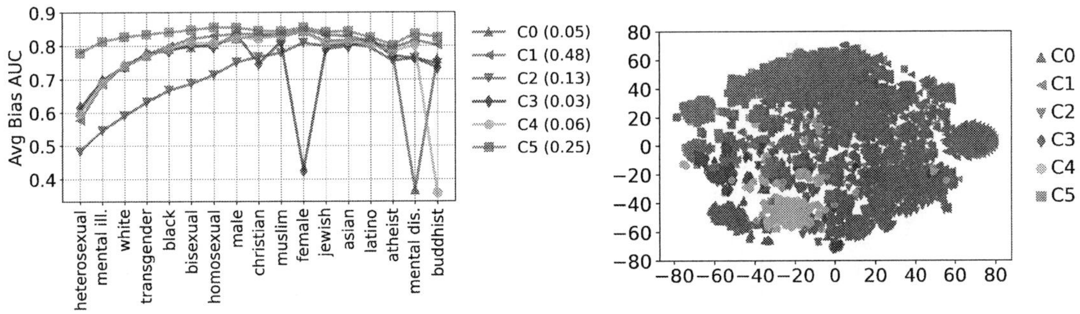

Figure 1: Left: Avg Bias AUC for each cluster centroid (between brackets, the population percentage). Right: t-SNE visualization of clusters in two dimensions.

that, we aggregate the three metrics according to Definition 2, resulting in a score for each rater for each sensitive identity.

To identify recurrent and recognizable groups of raters achieving similar identity scores, we then apply the KMeans clustering algorithm (Macqueen, 1967). We choose the k value for the number of clusters by evaluating the SSE score curve observed varying k. We adopt KMeans since we conduct a preliminary analysis, but more advanced clustering techniques could be used as alternatives. Finally, to visualize the clusters, we adopt the t-distributed Stochastic Neighbor Embedding (t-SNE) visualization (Van der Maaten and Hinton, 2008).

4. Preliminary Results and Discussion

This section reports the results of the preliminary analysis conducted.[9] As a first step, we focus on evaluating only raters who annotated at least 10 comments, aiming at finding as many identities in the texts as feasible. Thus, starting from the dataset containing $15,855,266$ annotations generated by $8,899$ raters, we filter for $15,847,581$ annotations for a total of $8,034$ raters.

Following the stages defined in the previous section, we calculate the metrics for all the 24 identities available. We then remove the values *other gender, other sexual orientation, other religion, other race or ethnicity, other disability*. Finally, we only keep the identities for which the missing values are lower than 30%, resulting in 17 residual identities. For the remaining identities, we fill the missing values with the average values of each identity.[10] We then apply the KMeans algorithm (Macqueen, 1967) on the data frame resulting from the process, i.e., having as columns the sensitive identities and as rows the annotators. The value of each cell is derived from the aggregated metrics as given in Definition 2. We identify 6 clusters, i.e., 6 different trends in annotators' rating behaviour. We test k in a range from 2 to 100, finding that for $k = 6$ the SSE does not decrease significantly. We report in Figure 1 the Avg Bias AUC for each of the cluster centroids, along side the percentage of the population size of each group. A cluster centroid is the most representative point of a group. Technically, it is calculated by averaging the identities of the *Avg Bias AUC* scores within that cluster. If an identity obtains a low value for this aggregated metric the cluster of annotators demonstrate a biased behaviour.

Generally, we recognize the utility of clustering annotators and display the metric calculated for subgroups. In fact, this setting contributes to the identification of critical disparities in accuracy that may be symptomatic of bias, demonstrated by a propensity to assign toxicity judgments in conjunction with particular identities.Noting the percentage of clusters population as a first aspect, we observe that the most populated are in order `clusters 1, 5,` and 2 (respectively of $0.48, 0.25$ and 0.13 percent). The remaining clusters have a population between 0.06 and 0.03 percent. `Cluster 5` proves to be the best for all identities w.r.t. the *Avg Bias AUC* scores obtained. For *heterosexual*, there is a disparity for the Avg Bias AUC metric between 0.2 and 0.3 points compared to the other clusters. Almost all clusters show an increasing trend for the central identities in the chart. It is interesting to focus on `clusters 0, 3` and 4, whose performance is good, tending to approach `cluster 1`, the best after `5`. Differently from the other clusters, `0, 3` and 4 register a significant drop for the *mental disability, female* and *buddhist* identities, respectively. These results highlight that groups of annotators register a divergent rating behaviour for specific identities, demonstrating a different sensibility w.r.t. the ground truth. The line that shows poor agreement for all identities, i.e., that deviates towards low levels on average, is with reference to `cluster 2`. This cluster represents the 0.13 percent of the annotators, i.e., $1,044$ on a total of $8,034$.

In Figure 1, we report the t-SNE visualization (Van der

[9] https://github.com/MartaMarchiori/Bias-Discovery-In-Human-Raters.

[10] We also tried replacing the missing values with the maximum and minimum values, and the results did not change. Thus, the replacement of the missing values is not affected by choice of this aggregation function.

Maaten and Hinton, 2008) in two dimensions. The plot highlights similar aspects of the previous one. Clusters achieving low scores for some identities are located in the lower-left area of the visualisation and have a rounded compact shape. In fact, `clusters 0, 3` and `4`, that differ a lot for some identities, create aggregations that depart from the central mass. `Cluster 5`, characterised by the highest scores, is located at the top and has an elongated shape, which implies a larger variability within it. The most populated cluster, i.e., `cluster 1`, is relatively scattered.

More individual annotations and comments dealing with sensitive topics would be needed for each rater to allow for a more appropriate assessment. However, we acknowledge the difficulty in real datasets to collect and organize this kind of data balancing minorities' frequency. More precisely, the distributions reflect online discourse, both in terms of identity presence and their unequal division within abusive versus non-abusive samples.

5. Conclusion and Future Work

In this paper we have proposed a preliminary approach for bias discovery of human raters by exploring individual ratings for specific sensitive topics annotated in the texts. Our analysis's object consisted of the Jigsaw dataset, a collection of comments aiming at challenging online toxicity identification. We measured the biases of raters through the *Bias AUCs* metrics. By dividing the annotators' behaviour into clusters, we assessed disparate treatments that occurred for particular sensitive identities, such as specific religions or disabilities. Therefore, the main inference drawn concerns the different levels of agreements registered by the clusters of annotators w.r.t. the ground truth evaluated separately for each diverse sensitive identity. Most trends show close alignment and consistency, except for isolated entities by a few clusters.

A first validation of our method would be to compare the resulting annotators groups identified through our clustering approach with other unsupervised strategies for annotator community grouping and analysis, such as the one presented by (Wich et al., 2020). An interesting experimental extension would consists of applying the proposed methodology to other datasets concerning toxicity detection.[11] It would require explicit sensitive identities mentioned in the texts and the disaggregated versions of individual annotations. The variety of sensitive identities do not constitute a limitation. In fact, the analysis could retrieve meaningful insights even by comparing a few (one or more) identities, e.g., comments grouped for the target of the text, addressing for example females or males. Instead, different thresholds regarding the number of comments needed for each sensitive identity and the least amount of annotations for each rater should be tested and evaluated on a case-by-case basis, i.e., depending on the size of datasets.

In addition, adopting the perspectivist's view would certainly be a good practice to ask data collectors and organizers for disaggregated versions of other similar sensitive tasks, encouraging a more responsible documentation process. One dimension to be explored further is to analyze the content of comments for which the datasets have multiple conflicting annotations. It would be helpful to detect a potential correlation between a given topic and a strong rater's disagreement to qualify the content of the comments that triggered the most controversy among annotators. Furthermore, adopting metrics to identify biases that don't need ground truth could release the analysis from the assumption of the robustness of a gold standard. Finally, having obtained a measure of bias for each rater, a critical experiment would be to construct an alternative version of the dataset that aggregates the annotations differently. Specifically, the annotation of a rater with a high bias score would have less weight for that specific sensitive identity than the judgment of a rater with a lower bias. A comparison between a classifier trained on the original and the weighted data could be an indicative test, focusing the analysis on the unintended bias of the models according to the metrics introduced by (Borkan et al., 2019).

Acknowledgements. This research was partially supported by TAILOR, a project funded by EU Horizon 2020 research and innovation programme under GA No 952215. The contents reflects only the author's view and the Commission is not responsible for any use that may be made of the information it contains.

6. Bibliographical References

Ball-Burack, A., Lee, M. S. A., Cobbe, J., and Singh, J. (2021). Differential tweetment: Mitigating racial dialect bias in harmful tweet detection. In *Proceedings of the 2021 ACM Conference on Fairness, Accountability, and Transparency*, pages 116–128.

Basile, V. (2020). It's the end of the gold standard as we know it. on the impact of pre-aggregation on the evaluation of highly subjective tasks. In *2020 AIxIA Discussion Papers Workshop, AIxIA 2020 DP*, volume 2776, pages 31–40. CEUR-WS.

Borkan, D., Dixon, L., Sorensen, J., Thain, N., and Vasserman, L. (2019). Nuanced metrics for measuring unintended bias with real data for text classification. In Sihem Amer-Yahia, et al., editors, *Companion of The 2019 World Wide Web Conference, WWW 2019, San Francisco, CA, USA, May 13-17, 2019*, pages 491–500. ACM.

Davidson, T., Bhattacharya, D., and Weber, I. (2019). Racial bias in hate speech and abusive language detection datasets. *CoRR*, abs/1905.12516.

[11] Examples could be the dataset proposed by (Sap et al., 2020), called Social Bias Inference Corpus or other collections published within the Perspectivist Data Manifesto.

Dixon, L., Li, J., Sorensen, J., Thain, N., and Vasserman, L. (2018). Measuring and mitigating unintended bias in text classification. In *Proceedings of the 2018 AAAI/ACM Conference on AI, Ethics, and Society*, pages 67–73.

Macqueen, J. (1967). Some methods for classification and analysis of multivariate observations. In *In 5-th Berkeley Symposium on Mathematical Statistics and Probability*, pages 281–297.

Ntoutsi, E., Fafalios, P., Gadiraju, U., Iosifidis, V., Nejdl, W., Vidal, M., Ruggieri, S., Turini, F., Papadopoulos, S., Krasanakis, E., Kompatsiaris, I., Kinder-Kurlanda, K., Wagner, C., Karimi, F., Fernández, M., Alani, H., Berendt, B., Kruegel, T., Heinze, C., Broelemann, K., Kasneci, G., Tiropanis, T., and Staab, S. (2020). Bias in data-driven artificial intelligence systems - an introductory survey. *Wiley Interdisciplinary Reviews: Data Mining and Knowledge Discovery*, 10(3).

Röttger, P., Vidgen, B., Hovy, D., and Pierrehumbert, J. B. (2021). Two contrasting data annotation paradigms for subjective NLP tasks. *CoRR*, abs/2112.07475.

Sap, M., Card, D., Gabriel, S., Choi, Y., and Smith, N. A. (2019). The risk of racial bias in hate speech detection. In *Proceedings of the 57th Annual Meeting of the Association for Computational Linguistics*, pages 1668–1678.

Sap, M., Gabriel, S., Qin, L., Jurafsky, D., Smith, N. A., and Choi, Y. (2020). Social bias frames: Reasoning about social and power implications of language. In *Proceedings of the 58th Annual Meeting of the Association for Computational Linguistics*, pages 5477–5490.

Sap, M., Swayamdipta, S., Vianna, L., Zhou, X., Choi, Y., and Smith, N. A. (2021). Annotators with attitudes: How annotator beliefs and identities bias toxic language detection. *CoRR*, abs/2111.07997.

Suresh, H. and Guttag, J. V. (2019). A framework for understanding unintended consequences of machine learning. *CoRR*, abs/1901.10002.

Van der Maaten, L. and Hinton, G. (2008). Visualizing data using t-sne. *Journal of machine learning research*, 9(11).

Wich, M., Kuwatly, H. A., and Groh, G. (2020). Investigating annotator bias with a graph-based approach. In Seyi Akiwowo, et al., editors, *Proceedings of the Fourth Workshop on Online Abuse and Harms, WOAH 2020, Online, November 20, 2020*, pages 191–199. Association for Computational Linguistics.

7. Language Resource References

Jigsaw. (2018). *Jigsaw Unintended Bias in Toxicity Classification*. distributed via Kaggle.

Proceedings of the 1st Workshop on Perspectivist Approaches to NLP @LREC2022, pages 32–36
Marseille, 20 June 2022

The Viability of Best-worst Scaling and Categorical Data Label Annotation Tasks in Detecting Implicit Bias

Parker Glenn[1,2], Cassandra L. Jacobs[1,3], Marvin Thielk[1], and Yi Chu[1]
1: Workhuman Inc., 2: Brandeis University, 3: University at Buffalo

Abstract

Annotating workplace bias in text is a noisy and subjective task. In encoding the inherently continuous nature of bias, aggregated binary classifications do not suffice. Best-worst scaling (BWS) (Louviere and Woodworth, 1991) offers a framework to obtain real-valued scores through a series of comparative evaluations, but it may be impractical to deploy to traditional annotation pipelines within industry. We present analyses of a small-scale bias dataset, jointly annotated with categorical annotations and BWS annotations and show that there is a strong correlation between observed agreement and BWS score (Spearman's r=0.72). We identify several shortcomings of BWS relative to traditional categorical annotation: (1) When compared to categorical annotation, we estimate BWS takes approximately 4.5x longer to complete; (2) BWS does not scale well to large annotation tasks with sparse target phenomena; (3) The high correlation between BWS and the traditional task shows that the benefits of BWS can be recovered from a simple categorically annotated, non-aggregated dataset.

Keywords: categorical annotation, best-worst scaling, scalability

1. Introduction

Social bias, or the preference for one class of people over another, is pervasive in our day-to-day interactions with the world. *Implicit bias* in language occurs when producers intentionally or unintentionally reveal their beliefs about a person or a group of people. The field of natural language processing has taken significant strides to eliminate biases from text (Bolukbasi et al., 2016; Garg et al., 2018; Zhao et al., 2017), though it is clear that producers are the source of the ultimate biases observable within corpora (Trix and Psenka, 2003; Blair, 2002).

In the present work, we present a novel data source from workplace interactions between employees in the same organization. The dataset contains instances of "social recognition" in which an employee (e.g., the *author*) praises a coworker (the *recipient*), such as for obtaining a career milestone such as a promotion, or for completing a difficult task successfully. We focus specifically on *workplace bias*, which we define as any language that detracts from the general positivity of the praise, such as instances of discrimination (e.g., "You're a great engineer for a woman!"), the promotion of unhealthy work-life balance (e.g., "Thanks for working until nighttime."), or self-centered praise.

However, because the bias is implicit, the linguistic phenomena that reflect workplace bias show considerable degrees of subjectivity. Along the *intersubjectivity spectrum* (Basile et al., 2021), annotating for specific categories of workplace bias relies considerably on the annotators' existing conceptualization of the classes. This makes the categorical labels effectively "projective latent content", lacking clear boundaries even with strong guidelines (Reidsma and op den Akker, 2008). In the context of bias identification, approaching the annotation process with a sense of distrust or hyperfocus on the raters' abilities to "correctly" annotate can quickly lead to erasure of diverse and valuable opinions in how bias is received (Basile et al., 2021). Indeed, it is partly due to this distrust that analyses of annotated data often aggregate across many raters, reducing the contribution of any single individual's biases.

In an effort to encode some of the nuance associated with highly subjective social phenomena, researchers have used Best-Worst Scaling (BWS) (Louviere and Woodworth, 1991) as one popular approach. (Mohammad, 2017; Pei and Jurgens, 2020). Kiritchenko and Mohammad (2017) verified the efficacy of BWS by obtaining judgments of positivity and negativity for 3,207 terms using both a 9-point rating scale and the BWS framework. They showed that using BWS produced more reliable annotations than rating scales (Kiritchenko and Mohammad, 2017).

We explore the potential viability of the BWS annotation procedure, which has been proposed in contrast to categorical data labeling in domains such as word affect intensity (Mohammad, 2017), intimacy (Pei and Jurgens, 2020), hate speech (Poletto et al., 2019), and sentiment (Kiritchenko and Mohammad, 2017), which are similar to our workplace bias dataset. However, the nuance of workplace bias makes it a distinct annotation problem, posing its own unique set of difficulties when implementing BWS at scale.

2. Methodology

As we aim to evaluate the viability of the BWS annotation procedure compared to traditional categorical labeling, we compile a jointly annotated dataset in both styles and analyze the results.

2.1. Dataset

For our study, we compile 50 social recognition messages between co-workers at various companies. Social recognition, or peer-to-peer recognition, is the act of employees empowering and acknowledging one another for great work. The messages are shared on the Workhuman online platform, where employees from a company write these peer-to-peer messages. For example, the following recognition is found in our dataset: *I want to appreciate you for working together and collaborating as a team in difficult times.*

Four trained linguists annotators rated 50 social recognition messages at the sentence level, where each message had on average 4.5 sentences ($sd = 1.3$). In total, the 50 messages yielded 227 categorically annotated sentences, with an average of 18.4 tokens ($sd = 12$). Of these, 107 sentences received a positive bias annotation, indicating the presence of some workplace bias category by at least one annotator, and thus went on to be annotated in the style of Best-Worst Scaling (BWS). Only these 107 jointly annotated sentences are included in the dataset. To our knowledge, this is the first analysis directly comparing BWS to parallel non-aggregated categorical labels. Before we introduce the BWS annotation procedure, we discuss the categorical annotation procedure.

2.2. Categorical Annotation

In our taxonomy, we define six categories for classifying instances of workplace bias. It is similar in nature to the typology of microaggressions described by Breitfeller et al. (2019). However, our implicit bias annotation task centers on nuanced language specific to the workplace. For legal reasons, we anonymize the bias categories in the present study to be of the form "Category {id}", in addition to "None" (the absence of any gold standard workplace bias category).

For each of the 227 sentences, annotators may identify multiple categories applying to a single sentence. The resulting average Fleiss' κ statistic across all categories is 0.32. This value represents low agreement in categorical annotation, but must be framed in the context of other difficult implicit bias annotation tasks, reporting κ values as low as 0.43 (Breitfeller et al., 2019)

For each datapoint, we find a single "gold standard" category by aggregating judgements and taking the most common category, where more than one annotator (at least 50% of the annotators) selected that category.

2.3. Best-Worst Annotation

Best-worst Scaling (BWS) is a method of annotation in which a series of comparative judgements are aggregated in order to produce real-valued scores corresponding to some criteria (Louviere and Woodworth, 1991). Rather than performing binary comparisons between all pairs of items in a dataset (N^2 complexity), the items are grouped into "tuples" of four datapoints, leveraging the transitivity property to maximize the information gained for each evaluation item. In our context, the criterion in question is "bias potency": how strong is the bias present in a given text? Being a subjective task capturing projective latent content, this annotation paradigm is intentionally ambiguous and category-agnostic, resulting in a lower cognitive overhead. However, our working definition of potency is a measure of the negative impact a text will have on both workplace culture and the individual recipient.

The final BWS scores are obtained using Counts Analysis (Orme, 2009). For each item a, the score is calculated as follows:

$$bws\_score(a) = \%best(a) - \%worst(a) \quad (1)$$

The final bws_score ranges from -1 (least potent workplace bias) to 1 (most potent workplace bias). An example of a BWS annotation item is shown in Figure 1.

We cannot apply traditional inter-annotator agreement algorithms like Alpha and Kappa to the set of BWS annotations, since all forms of disagreement will be penalized. However, disagreement that comes from two items having similar ratings is a useful signal in BWS, since these two items will ultimately be pushed towards having more similar real-valued scores (Mohammad, 2017). Instead, we calculate the split-half reliability correlation to ensure that the levels of disagreement are replicable across many random splits of annotations. Across 100 random splits, these tests yield a Spearman's r of 0.84, demonstrating high reliability in the annotations.

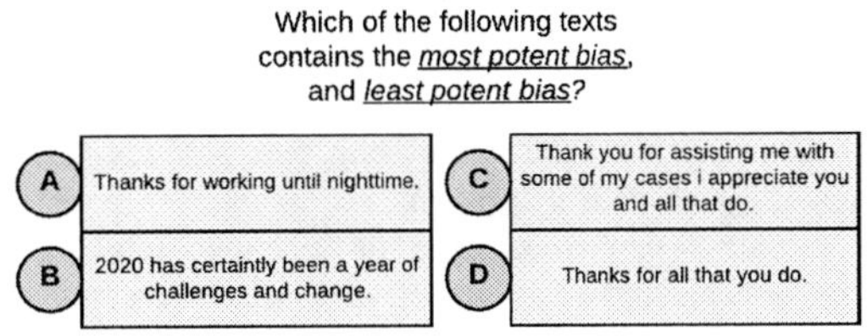

Figure 1: Example BWS item.

3. Analysis

Observed Agreement as Substitute for BWS

When calculating inter-annotator agreement on a traditional, categorically annotated dataset, a simple non-chance corrected metric used is observed agreement. Observed agreement is traditionally defined simply by the proportion of cases in which two raters agree. In our context, we slightly adapt this definition to reflect the direction of agreement, such that observed

Category	N	Coefficient	σ
None	47	-0.55	0.29
Category 1	11	0.25	0.36
Category 2	19	0.33	0.32
Category 3	11	**0.12**	**0.40**
Category 4	13	**0.03**	**0.36**
Category 5	1	0.13	0.0
Category 6	4	0.06	0.38

Table 1: Point biserial coefficients between category and BWS score, alongside standard deviations of BWS scores. In bold are notable examples where $N > 10$, and $\sigma - |\text{coefficient}| > 0.3$

agreement is *(number of annotators who identified any bias category in an item) / (total number of annotators for an item)*. The resulting values fall within the range of [0, 1], where 1 implies that all annotators agreed that some form of bias is present, and 0 implies that all annotators agreed that no bias is present.

Spearman's r between the observed agreement and the BWS scores is 0.72, demonstrating a strong positive correlation. Figure 2 plots a regression model fit between observed agreement scores and BWS scores.

Predicting Bias Potency

In examining the taxonomy of bias annotated for in the categorical annotations, it might seem fair to assume that certain categories inherently carry more bias potency than others. However, although the bias categories are indeed annotated as having higher degrees of bias than the "None" (no gold standard) category, there are no notable differences in the bias potency of different categories, which we show in Figure 3. Table 1 calculates the point biserial correlations and standard deviations with respect to each aggregated category, and "None". From the inferred confidence intervals in this table, it is clear that estimating bias potency through category alone is insufficient.

In order to examine the extent to which mental conceptions of implicit bias impact agreement on

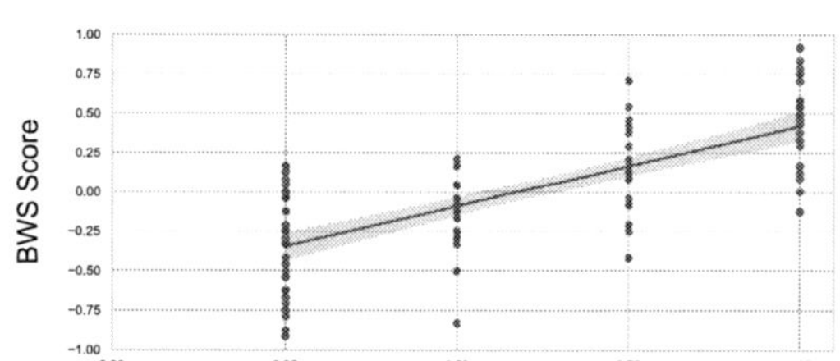

Figure 2: Regression plot between observed agreement and mean BWS scores. Note: Agreement scores of 0 were not used in the BWS annotation.

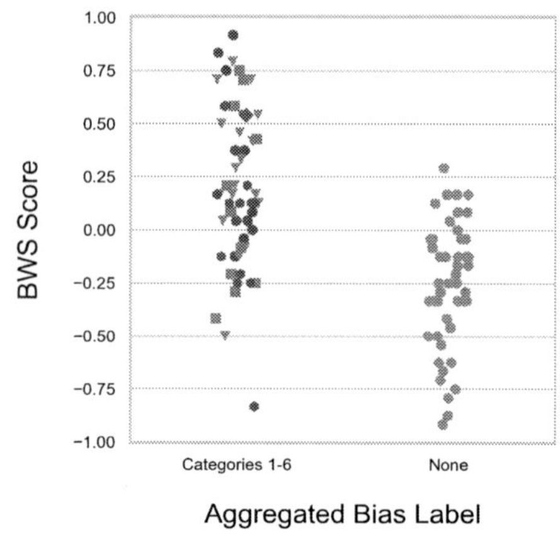

Figure 3: "Gold Standard" bias categories, plotted against BWS score. The hues correspond to specific bias categories.

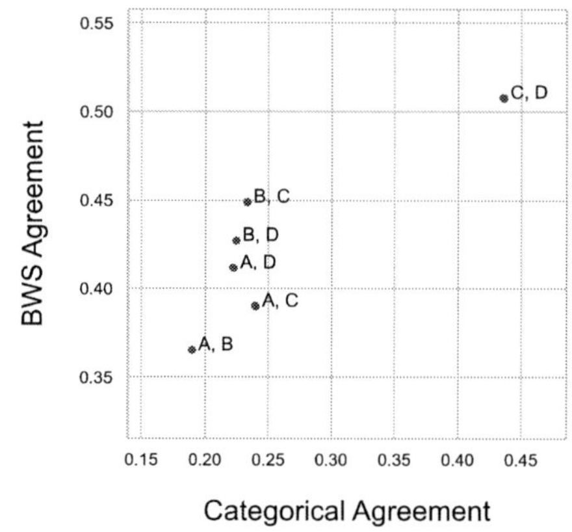

Figure 4: Agreement percentages for the BWS and categorical tasks between pairs of annotators A, B, C, and D.

the BWS and categorical task, we plot the observed agreement between pairs of annotators in Figure 4. For categorical annotations, agreement is the proportion of cases where the two raters' categorical judgements align. For BWS scaling, this is the proportion of best/worst judgements in which two annotators agree.

Annotating Sparse Phenomena with BWS

As seen in Figure 2, there are no observed agreement values equal to 0. This is a result of the data preprocessing we performed prior to BWS annotation; any sentence receiving less than two categorical annotations indicating the presence of some form of bias was discarded. This pre-processing is motivated by both practical annotation constraints and confounding linguistic considerations.

An internal dataset of 4,224 sentences from Workhuman social recognition data shows that only 452 (12%) of the sentences shows instances of perceived bias, according to our taxonomy. When confronted with a tuple of all-unbiased sentences, the random disagreement amongst annotators will likely produce relatively similar scores. However, annotating in the style of BWS when 88% of the data contain none of the target phenomena is costly and creates a massive overhead.

Surveying other applications of BWS in annotating social aspects of language shows that others do not employ similar pre-processing prior to BWS annotation. For example, Pei and Jurgens (2020) use BWS to annotate Reddit questions on intimacy levels, defined as the perceived independence, warmth, and willingness to share personally (Perlman and Fehr, 1987). For a social phenomenon as ubiquitous as intimacy, this lack of preprocessing might work well. However, for the annotation of a sparse phenomenon like bias, many datapoints will completely lack the trait in question (bias). Indiscriminate annotation of all datapoints in the BWS style may lead to unwanted priming, resulting in more positive annotations due solely to the rating environment or noisy linguistic cues in the prompt (Schuster et al., 2019). As shown in Figure 5, we observe a discrepancy between the percentage of data points that received the lowest score even with our preprocessing filtration, with 11.32% in the BWS task, and 33.02% in the categorical task. As a result, we see that BWS slightly skews judgements towards the biased side, similar to the conclusions made in Poletto et al. (2019).

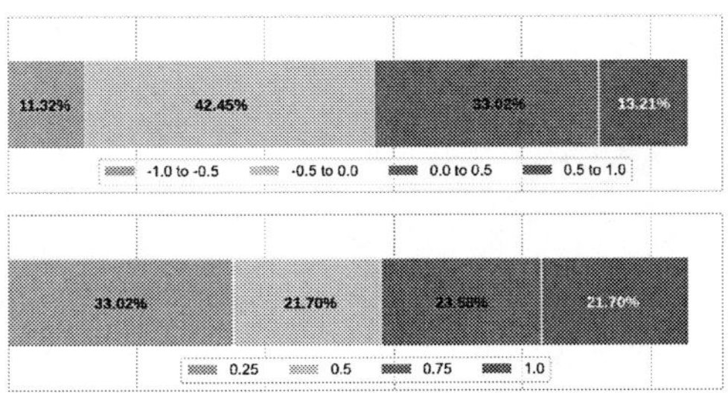

Figure 5: Label distribution for BWS and categorical annotation tasks.

Scaling to New Data

To annotate in the BWS style, a complete and final set of the data is required. If dataset A is annotated for bias potency in a BWS style, it may be realistic that dataset B becomes available at a later date. Since Figure 3 shows the difficulty in predicting distribution bias potency, there is no clear way to ensure the datasets are drawn from the same distribution of bias potency. As a result, a new annotation job must be created, based on a composite dataset of A + B.

This example highlights a major downside to deploying BWS at scale in an industry setting: the final scores are only interpretable in context of a reference dataset. However, the observed agreement of each data point is interpretable in isolation and shows a high correlation with the BWS scores.

Annotation Times

Additionally, annotation time must be considered when choosing a large-scale annotation pipeline. In the categorical annotation task, the annotators spent an average of 25 seconds per sentence. Annotating in the BWS style, annotators report spending an average of 60 seconds per tuple. These discrepancies in annotation times are highlighted when we consider the relative sizes of the datasets for annotation. In order to construct well-formed tuples which produce meaningful scores, the number of tuples is commonly made to be (at minimum) 1.5 times the size of the original dataset, though we note that Kiritchenko and Mohammad (2017) show that the reliability of BWS annotations is similar across 1N, 1.5N, and 2N tuples. As a result, the average annotator spent $\sim$ 45 minutes annotating 107 sentences in a categorical paradigm and $\sim$ 3.5 hours annotating 107 sentences in a BWS paradigm. While the overhead of training annotators to annotate in the categorical style must be considered, this substantial difference in annotation times makes categorical annotations better suited for scaling an annotation pipeline.

4. Conclusion and Future Work

In this work, we analyzed the relationship between non-aggregated categorical annotations and BWS annotations. Analyses of a novel dataset of workplace bias showed a strong correlation between observed agreement and the BWS score. Given the often-unmentioned pitfalls of annotation time and complications annotating on sparse social phenomena, we propose leveraging categorical annotations as a more realistic alternative for perspectivist modeling approaches. Additionally, we demonstrate the value of non-aggregated datasets.

We hope to see more datasets jointly annotated in this manner so that our results might be validated on a larger scale. In future work, we hope to leverage the observed agreement scores from non-aggregated categorical bias annotations to inform a form of soft loss learning Basile et al. (2021).

5. Acknowledgements

We would like to thank Kristen Frazier, Kaan Catalyurek, Mimi Zhang, Cassie Newland, and Cassidy Copeland, all with Workhuman, for their annotations on the dataset and invaluable conceptualization and development of the workplace bias categories.

6. Bibliographical References

Basile, V., Cabitza, F., Campagner, A., and Fell, M. (2021). Toward a perspectivist turn in ground truthing for predictive computing. *ArXiv*, abs/2109.04270.

Blair, I. V. (2002). The Malleability of Automatic Stereotypes and Prejudice. *Personality and Social Psychology Review*, 6(3):242–261, August. Publisher: SAGE Publications Inc.

Bolukbasi, T., Chang, K.-W., Zou, J. Y., Saligrama, V., and Kalai, A. T. (2016). Man is to Computer Programmer as Woman is to Homemaker? Debiasing Word Embeddings. In *Advances in Neural Information Processing Systems*, volume 29. Curran Associates, Inc.

Breitfeller, L., Ahn, E., Jurgens, D., and Tsvetkov, Y. (2019). Finding microaggressions in the wild: A case for locating elusive phenomena in social media posts. In *Proceedings of the 2019 conference on empirical methods in natural language processing and the 9th international joint conference on natural language processing (EMNLP-IJCNLP)*, pages 1664–1674.

Garg, N., Schiebinger, L., Jurafsky, D., and Zou, J. (2018). Word embeddings quantify 100 years of gender and ethnic stereotypes. *Proceedings of the National Academy of Sciences*, 115(16):E3635–E3644, April. Publisher: Proceedings of the National Academy of Sciences.

Kiritchenko, S. and Mohammad, S. M. (2017). Best-worst scaling more reliable than rating scales: A case study on sentiment intensity annotation. *arXiv preprint arXiv:1712.01765*.

Louviere, J. J. and Woodworth, G. G. (1991). Best-worst scaling: A model for the largest difference judgments. Technical report, Working paper.

Mohammad, S. M. (2017). Word Affect Intensities. *arXiv:1704.08798 [cs]*, April. arXiv: 1704.08798.

Orme, B. (2009). Maxdiff analysis: Simple counting, individual-level logit, and hb. *Sawtooth Software*.

Pei, J. and Jurgens, D. (2020). Quantifying intimacy in language. *arXiv preprint arXiv:2011.03020*.

Perlman, D. and Fehr, B. (1987). The development of intimate relationships.

Poletto, F., Basile, V., Bosco, C., Patti, V., and Stranisci, M. (2019). Annotating hate speech: Three schemes at comparison. In *6th Italian Conference on Computational Linguistics, CLiC-it 2019*, volume 2481, pages 1–8. CEUR-WS.

Reidsma, D. and op den Akker, R. (2008). Exploiting 'Subjective' Annotations. In *Coling 2008: Proceedings of the workshop on Human Judgements in Computational Linguistics*, pages 8–16, Manchester, UK, August. Coling 2008 Organizing Committee.

Schuster, S., Chen, Y., and Degen, J. (2019). Harnessing the linguistic signal to predict scalar inferences. *arXiv preprint arXiv:1910.14254*.

Trix, F. and Psenka, C. (2003). Exploring the Color of Glass: Letters of Recommendation for Female and Male Medical Faculty. *Discourse & Society*, 14(2):191–220, March.

Zhao, J., Wang, T., Yatskar, M., Ordonez, V., and Chang, K.-W. (2017). Men Also Like Shopping: Reducing Gender Bias Amplification using Corpus-level Constraints. In *Proceedings of the 2017 Conference on Empirical Methods in Natural Language Processing*, pages 2979–2989, Copenhagen, Denmark, September. Association for Computational Linguistics.

Proceedings of the 1st Workshop on Perspectivist Approaches to NLP @LREC2022, pages 37–45
Marseille, 20 June 2022

What if Ground Truth is Subjective?
Personalized Deep Neural Hate Speech Detection

Kamil Kanclerz, Marcin Gruza, Konrad Karanowski, Julita Bielaniewcz, Piotr Miłkowski, Jan Kocoń, Przemysław Kazienko
Department of Artificial Intelligence
Wrocław University of Science and Technology, Wrocław, Poland
{kamil.kanclerz, marcin.gruza, konrad.karanowski, julita.bielaniewicz, piotr.milkowski, jak.kocon, kazienko}@pwr.edu.pl

Abstract

A unified gold standard commonly exploited in natural language processing (NLP) tasks requires high inter-annotator agreement. However, there are many subjective problems that should respect users' individual points of view. Therefore, in this paper, we evaluate three different personalized methods for the task of hate speech detection. Our user-centered techniques are compared to the generalizing baseline approach. We conduct our experiments on three datasets including single-task and multi-task hate speech detection. For validation purposes, we introduce a new data split strategy, which prevents data leakage between training and testing. To better understand the behavior of the model for individual users, we carried out personalized ablation studies. Our experiments revealed that all models leveraging user preferences in any case provide significantly better results than most frequently used generalized approaches. This supports our general observation that personalized models should always be considered in all subjective NLP tasks, including hate speech detection.

Keywords: NLP, subjective NLP tasks, hate speech, offensive content, human bias, human representation

1. Introduction

At first glance, disagreement and nonregular annotations can be seen as noise that drags the performance of NLP task detection models down. As we know, the ability to think and perceive the environment differently is natural to humans as such. Therefore, it is crucial to include this observation while building predictive models in order to reflect the setup close to reality. As simple as this may seem, it is important to keep in mind that the key ideas behind NLP phenomenon detection, such as gold standard, agreement coefficients, or the evaluation itself need to be thoroughly analyzed and reconsidered especially for subjective NLP tasks like hate speech detection, prediction of emotional elicitation, sense of humor, sarcasm detection, or even sentiment analysis. Such NLP tasks come with each complexity of their own, especially within the aspect of subjectivity, therefore making them difficult to solve compared to non-subjective tasks.

The changes that need to be implemented do not only consist of acquiring of suitable annotated data, but also of the problem definition itself. The vast majority of methods related to hate speech detection focus on one generalized interpretation of the texts, usually called *ground truth* or *gold standard* (Basile, 2020a), that is, an assignment of a single *right* value to the textual content being labeled. This process could be supported by defining specific guidelines or by adding active learning methods (Huang et al., 2017) in order to adequately address the disagreement of annotations. We, however, follow another *personalized* direction, in which model prediction is individualized for every user.

Our contribution is, inter alia, comprehensive experimental studies on hate speech for three datasets (suitable for both multi-task and single-task) and various personalized architectures (section 3). This data diversity helps us to accurately grasp the accuracy in the subjective setup, regardless of the characteristics of the datasets themselves. We have also decided to compare the fine-tuned and non-fine-tuned models in order to uncover possible errors in the assessment of the scores. Another valuable comparison was performed between collaborative filtering and the transformer-based architecture. Data extraction methods were evaluated side by side with information extraction methods based on data related to attention. As the key personalization ideas needed a new definition, we have managed to formulate a new data split and validation strategy, see Fig. 3. Such enhancements in the fundamental processes and concepts of deep neural solutions to NLP tasks turned out to be more accurate in terms of capturing the subjectivity of a single user, performing a legitimate personalization of user opinions in terms of their sensitivity to hate speech, both as a receiver and as an addressee (Fig. 1). Compared to the generalized approach, we have achieved results that greatly exceed the more common process of gratifying the majority, as seen in Section 6. To magnify and secure the scores achieved, we performed an ablation study, as well as a detailed analysis of the lower performance values in our models.

2. Related work

The number of tasks included in the natural language processing research areas is constantly growing. This phenomenon has potential that will even-

Figure 1: Personalization as an interesting alternative to majority voting.

tually help with the tasks where consumers' opinions will be prioritized. The use of a perspectivist approach performs well in many NLP detection tasks, such as hate speech (Rajadesingan et al., 2015; Zhang et al., 2016; Amir et al., 2016; Gong et al., 2017; Chetty and Alathur, 2018; Fortuna and Nunes, 2018; Gultchin et al., 2019; Kamal and Abulaish, 2019; Kocoń et al., 2021; Mondal and Sharma, 2021). To accurately grasp the idea behind uncovering the universal emotional characterization of the data annotated by users, we first need to define what that gold standard truly is in our case. The authors of the work (Aroyo and Welty, 2015) claim that the truth is completely relative and is more closely related to agreement and consensus. In *Seven Myths*, the myth of One Truth is debunked through various examples, indicating that the *correct* interpretation of the sentence is a matter of opinion, and therefore there is no one true interpretation. This statement is a high-level look at the domain of NLP. However, there are other approaches. As such, the most common is represented through the generalized approach. This method suggests that the majority is the gold standard and the authors of the work (Liu et al., 2019) imply that specific label aggregation methods can help provide reliable representative semantics at the population level. In the domain of detecting and labeling hate speech, recent work (Akhtar et al., 2020) presents an approach that creates different gold standards, one per chosen group. Experiments indicate that supervised models that include different perspectives on a certain topic outperform a baseline model that was trained on fully aggregated data. Similar results exposing these phenomena were presented in (Weerasooriya et al., 2020), which included the size of each group. The authors processed the annotation collection for each data item as a sample of the opinions of a population of human annotators. Among each group of individuals, disagreement was a natural and expected occurrence. Therefore, a standard training set may contain a large number of very small samples, one for each data item, none of which, by itself, is large enough to be considered representative of the beliefs of the underlying population about each topic. Another crucial aspect in the phenomena detection in texts, is the agreement coefficients. Some of them were shown in the work (Artstein and Poesio, 2008) in which the authors exposed the underlying assumptions of the agreement coefficients, covering Krippendorff's alpha, Scott's pi, and Cohen's kappa. They discussed the use of coefficients in various annotation tasks and argued that weighted alpha-like coefficients, traditionally less used than kappa-like measures in computational linguistics, may be more appropriate for many corpus annotation tasks. However, a certain problem with Cohen's Kappa has been found, as described in (Powers, 2012). Deploying a system in a context which has the opposite skew from its validation set can be expected to approximately negate Fleiss's Kappa and halve Cohen's Kappa, but leave Powers Kappa unchanged. For most performance evaluation purposes, the latter is, therefore, most appropriate. Some annotators choose bad labels to maximize their pay. To avoid manual identification, a response model item named MACE (Multi-Annotator Competence Estimation) was introduced in (Hovy et al., 2013). It learns in an unsupervised fashion to identify which annotators are trustworthy and predict the correct underlying labels. The process of matching the performance of more complex state-of-the-art systems performs well even under adversarial conditions. On the other hand, a low level of agreement between annotators can have a positive effect on the performance of the models (Leonardelli et al., 2021). (Plank et al., 2014) present an empirical analysis of part-of-speech annotated data sets that suggests that disagreements are systematic across domains and, to some extent, also across languages. A quantitative analysis of tag confusions reveals that most disagreements are due to linguistically debatable cases rather than annotation errors. And the final key element is the evaluation itself. Although not largely analyzed, it may expose some of the less obvious issues. The work (Basile, 2020b) suggests that majority-driven gold standards can be undone in time, and the coming progress in NLP is headed towards an inclusive approach that may preserve the personal opinions and perspectives of annotators. The same author appeared in the work (Basile et al., 2021) and expressed disagreement with practices such as minimizing disagreement or creating cleaner datasets. That simplification is said to result in oversimplified models for end-to-end tasks. Therefore, there exists a need for improvement evaluation practices in order to better grasp such a disagreement.

3. Datasets

The data we used were collected from three datasets: Measuring Hate Speech, Wikipedia Detox Aggression, and Unhealthy Conversations. All datasets contain texts that are related to offensive speech, yet differ significantly from each other to a degree that accurately displays the universal nature of the evaluated methods; see Tab. 1 for a detailed data profile.

3.1. Measuring Hate Speech (MHS) dataset

The Measuring Hate Speech dataset (Kennedy et al., 2020) consists of 39,565 comments acquired from YouTube, Twitter, and Reddit. These comments are annotated by 7,912 Amazon Mechanical Turk workers from the United States. The annotators focused on measuring the intensity of various types of offensiveness. It means that a given user annotated a text with the level of each of ten types: (1) disrespect, (2) insult, (3) humiliation, (4) sentiment, (5) attacking or defending nature of the post, (6) dehumanization, (7) inferiority of the status, (8) hate speech, (9) violence, and (10) genocide. Each type was treated by us as another NLP task – a distinct output of the model. The correlations between the annotations for the different types (tasks) are shown in Fig. 2.

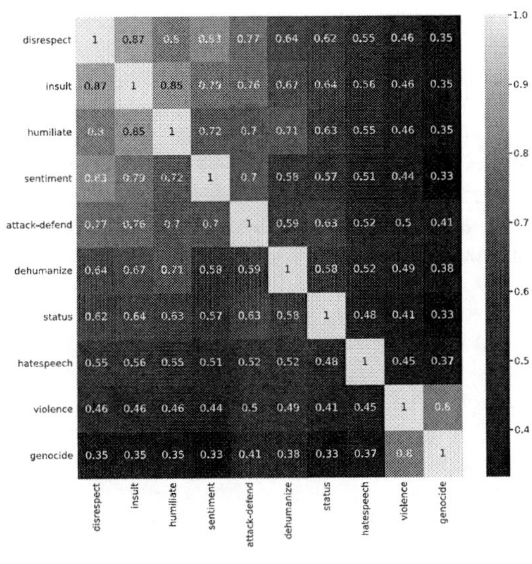

Figure 2: Correlation between real values of the hate speech types (tasks) for the same text in the MHS dataset

3.2. Wikipedia Detox: Aggression

The data available in Wikipedia Detox: Aggression dataset was accumulated during the Wikipedia Detox project [1] that took place between 2001 and 2015. It consists of 116k texts from the Wikipedia forum that were labeled by more than 4k annotators. Each human annotator marked the level of aggression from -3 to 3, where the value -3 defines a highly aggressive text and 3 implies a complete lack of aggression in the labeled text. We have simplified the values to range from -1 to 1, where negative or zero values correspond to the highly aggressive label, whereas the values greater than 0 to the non-aggressive one.

[1] https://meta.wikimedia.org/wiki/Research:Detox/Data_Release

3.3. Unhealthy Conversations

The Unhealthy Conversations dataset (Price et al., 2020) was made publicly available in October 2020. It contains 44k unique comments of 250 characters or less from Globe and Mail opinion articles sampled from the Simon Fraser University Opinion and Comments Corpus dataset (Kolhatkar et al., 2020). Each comment was coded by at least three annotators with at least one of the following class labels: *antagonize*, *condescending*, *dismissive*, *generalization*, *generalization unfair*, *healthy*, *hostile*, and *sarcastic*. The comments were presented in isolation to the annotators, without the surrounding context of the news article and other comments, thus possibly reducing bias.

4. Methods

To investigate the impact of subjectivity on the modeled tasks, we compare four different neural-based models: one non-personalized (TXT-Baseline) and three personalized (HuBi-Formula, HuBi-Medium and UserId). All the described models are neural networks trained using a backpropagation algorithm.

- **TXT-Baseline** (Kocoń et al., 2021) – the baseline model that uses only the language model vector representation for the prediction. This model is used in most NLP tasks, where it is assumed that there is only one ground truth for each text and the prediction is not dependent on the person. The model consists of one linear layer that projects the text vector representation into the desired prediction dimension.
- **HuBi-Formula** (Kocoń et al., 2021) – the simplest personalization model which uses additional statistical features of a person to improve the quality of model predictions. The features of the person are their Z-scores of annotations for each class calculated from the training dataset. The person's Z-score can be interpreted as their standarized deviation from mean labels of texts that he annotated, which allows the model to learn that the person is more or less likely to annotate given label. The architecture of the model is similar to TXT-Baseline, with the difference that Z-scores are concatenated to textual vector representations before the projecting linear layer.
- **HuBi-Medium** (Kocoń et al., 2021) – inspired by collaborative filtering methods, this model learns a personal latent vector which captures personal beliefs about the modeled task. As in the neural collaborative filtering model (He et al., 2017), the personal latent vector is multiplied element-wise with the textual vector, and the resulting vector is further fed to linear layers. Vectors are initialized randomly and learned through backpropagation.

	Measuring Hate Speech	Wiki Detox Aggression	Unhealthy Conversations
Textual content profile	comments	comments & discussions	comments & discussions
Tasks	disrespect, insult, humiliate, sentiment, attack-defend, dehumanize, status, hatespeech, violence, genocide	aggression	antagonize, condescending, dismissive, generalization, unfair generalization, healthy, hostile, sarcastic
Labels / values	$\{0, \ldots, 4\}$	$\{0, 1\}$	$\{0, 1\}$
Output / ML task	10*regression	binary classification	8*binary classification
Number of texts	39,565	115,864	44,355
Number of annotations	135,556	1,365,217	244,468 (227,975 valid)
Number of annotators	7,912	4,053	558
Avg. annotations per text	3.43	11.78	4.66
Avg. annotations per annotator	17.13	336.84	387.71
Language	English	English	English

Table 1: Dataset profiles.

- **UserId** (Kocoń et al., 2021) – this model encodes the information about a person by appending a user ID token to the beginning of the annotated text. The text with the user ID is then encoded with the transformer model into a vector representation. As an extension of the original model, to prevent the tokenizer from splitting the user ID tokens, we manually add them to models' special tokens set. In this model, the transformer weights are trained with the whole model to learn the dependencies between the user and the text.

5. Experimental Setup

To provide a comparison between the generalized approach and personalized methods, we choose the TXT-Baseline architecture as our baseline. It provides the same unified prediction for a given text. It does not take into account the existence of individual users at all. However, to enable comparability of the results, we trained the baseline model in the same setup as the personalized architectures, i.e. treating each annotation concerning a given text and made by a specific user as a separate training sample.

To counteract the possible imbalance between text relevance, we applied the text-based data split and the 10-fold cross-validation shown in Fig. 3.

Due to the various text lengths in each dataset described in Sec. 3 we limited each text to 128 tokens. The WikiDetox Aggression dataset required additional preprocessing, including the removal of the new-line sign from each text. On the other hand, we used multi-objective regression for the MHS dataset and scaled the sample labels to the range $[0, 1]$.

To obtain the vector representations of the texts in each dataset, we leveraged the XLM-RoBERTa (XLM-R) (Conneau et al., 2020) model and its tokenizer. We used the implementation provided by the HuggingFace library (Wolf et al., 2020).

For the TXT-Baseline, HuBi-Formula, and HuBi-Medium models, our experimental setup consists of two phases: generating embeddings and training classifiers. The first phase involves splitting the texts of the training samples into tokens and then generating their embeddings via the language model. On the contrary, we could include the language model in the training process. This would improve the performance of each model, but also significantly increase the learning time, because of the performing the forward and the backward propagation through the layers of the language model, which in our case consists of a very large number of parameters. This setup would be too expensive, taking into account multiple model architectures and the 10-fold cross-validation. The main objective of our work is to show the impact of personalization on the performance of reasoning methods. Another advantage of this approach is a more robust comparison of different model architectures, highlighting the best extraction of user knowledge.

To obtain a vector representation of the text, we averaged the embeddings of all tokens. Our technique differs from the standard approach of focusing on a CLS token that contains a representation of the entire text. During the initial experiments, we found that embedding of the entire text based on the averaged vector representation of the tokens yields better results than the standard technique using the CLS token embedding.

In the case of the UserId model, each text is tokenized and encoded with the transformer in each epoch during the training procedure. This approach results in significantly increased training time. However, it enables fine-tuning of the transformer weights in order to achieve a better quality of the predictions.

In the training process, we used Adam optimizer (Kingma and Ba, 2015) and set the cross-entropy (Zhang and Sabuncu, 2018) as our loss function. The hyperparameter values including the learning rate, the number of epochs, and the size of the training batch were optimized separately for each dataset. *HuBi-Medium* model contains additional hyperparameters related to user representation. The size of the user embedding is set to 50. We initialized the weights of the embedding layer with the values we acquired from the uniform distribution within the range $(-0.01, 0.01)$.

In the case of classification tasks performed on the WikiDetox Aggression dataset, we measured the macro f1-score (F1). For the regression tasks performed on the MHS dataset, we used the R^2 measure. To measure the significance of the difference between different experiment configurations, we performed statistical tests. After ensuring that the test assumptions are met, we applied the independent samples t-test with the Bonferroni correction. If the assumptions could not be fulfilled, we used the Mann-Whitney U test.

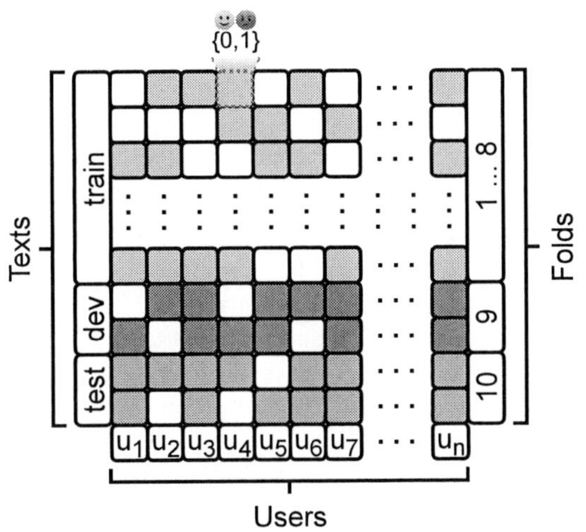

Figure 3: Data split strategy used for each dataset using the example of the WikiDetox Aggression dataset. White blocks are texts, which are not annoated by a specific user.

6. Results

Experiments were carried out for each set presented in Tab. 1. For the Measuring Hate Speech dataset, the results of the model that predict the exact value of each dimension are presented in Tab. 2. For 9 out of 10 dimensions, we see a strong predominance for the UserId model. Thus, it also occurred in the average score for the entire model, 48.67% vs 40.95% (the second-best model, HuBi-Medium). HuBi-Formula and HuBu-Medium models compared to the TXT-Baseline perform significantly better in 5 out of 10 dimensions. They were also superior to UserId on the *dehumanize* dimension. When comparing the score of TXT-Baseline (generalized approach) and HuBi-Medium (personalized approach), we see an analogous jump in the average score as between HuBi-Medium and UserId. The average scores for these two models are 35.45% (TXT-Baseline) and 40.95% (HuBi-Medium), respectively. HuBi-Formula (37.90%) compared to TXT-Baseline (35.45%) also performs slightly better. The most problematic dimension for all models was the *status* dimension. The results for each architecture were at least one third worse than for the other dimensions.

For the second dataset, WikiDetox: Aggresion, the results are shown in Tab. 3. In this case, we are looking at a classification task. The UserId model proved to be the best for the positive class and the macro scale. For the cases where we had no aggression, all 4 models achieved similar results. For a simple binary determination of the content of an utterance type in a text, the differences between the models were no longer as apparent as for the first dataset. The most visible and significant differences for the positive class are around the same values. These are 52.72% (TXT-Baseline), 60.54% (HuBi-Formula), 65.46% (HuBi-Medium), and 69.99% (UserId), respectively. The macro difference between the generalized approach (TXT-Baseline, 72.60%) and the best personalized approach (UserId, 81.91%) is 9.31%. However, between the second best personalized model (HuBi-Medium, 79.49%) and the best personalized model (UserId, with a score of 81.91%), the difference, although significant, is already marginal with respect to the computational complexity of the model and is 2.42%.

The bivariate histogram showing the difference between the regression results obtained for the HuBi-Medium and the TXT-Baseline models is presented in Fig. 4. The points in the upper left half of the diagram (above the red line) are users for whom the personalized HuBi-Medium architecture achieved better results than the generalized baseline. However, the points located in the lower right half of the histogram (under the red line) are the users whose annotations were better predicted by the TXT-Baseline model. It can be seen that the personalized model (HuBi-Medium) achieves the best results in all tasks. The use of personalization improved the performance of the model in the tasks: *humiliate*, *dehumanize*, *violence*, and *genocide*.

For the last dataset, Unhealthy Conversations, the results are presented in Tab. 4. As a consequence of the unbalanced dataset (almost 80% are cases of healthy statements), this is the most difficult dataset presented from a prediction quality perspective. In this case, the model based on the fine-tuned transformer showed tremendous gains. The differences between the other architectures here were as much as tens of percent (e.g. 74.25% vs 46.10% for the *antagonize* dimension in the case of TXT-Baseline). The HuBi-Formula model showed almost no gains relative to the TXT-Baseline model. For the HuBi-Medium architecture for 2 of the 8 classes, we had statistically significant improvements over TXT-Baseline. These were 49.65% vs 46.10% for the *antagonize* dimension and 52.85% vs 44.11% for the *healthy* dimension.

7. Discussion

The architectures evaluated during the experiments are characterized not only by different structures, but also at the level of information extraction. The *HuBi-Formula* model focuses on single-valued human bias (*HB*). It measures how much a user distinguishes themselves from other users based on their decisions. It can be calculated before the training procedure. The *HuBi-*

	respect	insult	humiliate	sentiment	attack-defend	dehumanize	status	hatespeech	violence	genocide	mean
TXT-Baseline	48.03±7.01	43.53±6.96	38.74±6.38	50.17±6.00	34.67±6.19	27.18±5.97	22.79±6.95	32.74±5.81	30.23±6.78	17.98±8.93	34.54±4.39
HuBi-Formula	47.38±6.44	43.20±5.95	41.69±5.44	49.23±5.88	35.19±4.82	**38.77**±3.51	26.58±4.87	35.48±4.32	36.91±6.62	25.19±10.84	37.90±2.85
HuBi-Medium	48.53±6.07	44.45±5.77	**43.52**±4.83	49.80±6.30	36.66±4.58	**42.29**±4.11	**29.73**±6.01	39.10±4.48	**42.57**±9.51	**33.42**±14.36	**40.95**±3.48
UserId	**60.73**±5.24	**55.44**±5.44	**48.86**±5.52	62.76±5.05	**48.00**±4.56	37.27±5.36	**34.21**±5.10	**46.78**±6.22	**48.80**±11.53	**43.81**±15.39	**48.67**±8.70

Table 2: R^2 measure values for the Measuring Hate Speech dataset. The values in **bold** are significantly better than the values of other classifiers (rows). Underlined values are significantly better than in other tasks (columns).

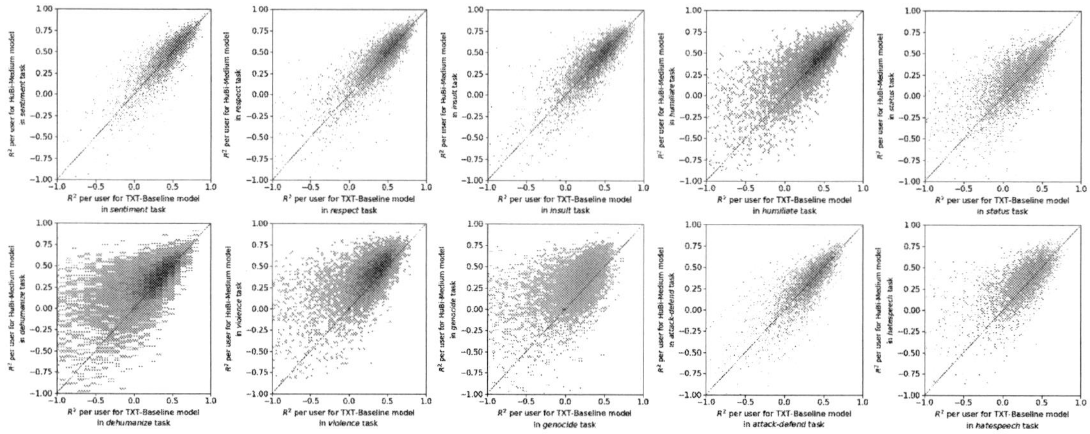

Figure 4: Bivariate histogram of the results R^2 obtained by the HuBi-Medium and TXT-Baseline models for individual users for each of the tasks in the Measuring Hate Speech Dataset. The area was narrowed down to [-1, 1] because at least 95% of users obtained this result on each task.

	F1 negative	F1 positive	Macro F1
TXT-Baseline	92.21 ± 0.36	52.72 ± 1.64	72.60 ± 0.94
HuBi-Formula	92.91 ± 0.34	60.54 ± 1.05	76.82 ± 0.56
HuBi-Medium	93.38 ± 0.31	65.46 ± 0.96	79.49 ± 0.39
UserId	**93.83** ± 0.16	**69.99** ± 0.94	**81.91** ± 0.43

Table 3: Classification results for WikiDetox: Aggression dataset. Values in **bold** are significantly better than other classifiers (rows). Underlined values are significantly better than the performance of the given model in other tasks (columns). Metrics: F1 negative – F1 score for the nonaggressive class (0); F1 positive – F1 score for the aggressive class (1); Macro F1 – the macro average of the F1 scores for each class.

Medium model involves the user representation obtained during the training procedure through the backpropagation procedure. On the other hand, the *UserId* model takes advantage of the transformer-based architecture with masked language modeling and self-attention. Those two are different ways of information extraction, including the user representation generation procedure.

The *UserId* model achieved the best result on the vast majority of tasks in each of the evaluated datasets. This may be related to its much more complex structure compared to the other classifiers. The fine-tuned transformer architecture combined with self-attention mechanism allowed for a better understanding of the text and improved the ability to extract additional knowledge about the user preferences.

The greatest gains in the case of WikiDetox: Aggression dataset were observed for the *aggressive* class (1). This may be due to the much more subjective nature of this label.

Applying the 10-fold cross-validation allowed conducting statistical tests, and measuring the standard deviation between each model performance on specific folds provided information about its stability. Moreover, fine-tuning the language model in this setup would be much more expensive.

In addition to individual user annotations, metadata such as the context of texts, comments, and information about the author may allow the extraction of additional knowledge.

8. Conclusions and Future Work

The experiments carried out on three datasets allowed us to observe some interesting phenomena. The task of detecting hate speech is difficult due to its complex context. The first significant issue is the lack of the possibility of application of simple dictionary analysis because wordplay really matters in hate interpretation. For this reason, we have shown that using appropriate architectures and state-of-the-art solutions extracts representations containing complete knowledge from text.

The second problem is that each user may have very different perception of offensiveness. The personalized approach allowed us to substantially increase the prediction quality compared to the generalized approach.

This leads us to the general conclusion presented in Fig. 5: *the ground truth* is *subjective*. Therefore, we

	antagonize	condescending	dismissive	generalisation	unfair generalisation	healthy	hostile	sarcastic
TXT-Baseline	46.10 ± 0.21	45.80 ± 0.14	46.74 ± 0.20	47.99 ± 0.23	48.23 ± 0.20	44.11 ± 0.32	47.10 ± 0.15	46.31 ± 0.22
HuBi-Formula	46.15 ± 0.19	45.85 ± 0.17	46.76 ± 0.20	47.99 ± 0.23	48.23 ± 0.20	44.30 ± 0.34	47.11 ± 0.15	46.32 ± 0.22
HuBi-Medium	49.65 ± 2.49	48.03 ± 1.54	47.25 ± 0.43	47.99 ± 0.23	48.23 ± 0.20	52.85 ± 4.69	47.17 ± 0.19	46.37 ± 0.23
UserId	**74.25** ± 1.77	**71.88** ± 3.14	**67.87** ± 4.18	**68.72** ± 4.20	**67.78** ± 4.37	**66.68** ± 1.86	**70.40** ± 2.62	**65.96** ± 2.99

Table 4: Classification results for Unhealthy Conversations dataset. The values in **bold** are significantly better than other classifiers (rows). Underlined values are significantly better than the performance of the given model in other tasks (columns). Metrics: Macro F1 – the macro average of the F1 scores for each class.

Figure 5: Meme representing the moment of sudden realization that the ground truth we were all looking for is subjective and we cannot use approaches based on generalization.

should gather and incorporate knowledge about annotators into the reasoning models.

Our validation of three personalized architectures on three distinct datasets revealed that the UserId model usually performs best even though it requires the user to be precisely identified before the training process.

The code for all methods and experiments is publicly available on GitHub[2] under the MIT license.

Overall, we strongly believe that architectures capable of representing the user beliefs in the comprehensive way appear to be the future of inference for subjective NLP tasks including hate speech detection.

Based on our experiments on the Unhealthy Conversations dataset, we want to address the problem of dimensional imbalance in our future work. Only 20% of this dataset corresponds to instances with unhealthy speech. Thus, seven dimensions are massively underrepresented in relation to the healthy speech cases.

[2] https://github.com/CLARIN-PL/personalized-nlp/releases/tag/2022-lrec-nlperspectives

9. Acknowledgements

This work was financed by (1) the National Science Centre, Poland, project no. 2019/33/B/HS2/02814 and 2021/41/B/ST6/04471; (2) the Polish Ministry of Education and Science, CLARIN-PL; (3) the European Regional Development Fund as a part of the 2014-2020 Smart Growth Operational Programme, CLARIN – Common Language Resources and Technology Infrastructure, project no. POIR.04.02.00-00C002/19; (4) the statutory funds of the Department of Artificial Intelligence, Wroclaw University of Science and Technology.

10. Bibliographical References

Akhtar, S., Basile, V., and Patti, V. (2020). Modeling annotator perspective and polarized opinions to improve hate speech detection. In *Proceedings of the AAAI Conference on Human Computation and Crowdsourcing*, volume 8, pages 151–154.

Amir, S., Wallace, B. C., Lyu, H., and Silva, P. C. M. J. (2016). Modelling context with user embeddings for sarcasm detection in social media. *arXiv preprint arXiv:1607.00976*.

Aroyo, L. and Welty, C. (2015). Truth is a lie: Crowd truth and the seven myths of human annotation. *AI Magazine*, 36(1):15–24.

Artstein, R. and Poesio, M. (2008). Inter-coder agreement for computational linguistics. *Computational linguistics*, 34(4):555–596.

Basile, V., Fell, M., Fornaciari, T., Hovy, D., Paun, S., Plank, B., Poesio, M., Uma, A., et al. (2021). We need to consider disagreement in evaluation. In *1st Workshop on Benchmarking: Past, Present and Future*, pages 15–21. Association for Computational Linguistics.

Basile, V. (2020a). It's the end of the gold standard as we know it. In *International Conference of the Italian Association for Artificial Intelligence*, pages 441–453. Springer.

Basile, V. (2020b). It's the end of the gold standard as we know it. on the impact of pre-aggregation on the evaluation of highly subjective tasks. In *2020 AIxIA Discussion Papers Workshop, AIxIA 2020 DP*, volume 2776, pages 31–40. CEUR-WS.

Chetty, N. and Alathur, S. (2018). Hate speech review in the context of online social networks. *Aggression and violent behavior*, 40:108–118.

Conneau, A., Khandelwal, K., Goyal, N., Chaudhary, V., Wenzek, G., Guzmán, F., Grave, E., Ott, M.,

Zettlemoyer, L., and Stoyanov, V. (2020). Unsupervised cross-lingual representation learning at scale. In *Proceedings of the 58th Annual Meeting of the Association for Computational Linguistics*, pages 8440–8451, Online, July. Association for Computational Linguistics.

Fortuna, P. and Nunes, S. (2018). A survey on automatic detection of hate speech in text. *ACM Computing Surveys (CSUR)*, 51(4):1–30.

Gong, L., Haines, B., and Wang, H. (2017). Clustered model adaption for personalized sentiment analysis. In *Proceedings of the 26th International Conference on World Wide Web*, pages 937–946.

Gultchin, L., Patterson, G., Baym, N., Swinger, N., and Kalai, A. (2019). Humor in word embeddings: Cockamamie gobbledegook for nincompoops. In *International Conference on Machine Learning*, pages 2474–2483. PMLR.

He, X., Liao, L., Zhang, H., Nie, L., Hu, X., and Chua, T.-S. (2017). Neural collaborative filtering. In *Proceedings of the 26th international conference on world wide web*, pages 173–182.

Hovy, D., Berg-Kirkpatrick, T., Vaswani, A., and Hovy, E. (2013). Learning whom to trust with mace. In *Proceedings of the 2013 Conference of the North American Chapter of the Association for Computational Linguistics: Human Language Technologies*, pages 1120–1130.

Huang, S.-J., Chen, J.-L., Mu, X., and Zhou, Z.-H. (2017). Cost-effective active learning from diverse labelers. In *Proceedings of the 26th International Joint Conference on Artificial Intelligence*, IJCAI'17, page 1879–1885. AAAI Press.

Kamal, A. and Abulaish, M. (2019). Self-deprecating humor detection: A machine learning approach. In *International Conference of the Pacific Association for Computational Linguistics*, pages 483–494. Springer.

Kennedy, C. J., Bacon, G., Sahn, A., and von Vacano, C. (2020). Constructing interval variables via faceted Rasch measurement and multitask deep learning: a hate speech application. *arXiv e-prints*, page arXiv:2009.10277, September.

Kingma, D. P. and Ba, J. (2015). Adam: A method for stochastic optimization. In *ICLR (Poster)*.

Kocoń, J., Gruza, M., Bielaniewicz, J., Grimling, D., Kanclerz, K., Miłkowski, P., and Kazienko, P. (2021). Learning personal human biases and representations for subjective tasks in natural language processing. In *2021 IEEE International Conference on Data Mining (ICDM)*, pages 1168–1173. IEEE.

Kocoń, J., Figas, A., Gruza, M., Puchalska, D., Kajdanowicz, T., and Kazienko, P. (2021). Offensive, aggressive, and hate speech analysis: From data-centric to human-centered approach. *Information Processing & Management*, 58(5):102643.

Kolhatkar, V., Wu, H., Cavasso, L., Francis, E., Shukla, K., and Taboada, M. (2020). The sfu opinion and comments corpus: A corpus for the analysis of online news comments. *Corpus Pragmatics*, 4(2):155–190.

Leonardelli, E., Menini, S., Palmero Aprosio, A., Guerini, M., and Tonelli, S. (2021). Agreeing to disagree: Annotating offensive language datasets with annotators' disagreement. In *Proceedings of the 2021 Conference on Empirical Methods in Natural Language Processing*, pages 10528–10539, Online and Punta Cana, Dominican Republic, November. Association for Computational Linguistics.

Liu, T., Venkatachalam, A., Sanjay Bongale, P., and Homan, C. (2019). Learning to predict population-level label distributions. In *Companion Proceedings of The 2019 World Wide Web Conference*, pages 1111–1120.

Mondal, A. and Sharma, R. (2021). Team_KGP at SemEval-2021 task 7: A deep neural system to detect humor and offense with their ratings in the text data. In *Proceedings of the 15th International Workshop on Semantic Evaluation (SemEval-2021)*, pages 1169–1174. Association for Computational Linguistics, August.

Plank, B., Hovy, D., and Søgaard, A. (2014). Linguistically debatable or just plain wrong? In *Proceedings of the 52nd Annual Meeting of the Association for Computational Linguistics (Volume 2: Short Papers)*, pages 507–511.

Powers, D. M. W. (2012). The problem with kappa. In *Proceedings of the 13th Conference of the European Chapter of the Association for Computational Linguistics*, pages 345–355.

Price, I., Gifford-Moore, J., Fleming, J., Musker, S., Roichman, M., Sylvain, G., Thain, N., Dixon, L., and Sorensen, J. (2020). Six attributes of unhealthy conversation. *arXiv preprint arXiv:2010.07410*.

Rajadesingan, A., Zafarani, R., and Liu, H. (2015). Sarcasm detection on twitter: A behavioral modeling approach. In *Proceedings of the eighth ACM international conference on web search and data mining*, pages 97–106.

Weerasooriya, T. C., Liu, T., and Homan, C. M. (2020). Neighborhood-based pooling for population-level label distribution learning. *arXiv preprint arXiv:2003.07406*.

Wolf, T., Debut, L., Sanh, V., Chaumond, J., Delangue, C., Moi, A., Cistac, P., Rault, T., Louf, R., Funtowicz, M., Davison, J., Shleifer, S., von Platen, P., Ma, C., Jernite, Y., Plu, J., Xu, C., Le Scao, T., Gugger, S., Drame, M., Lhoest, Q., and Rush, A. (2020). Transformers: State-of-the-art natural language processing. In *Proceedings of the 2020 Conference on Empirical Methods in Natural Language Processing: System Demonstrations*, pages 38–45, Online, October. Association for Computational Linguistics.

Zhang, Z. and Sabuncu, M. (2018). Generalized cross entropy loss for training deep neural networks with noisy labels. *Advances in neural information processing systems*, 31.

Zhang, M., Zhang, Y., and Fu, G. (2016). Tweet sarcasm detection using deep neural network. In *Proceedings of COLING 2016, the 26th International Conference on Computational Linguistics: technical papers*, pages 2449–2460.

Proceedings of the 1st Workshop on Perspectivist Approaches to NLP @LREC2022, pages 46–55
Marseille, 20 June 2022

StudEmo: A Non-aggregated Review Dataset for Personalized Emotion Recognition

Anh Ngo[1], Argi Candri[1], Teddy Ferdinan[1], Jan Kocoń[2], Wojciech Korczyński[2]
Wrocław University of Science and Technology, Wrocław, Poland
[1]{269588, 268894, 268893}@student.pwr.edu.pl
[2]{jan.kocon, wojciech.korczynski}@pwr.edu.pl

Abstract

Humans' emotional perception is subjective by nature, in which each individual could express different emotions regarding the same textual content. Existing datasets for emotion analysis commonly depend on a single ground truth per data sample, derived from majority voting or averaging the opinions of all annotators. In this paper, we introduce a new non-aggregated dataset, namely StudEmo, that contains 5,182 customer reviews, each annotated by 25 people with intensities of eight emotions from Plutchik's model, extended with valence and arousal. We also propose three personalized models that use not only textual content but also the individual human perspective, providing the model with different approaches to learning human representations. The experiments were carried out as a multitask classification on two datasets: our StudEmo dataset and GoEmotions dataset, which contains 28 emotional categories. The proposed personalized methods significantly improve prediction results, especially for emotions that have low inter-annotator agreement.

Keywords: emotion recognition, personalization, non-aggregated dataset, learning human representation

1. Introduction

Emotions play an essential role in human communication. We can observe an increasingly high demand in studies of emotion recognition within natural language processing (NLP) due to its applicability in multiple domains. Emotion perception is naturally subjective and varies regarding each individual due to the differences in personal backgrounds, such as culture, gender, and age, which leads to the problem of low inter-annotator agreement in the existing datasets.

Recent studies have shown that different reviewers may classify the same object differently, but that unnecessarily means they're wrong, as they merely have different sentiments about the same thing (Basile et al., 2021). Those studies also identified the increased demand for new datasets related to personal perspectives on subjective NLP tasks. However, almost all available datasets for emotion recognition provide only limited information on the annotators. Moreover, to solve the problem of low inter-annotator agreement, only a few of them retain multiple annotations per sample. One of the most popular approaches is to use majority voting to obtain a single ground truth for each data sample. Another common approach is to collect the annotation from experts. Both methods consider only one correct label for a given text sample.

Existing solutions for emotion recognition do not consider involving individual perspectives, which rely on using only one ground truth to train the emotion recognizer. In addition, current personalization approaches include human representation generated from personal characteristics. However, these methods do not take into account the relationship between each annotator and the specific features of the text.

In this work, we introduce StudEmo, a non-aggregated dataset of 5,182 customer reviews in English, labeled for eight basic emotions from Plutchik's model, along with valence and arousal. Our dataset provides the annotations from 25 unique annotators who are students from different countries with different cultures, ages, and characteristics. The annotation strategy followed the procedures proposed by Janz et al. (2017) and Zaśko-Zielińska and Piasecki (2018).

Additionally, we propose personalized methods for emotion recognition tasks on textual data that take into account both textual content and how the raters react to that content. The approach is inspired by the idea of involving personal human bias and representation (Kocoń et al., 2021b), which is based on optimizing a multidimensional latent vector that represents the perspective of each annotator in a targeted text. Here, we propose extensions to these models by finetuning the entire architecture, which yields a significant quality improvement over the methods presented in (Kocoń et al., 2021b).

2. Related Work

Recent studies have highlighted the advantages of integrating the opinions and perspectives of individual annotators involved in subjective NLP tasks (Basile et al., 2021; Kocoń et al., 2021b). However, most current methods do not consider involving multiple annotator perspectives, in which neural network models such as CNN, Bi-LSTM, GRU (Abdullah et al., 2018) are combined with a separate model to extract text embeddings, such as transformer-based (Ghosh and Kumar, 2021; Chiorrini et al., 2021; Wang and Tong, 2021); GloVE, and ELMo (Lee et al., 2020). Akhtar et al. (2020a) proposed a stacked ensemble architecture for the recognition of the intensity of emotions, while Li and Xu (2014) involved emotional causes extracted from expert knowledge.

Dealing with tasks related to subjectivity in text perception is difficult due to the high variability in different points of view. One of the common approaches to representing multiple annotators without losing individual perspectives is to utilize a multitask or ensemble architecture that treats predicting annotator decisions as separate subtasks (Fayek et al., 2016; Davani et al., 2022). Another idea is to use the attention mechanism to introduce human representation, which considers personal characteristics, into emotion modeling. Although Li and Lee (2019) used the feature *Linguistic Inquiry Word Count* to create personal profile embeddings, a valuable idea was presented in (Kamran et al., 2021), where the authors demonstrated the correlation between personal cognitive factors and emotions from textual data. Furthermore, Akhtar et al. (2020b) considered a group-based personalized method and tried to maximize the polarity index between two groups.

The problem of the scarcity of non-aggregated datasets is discussed by Basile et al. (2021), since most current datasets for emotion recognition are aggregated by majority voting, best-worst scaling (Mohammad and Bravo-Marquez, 2017), or using a hybrid rule-based automated system (Krommyda et al., 2021). As mentioned by Hernandez et al. (2021) collecting high-quality emotional data is difficult and expensive which limits the availability of generalizable data. Only a few non-aggregated datasets exist, such as Measuring Hate Speech (Kennedy et al., 2020), Offensive Language Datasets with Annotators' Disagreement (Leonardelli et al., 2021). Specifically, we have found only three datasets for the emotion recognition task that preserve each annotator's opinions without combining them, including GoEmotions Datasets (Demszky et al., 2020), Emotion Meanings dataset (Wierzba et al., 2021), and Sentimenti database (Kocoń et al., 2019).

3. Datasets

3.1. StudEmo Dataset

Our dataset consists of 5,182 reviews in English. It is available on the DSpace CLARIN-PL repository under a CC BY-NC-ND 4.0 license[1]. These reviews were acquired from the MultiEmo dataset (Kocoń et al., 2021), which is a benchmark dataset for multilingual sentiment analysis containing consumer reviews from four different domains: hotels, medicine, products, and university. Since the original texts were written in Polish, the translation to English was performed using DeepL which is a translation system based on deep neural networks. The tool's producers present it as the best existing translation system[2]. Its superiority or similar performance in comparison to other existing tools, e.g, Google Translate, is proved by some recent studies: (Cambedda et al., 2021), (Hidalgo-Ternero, 2021) and (Bellés-Calvera and Quintana, 2021).

It is not easy to determine if emotions and sentiment are preserved after translation. Nevertheless, sentiment classification results for the original and translated texts (Kocoń et al., 2021) are very similar what suggests that translation quality is good enough to express similar sentiment.

The texts are annotated by 25 unique English-speaking annotators who are international students from different countries and cultural backgrounds studying at the master's degree level. They were not remunerated, annotators were only graded based on number of annotations during one of the study tutorials. The annotation schema was based on the procedures used in (Janz et al., 2017; Zaśko-Zielińska and Piasecki, 2018). Each annotator received a subset of 400 reviews and was asked to annotate it according to their own personal emotional reaction to the given text. Each annotator was allowed to annotate a given text with multiple emotion labels.

The resulting annotated data consist of ten categories: eight basic emotion categories from Plutchik's Wheel of Emotions: joy, trust, anticipation surprise, fear, sadness, anger, and disgust. Two additional dimensions were valence and arousal. Each basic emotion category and arousal has an intensity range of [0,3]. Meanwhile, valence has a range of [-3,+3]. Finally, a total of 7,463 annotations were acquired. The average annotation distribution for each basic emotion category is shown in Figure 1.

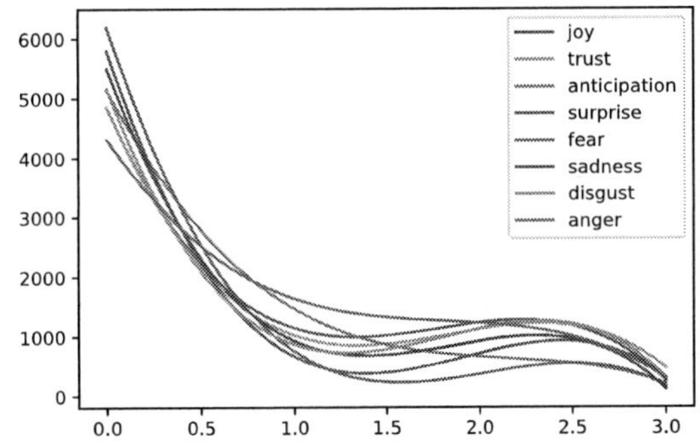

Figure 1: Data distribution of basic emotions in the StudEmo dataset. The x-axis is the intensity levels of emotions, while the y-axis is the number of annotations.

Of the 5,182 texts in the dataset, 2,901 were annotated by one annotator, and 2,281 were annotated by two annotators. There are 1,701 texts in which both annotators agree on the existence of at least one emotion category regardless of the intensity level. If the intensity level is considered, there are 1,011 texts where both

[1] http://hdl.handle.net/11321/895

[2] https://www.deepl.com/en/blog/20200206

annotators agree on at least one emotion category with the same intensity level.

On texts that received two annotations, the inter-annotator agreement was measured using the weighted Cohen's kappa coefficient to take into account the degree of disagreement, as the intensity levels in each category are ordered. The average weighted Cohen's kappa is 0.26. The weighted Cohen's kappa value for each category is as follows: Joy 0.33, Trust 0.33, Anticipation 0.22, Surprise 0.09, Fear 0.08, Sadness 0.21, Disgust 0.25, Anger 0.40, Valence 0.52, Arousal 0.12.

3.2. GoEmotions Dataset

The GoEmotions dataset from (Demszky et al., 2020) consists of 58,011 texts with 28 labels (27 emotion categories and 1 neutral category). The texts were carefully selected from Reddit. Each emotion category only has two possible values, 0 or 1. However, the texts are multi-labeled so that a given text may be annotated with more than one emotion category.

The texts were annotated by 82 unique annotators, each of them having 1-5 annotations. A total of 211,225 annotations are available; the average annotation distribution for each emotion category is shown on Figure 2.

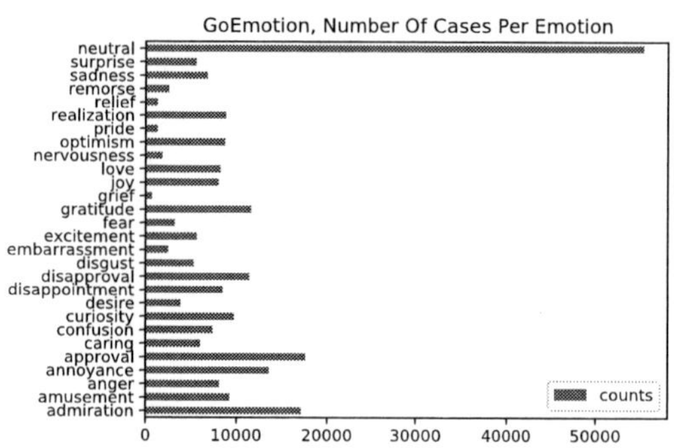

Figure 2: Data distribution of emotion categories in the GoEmotions dataset. The x-axis is the emotion categories, while the y-axis is the number of annotations.

The inter-annotator agreement in this dataset is somewhat high. There are 54,263 (94%) texts in which two or more annotators agree on at least one emotion category. However, there are only 17,763 (31%) texts in which three or more annotators agree on at least one emotion category. One reason for the relatively high inter-annotator agreement is that this dataset does not consider the intensity levels of the emotions, only their presence.

4. Dataset Splitting

Our dataset splitting strategy is based on (Miłkowski et al., 2021) and is depicted by Figure 3. The dataset was divided into columns (texts) and rows (annotators/users). The dataset was then partitioned with respect to the *texts* axis into Past (15%), Present (55%), Future1 (15%), and Future2 (15%). Meanwhile, the user-based split into the train, dev, and test sets was performed with the 10-fold cross-validation schema. All of the annotators/users are seen, which means that the models already learned all users before making the predictions.

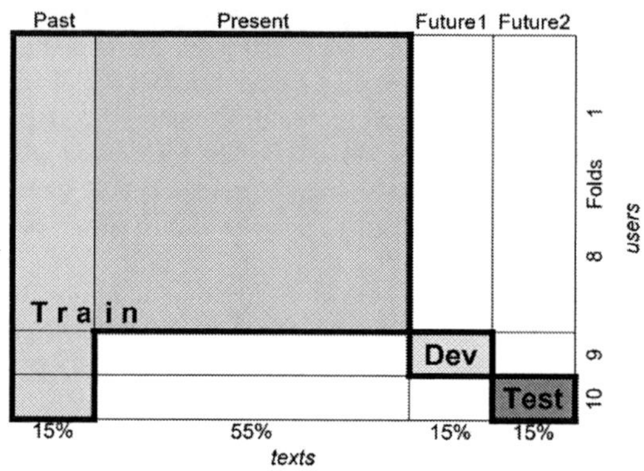

Figure 3: Dataset splitting strategy.

The dataset is split into *Past*, *Present*, and *Future* partitions to simulate data that is available in a working emotion prediction system. We assume the *Past* partition as texts that users have previously annotated (i.e. when these users started using the system, they were asked to annotate several texts for the purpose of calibrating the system); this *Past* partition is used to estimate individual user beliefs and biases. The *Present* partition represents texts and annotations that come up during the usage of the emotion prediction system, and it allows us to train the reasoning model. The *Future* partition is used for evaluation and test purposes.

The models were trained on the *Past* partition of 100% of all users and the *Present* partition of 80% of all users. In the case of personalization methods, the *Past* partition signifies some background knowledge about the users, and it was used to calculate the Human Bias (HuBi) measure of each user. On the other hand, *Present* partition signifies the general view of the texts and was used to train the reasoning of a personalized model. In the case of the baseline methods, both the *Past* and *Present* partitions were used for training but without considering the biases of the users.

The models were validated with the *dev* split, which uses the *Future1* partition of a different user fold. Therefore, *dev* contains about 10% of all users and 15% of all texts. It is important to note that *dev* is disjoint from *train*, which means that the models were validated on annotations never seen before.

The models were tested with the *test* split, which uses the *Future2* partition of yet another different user fold. Hence, the *test* split also contains about 10% of all users and 15% of all texts. Similarly, *test* is disjoint from *train* and *dev*, which means that the models were tested on annotations never seen before during training or validation.

5. Models

With the objective of emotion recognition based on individual's perspectives, we decided to exploit four different sources of information about annotators and text, including embedding of the considered text, user id, embeddings of annotated texts with annotations, and human bias. The text embeddings are generated by the pre-trained Transformer language model, in which the parameters are either finetuned or frozen during the training process. We started with the two variants, AVG-ANN and SINGLE-ANN, of the baseline models, which used only text embeddings as input. Next, we proposed and compared three new deep learning architectures that utilized the annotator's information, including the following:

1. User-ID – modeling the user id as a special token in text embedding,
2. Past-Embedding – the model uses embeddings of a few texts from Past split with user annotations,
3. HuBi-medium – the model using learned human embedding and word biases.

5.1. AVG-ANN Baseline

The AVG-ANN Baseline model adapts a simple approach in which it receives the evaluated text embeddings as input and compares the mean value of annotations of all texts to the target values. The method is similar to the majority voting calculation in which the annotations are also aggregated.

5.2. SINGLE-ANN Baseline

The SINGLE-ANN Baseline model implements a commonly investigated approach known in NLP with one unified output for all users. The model receives the evaluated text embeddings as input and trained on each users annotation.

5.3. User-ID

User-ID is a simpler personalization approach that is adapted from (Kocoń et al., 2021a). This approach was briefly mentioned in Dudy et al. (2021), in which it was argued that user-level personalization on language models can be done by conditioning textual generation on different users. With the User-ID approach, the annotator was simply represented as a one-hot vector that was concatenated to the text embeddings. However, one potential issue with that approach is that the dimension of the vector can become quite large with an increase in the number of annotators. Hence, in User-ID method, the annotator is represented by a special token that is added to the text embedding; and in the case of BERT, the special token gets its own embedding.

5.4. Past-Embedding

In Past-Embedding model, personalization is ensured by adding an extra input composed of embeddings of a few texts from Past split along with their annotations given by a user. It is an adaptation of the *Class-based* model from (Kanclerz et al., 2021). These embeddings and annotations form a vector that constitutes a representation of the user beliefs. It is concatenated with an embedding of a currently processed text. This concatenation forms an input to the final classification layer. Embeddings of annotated past texts come from frozen pre-trained language model.

5.5. HuBi-medium: Learned Human Embedding Model

HuBi-medium model is derived from the approach introduced by Kocoń et al. (2021b), in which the multidimensional latent vector of an annotator is optimized for multi-dimensional modeling user subjectivity. This approach is based on the concept of Neural Collaborative Filtering (NFC) in recommender systems (He et al., 2017). A typical issue when directly applying NFC to personal perspective modeling is a cold start, which is a consequence of the small number of annotations assigned for each text, making it difficult to obtain a good representation from scratch. To deal with this problem, we propose an alternative hybrid model that utilizes text representations from language models and optimizes only the annotator's latent vector. Figure 4 illustrates the HuBi-medium architecture to capture the relationship between the annotator and the targeted text, in which the product of element-wise multiplication between the annotator embedding and the text embedding is passed on to the fully connected layer for the final prediction. The prediction is defined as follows:

$$y(t,a) = W_{TU}(a(W_T x_t) \otimes a(W_U x_u)) + \sum_{word \in t} b_{word}$$

where t and u: evaluated text and user; b: a vector of biases indexed with words; x_t, x_u: text embedding of the evaluated text t and embedding of user u, respectively; W_{TA}, W_T, W_A: weights of the fully-connected layers; a: the activation function.

6. Experimental Setup

We formulated all experiments as a multitask classification, in which each task was to predict an accurate label for each emotional category, including one over four classes for arousal and eight emotion types, and one over seven classes for valence. To handle the class imbalance problem, in which other labels are dominated by label '0', the macro F1-score was used for model evaluation. The 10-fold cross-validation is applied to randomly divide the dataset into 10 subsets of the same size.

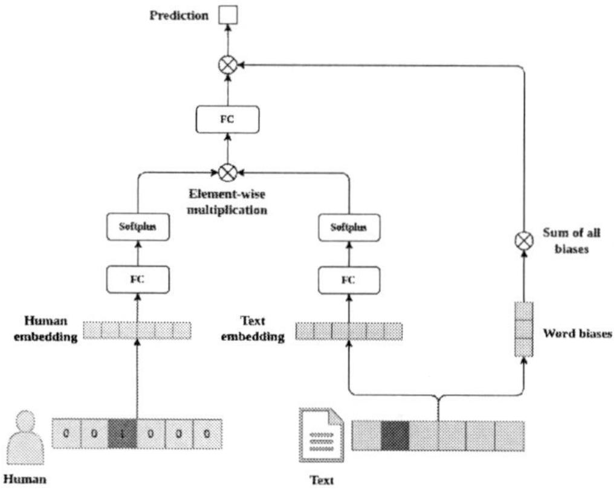

Figure 4: HuBi-medium: learned human embedding model architecture.

6.1. Language Models

A proposed architectures utilize RoBERTa (Liu et al., 2019), a Transformer-based language model, to obtain a representation of text. RoBERTa is an extension of BERT (Devlin et al., 2019) with additional key modifications introduced above BERT's pretraining procedure, including removing the next sentence prediction objective and changing the masking pattern applied to training data dynamically.

All experiments were performed on both the *original* RoBERTa model (*non-finetuned*) and the *finetuned* model. In the non-finetuned scenario, the text embeddings are generated from the pre-trained Transformer's RoBERTa, while in finetuning, the entire pre-trained model was unfrozen, and the entire pre-trained weights are updated during further training on our dataset.

6.2. Hyperparameter Settings

For both scenarios (non-finetuned and finetuned), the optimal values for hyperparameters were obtained for each model separately, in which the optimal learning rate for two baselines was 5e-5, for both User-ID and HuBi-medium was 3e-5, and 1e-5 for Past-Embedding. We used the Adam optimizer and cross-entropy as a loss function. For the *finetuning* scenario, the weight decay was 0.01, and we used the learning rate schedule with a warm-up proportion of 0.1. All models were trained for 20 epochs in both training scenarios, except for finetuned Past-Embedding, where the trained epochs were 10.

In addition, Past-Embedding requires the parameter to control the number of texts in the annotator's past embedding, which is equal to 4. Since the HuBi-medium model extends the standard architecture with human embedding, it requires additional hyperparameters, including the annotator embedding size of 50 and the hidden size of 100 for the classifier's last fully connected layer. A dropout layer with a rate of 0.25 was added to prevent overfitting.

Similar experiments were performed on the GoEmotions dataset, in which we utilized the same parameters, except for learning rates and the number of trained epochs. While the learning rate for both baseline models and HuBi-medium was 3e-5, User-ID was trained with a learning rate of 1e-3, in both non-finetuning and finetuning scenarios. For Past-Embedding, they are 1e-4 and 1e-5, respectively. The epoch number was 10, since it preserves a stable learning curve for all models, except for Past-Embedding, in which we employed 20 epochs without finetuning and 5 epochs on finetuning.

6.3. Statistical Testing

To determine the significance of the differences found in the models' results, statistical tests are performed. The normality of the distribution of the results is checked using Q-Q plots and Shapiro-Wilk test with significance level $\alpha = 0.05$. Depending on that, an appropriate statistical hypothesis test is chosen.

For data with a normal distribution, *independent samples t-test* is used. Since the results are acquired from different models, the assumption that the groups are independent is fulfilled. The homogeneity of the variance is tested using the Levene test. In case the data do not have homogeneous variances, the independent samples t-test is performed using the Welch-Satterthwaite adjusted method.

The independent samples t-test is performed with $\alpha = 0.1$ on results for each emotional category. If $p\_value > \alpha$, then we cannot reject the null hypothesis, which means that there is no significant difference between the results of the two models. If $p\_value \leq \alpha$, then the null hypothesis is rejected, which means that there is a significant difference between the results of the two models.

7. Results

The results of the StudEmo experiment scenarios for each emotional category are presented in Table 1-p.6 for the *non-finetuning* scenario and Table 2-p.6 for the *finetuning* scenario. The results of GoEmotions experiment scenarios for each emotional category are presented in Table 3-p.7 for the *non-finetuning* scenario and in Table 4-p.7 for the *finetuning* scenario. Figure 5-p.6 presents boxplots of the averaged macro F1-scores among all categories for all experiment scenarios on the StudEmo dataset. The analogous plot for the GoEmotion experiments is shown in Figure 6-p.7.

Generally, the differences in results for HuBi-medium and Past-Embedding are not significant in most cases. For StudEmo dataset, the latter achieved slightly better results and vice-versa for GoEmotions dataset. However, the difference is not drastic, only about 1.3 - 1.8 pp, which shows the stability in the performance of Past-Embedding. The only exception is observed in non-finetuned models on StudEmo, in which HuBi-medium is 8.4% behind Past-Embedding. This phenomenon may arise because the HuBi medium benefits more from finetuning and a larger dataset. For larger datasets like GoEmotions, Past-Embedding also took advantage of finetuning considerably much higher than with small datasets like StudEmo, in which there is no significant difference between the two strategies.

7.1. StudEmo

Overall, the best results were obtained for the Past-Embedding method in both non-finetuned and finetuned scenarios, with the mean macro F1-score of 34.4% and 34.3%, respectively (Table 1, Table 2). Statistical tests reveal no statistical significance between these two scenarios, which shows that Past-Embedding does not benefit from finetuning. Additionally, Figure 5 shows that the finetuned Past-Embedding results have a broader range than the original accompanying slightly positive skewing and outliers. It indicates a larger data dispersion and instability for the finetuned variant of Past Embedding.

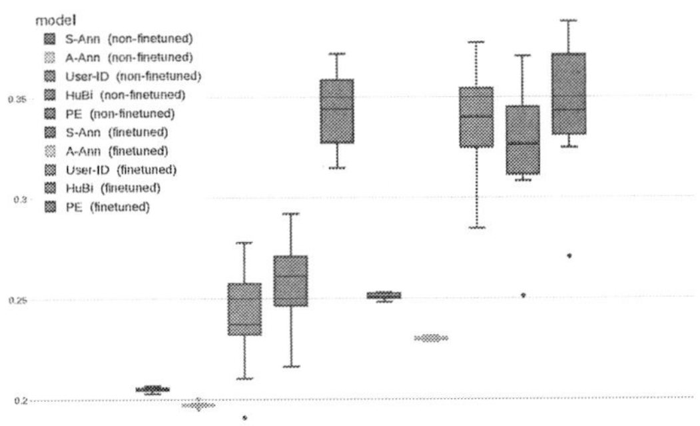

Figure 5: Test macro F1 mean results from non-finetuned and finetuned models, run on StudEmo dataset. S-Ann: SINGLE-ANN, A-Ann: AVG-ANN, HuBi: HuBi-medium, PE: Past-Embedding.

Emotions	S-Ann	A-Ann	User-ID	HuBi	PE
anger	19.1%	19.5%	20.7%	29.4%	**40.7%**
anticipation	20.3%	20.6%	21.3%	22.4%	**29.8%**
arousal	20.7%	19.5%	23.5%	26.6%	**37.8%**
disgust	20.9%	20.9%	20.5%	21.7%	**30.9%**
fear	22.7%	23.0%	29.8%	29.8%	**33.6%**
joy	19.5%	19.6%	20.9%	23.4%	**34.1%**
sadness	21.5%	21.7%	24.5%	24.5%	**30.0%**
surprise	21.9%	21.8%	21.6%	21.6%	**24.6%**
trust	19.4%	19.2%	19.7%	21.0%	**33.6%**
valence	18.8%	11.5%	36.5%	39.1%	**49.5%**
Mean	20.5%	19.7%	23.9%	26.0%	**34.4%**

Table 1: Test macro F1 results for models in *non-finetuned* scenario run on StudEmo dataset. S-Ann: SINGLE-ANN, A-Ann: AVG-ANN, HuBi: HuBi-medium, PE: Past-Embedding. The best model for a specified emotion is marked in bold.

For the *non-finetuned* scenario, there are remarkable differences between the three personalized models. The gap between the best (Past-Embedding) and the worst (User-ID) is approximately 10.5 pp. HuBi-medium with 26% of macro F1-score on average is situated between them. Table 1 demonstrates that Past-Embedding and HuBi-medium outperformed User-ID on all emotions, except fear, sadness, and surprise, for which HuBi-medium and User-ID resulted similarly.

In contrast, an interesting phenomenon was observed for the *finetuned* scenario, in which both User-ID and HuBi-medium took advantage of finetuning. User-ID achieved 34% of macro F1-score on average, which is 10.1 pp higher than the non-finetuned User-ID and only 0.3 pp lower than Past-Embedding, followed by HuBi-medium, which increased from 26% to 32.5%. Furthermore, statistical tests showed almost no significance in the differences between these three finetuned personalized models, indicating that they are all comparable.

Emotions	S-Ann	A-Ann	User-ID	HuBi	PE
anger	30.9%	24.0%	**45.2%**	43.9%	44.3%
anticipation	23.4%	20.9%	**29.2%**	26.9%	28.8%
arousal	27.2%	28.9%	29.1%	27.5%	**30.2%**
disgust	22.7%	20.9%	**31.8%**	30.0%	30.9%
fear	22.7%	23.0%	28.2%	**29.8%**	**29.8%**
joy	25.9%	21.9%	36.9%	35.5%	**39.3%**
sadness	21.5%	21.7%	28.4%	24.6%	**29.6%**
surprise	**21.9%**	21.8%	21.6%	21.6%	21.6%
trust	22.3%	19.7%	**43.0%**	38.8%	40.0%
valence	32.5%	27.4%	46.6%	46.1%	**48.6%**
Mean	25.1%	23.0%	34.0%	32.5%	**34.3%**

Table 2: Test macro F1 results for models in *finetuned* scenario run on StudEmo dataset. S-Ann: SINGLE-ANN, A-Ann: AVG-ANN, HuBi: HuBi-medium, PE: Past-Embedding. The best model for a specified emotion is marked in bold.

However, Figure 5 exhibits a moderately wide range in User-ID's macro F1-score distribution compared to the other personalized models, implying a broader dispersion of predictions. In terms of that comparison, Past-Embedding, and HuBi-medium have shown more stable and less scattered predictions.

Detailed studies of the results for particular emotions demonstrate some differences among personalized methods, even though they are relatively comparable on average. Past-Embedding outperformed the other models in predicting four emotions, including arousal, joy, sadness, and valence. Meanwhile, User-ID achieved the best results in predicting anger, anticipation, disgust, and trust. Both HuBi-medium and Past-Embedding got the same score on *fear*. Exceptionally, the best result for *surprise* came from the SINGLE-ANN baseline with 21.9%, while all personalized methods got slightly lower at 21.6%. Interestingly, except for the original Past-Embedding, which achieved 24.6% for *surprise*, all other experiments got almost identical results of approximately 21% on that emotion. The high imbalance of classes distribution for that emotion (value 0 is nearly 20 times more frequent than value 3), together with the low annotator agreement of 0.09 on the Cohen's kappa coefficient, could be the reason to explain this phenomenon. A similar case can also be be seen for *fear*, in which all the non-finetuned and finetuned baselines resulted in the same score of 23%, while finetuned HuBi-medium could achieve 29.8%, and the non-finetuned Past-Embedding obtained 33.6%. *Fear* is also a contentious emotion that got only 0.08 of Cohen's kappa coefficient and was affected by a high imbalance. These phenomena strengthen the benefits of the personalized methods on high-controversial emotions, such as *fear* and *surprise*.

The highest results were obtained for *valence* (49.5% with non-finetuned Past-Embedding method), *anger* (45.2% with finetuned User-ID), and *trust* (43% with finetuned User-ID). The Cohen's kappa coefficient for *valence* is relatively high and equals 0.52, which can explain the higher performance. However, in contrast to personalized approaches, without finetuning, two baselines performed the worst on valence, especially the AVG-ANN, which got to the bottom at 11.5% on predicting valence (Table 1). It demonstrates that even for less controversial emotions, the application of the personalized methods give performance gain.

7.2. GoEmotions

In the case of GoEmotions, the best performing baseline model is the finetuned AVG-ANN, with an average macro F1-score of 50.9%. Meanwhile, the best personalized model is the finetuned HuBi-medium, with an average macro F1-score of 66.1%. In Figure 6, we can see that the best personalized model outperformed the best baseline in both non-finetuned and finetuned scenarios. Statistical testing also proved that the differences between the best personalized model and the best baseline are statistically significant.

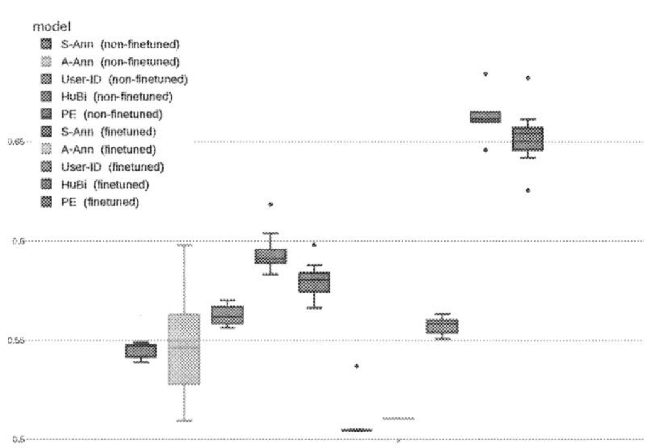

Figure 6: Test macro F1 mean results from non-finetuned and finetuned models, run on GoEmotions dataset. S-Ann: SINGLE-ANN, A-Ann: AVG-ANN, HuBi: HuBi-medium, PE: Past-Embedding.

The non-finetuned baseline AVG-ANN model exhibited an interesting behavior, which can be seen in Table 3., and *relief* emotions. For *nervousness*, *pride*, *remorse*, *desire*, and *grief* it obtained macro F1-score median of around 0.49, but outliers could reach a macro F1-score of 1.0. In the case of *grief* and *relief*, the macro F1-score median was 1.0 with a mean value of about 0.8, yet the distribution was very wide. Consequently, the mean of the macro F1-score of the non-finetuned AVG-ANN became abnormally high in these emotions.

Emotions	S-Ann	A-Ann	User-ID	HuBi	PE
desire	52.7%	55.0%	54.9%	**59.4%**	56.3%
nervousness	49.8%	**65.0%**	50.7%	50.3%	50.9%
pride	49.9%	**65.0%**	51.1%	52.0%	52.3%
remorse	57.8%	55.0%	59.9%	61.8%	**63.3%**
grief	50.3%	**85.0%**	55.2%	51.6%	55.9%
relief	49.8%	**80.0%**	50.4%	50.2%	50.4%
gratitude	82.2%	78.8%	84.1%	**87.9%**	83.5%
fear	54.5%	49.9%	59.1%	**60.6%**	59.1%
embarrassment	49.7%	50.0%	50.2%	50.0%	**50.4%**
joy	52.0%	49.9%	54.7%	**59.2%**	55.5%
disgust	51.0%	49.9%	52.6%	**55.2%**	52.9%
sadness	53.9%	49.9%	55.9%	**58.8%**	56.2%
surprise	52.5%	49.9%	54.9%	**56.7%**	55.0%
Mean	54.5%	54.7%	56.3%	**59.4%**	58.1%

Table 3: Test macro F1 results for models in *non-finetuned* scenario run on GoEmotions dataset. S-Ann: SINGLE-ANN, A-Ann: AVG-ANN, HuBi: HuBi-medium, PE: Past-Embedding. The best model for a specified emotion is marked in bold.

Furthermore, it was found that the model was never detecting the considered emotions; it always predicts the lack of these emotions. Meanwhile, there is a remarkably high imbalance in these categories (class *0* is present 312 times more frequently than class *1*). These emotion categories are so rare that they are not available in some test folds, giving a perfect F1-score even though the model was always predicting zero. However, the finetuned baseline AVG-ANN showed a much more stable behavior and greatly reduced outliers.

Emotions	S-Ann	A-Ann	User-ID	HuBi	PE
desire	49.7%	50.0%	54.3%	63.9%	**65.2%**
nervousness	49.8%	50.0%	50.7%	**55.5%**	53.6%
pride	49.8%	50.0%	51.5%	**58.8%**	52.3%
remorse	50.6%	50.0%	59.7%	67.8%	**73.1%**
grief	49.9%	50.0%	53.8%	**57.2%**	50.5%
relief	49.8%	50.0%	50.5%	**55.8%**	51.2%
gratitude	74.9%	74.0%	84.1%	89.8%	**90.3%**
fear	49.7%	49.9%	58.2%	72.8%	**73.7%**
embarrassment	49.7%	50.0%	50.0%	61.9%	**62.1%**
joy	49.2%	49.9%	54.2%	64.5%	**64.9%**
disgust	49.4%	49.9%	51.4%	**63.5%**	61.8%
sadness	49.6%	49.9%	55.3%	66.9%	**68.7%**
surprise	49.5%	49.9%	54.4%	67.9%	**68.6%**
Mean	50.8%	50.9%	55.8%	**66.1%**	65.3%

Table 4: Test macro F1 results for models in *finetuned* scenario run on GoEmotions dataset. S-Ann: SINGLE-ANN, A-Ann: AVG-ANN, HuBi: HuBi-medium, PE: Past-Embedding. The best model for a specified emotion is marked in bold.

HuBi-medium benefits significantly from finetuning in the case of the GoMEotions dataset. Statistical testing showed that there is a significant difference between the non-finetuned and the finetuned model for every category, with a macro F1-score difference of about 6.7 pp on average.

Past-Embedding also conveyed good performance on GoEmotions. Without finetuning, it reached an average macro F1-score of 58.1%, only 1.3% behind HuBi-medium. With finetuning, it reached 65.3%, 1.2% behind the HuBi-medium. It shows the model benefits a lot from finetuning. Nevertheless, despite the relatively small difference with HuBi-medium, statistical testing showed that the difference is significant.

In the finetuned scenario, Past-Embedding is actually the best-performing model for the most of emotions. However, the differences with comparison to HuBi-medium are minimal. On the other hand, HuBi-medium is the best model for the remaining categories with considerable advantages for some of them.

The other personalized method, i.e. User-ID was not as good as HuBi-medium or Past-Embedding, and it was greatly outperformed by HuBi-medium and Past-Embedding on almost every category. However, it still was statistically better compared to both baselines.

We assume User-ID method was struggling more than the other personalized models because of the high number of annotators in the dataset. There are 82 annotators, which is three times more than in the StudEmo dataset. Thus it is harder for the model to learn the user special tokens. It would require more time to learn them properly. Having too many tokens without enough training may lead to a generalization problem, hence the lower performance.

Nevertheless, there are a few categories where User-ID and Past-Embedding performed almost similarly, namely *nervousness* (2.9 pp difference), *pride* (0.8 pp difference), and *relief* (0.7 pp difference). These categories are affected by high data imbalance. It appears that HuBi-medium is able to deal with the high data imbalance the best, while User-ID and Past-Embedding are less efficient in dealing with the issue.

The experiments for the GoEmotions dataset revealed again that the performance of the personalized approaches is much better than for the baselines. In that case, the best model was the HuBi-medium.

8. Conclusions and Future Work

In this work, we present StudEmo, a non-aggregated, manually annotated review dataset for personalized emotion recognition. We also provide detailed information about the source of the texts and annotations, along with the data characteristics including data distribution, number of annotators, and inter-annotator agreement. The dataset keeps all the decisions of the annotators without aggregating or combining them in any way. Thanks to that, it can be used as a benchmark for personalized NLP methods.

That dataset was used to compare the personalized methods with non-personalized baselines. Additional experiments were also performed on the GoEmotions dataset. Two baseline methods were considered: the AVG-ANN baseline which represents the aggregated approach, and the SINGLE-ANN baseline, which represents the non-personalized approach where the model learns individual annotations without any further information about the annotators. Three personalized methods were analyzed: User-ID, where the model is provided with information about the user in the form of a special token; Past-Embedding, where the user beliefs are represented by a vector of the text embeddings and annotations, and HuBi-medium, where additional human embeddings and word biases are learned. For both datasets, the results showed that the personalized methods deliver significantly higher performance compared to baselines.

In StudEmo, the Past-Embedding method featured the highest performance. Without finetuning, it was considerably better compared to not only the baselines, but also the other two personalized models. However, with finetuning, there is no significant difference in the results from User-ID, Past-Embedding, and HuBi-medium. It was shown that finetuning leads to large performance gain for HuBi medium and User-ID methods. The bigger difference between the personalized and non-personalized methods is observed for some controversial emotions. Extra knowledge about user beliefs allows the model to make more appropriate and personalized decisions.

On GoEmotions, HuBi-medium showed the greatest performance with a significant margin. It is slightly better than Past-Embedding, and remarkably better than User-ID and the baselines. We assume that User-ID did not perform as well because a large number of special tokens were injected into the language model. HuBi-medium and Past-Embedding benefit significantly from finetuning.

In future work, the effect of the number of texts in the *Past* split needs to be investigated further because it determines how much knowledge about a user is known to the model. We also would like to see if some ordering of these past texts, such as ranking them by controversy, can further improve the performance.

9. Acknowledgements

This work was financed by (1) the National Science Centre, Poland, project no. 2019/33/B/HS2/02814 and 2021/41/B/ST6/04471; (2) the Polish Ministry of Education and Science, CLARIN-PL; (3) the European Regional Development Fund as a part of the 2014-2020 Smart Growth Operational Programme, CLARIN – Common Language Resources and Technology Infrastructure, project no. POIR.04.02.00-00C002/19; (4) the statutory funds of the Department of Artificial Intelligence, Wroclaw University of Science and Technology.

10. Bibliographical References

Abdullah, M., Hadzikadicy, M., and Shaikhz, S. (2018). Sedat: Sentiment and emotion detection in arabic text using cnn-lstm deep learning. In *2018 17th IEEE International Conference on Machine Learning and Applications (ICMLA)*, pages 835–840.

Akhtar, M. S., Ekbal, A., and Cambria, E. (2020a). How intense are you? predicting intensities of emotions and sentiments using stacked ensemble [application notes]. *IEEE Computational Intelligence Magazine*, 15(1):64–75.

Akhtar, S., Basile, V., and Patti, V. (2020b). Modeling annotator perspective and polarized opinions to improve hate speech detection. *Proceedings of the AAAI Conference on Human Computation and Crowdsourcing*, 8(1):151–154, Oct.

Basile, V., Cabitza, F., Campagner, A., and Fell, M. (2021). Toward a perspectivist turn in ground truthing for predictive computing. *ArXiv*, abs/2109.04270.

Bellés-Calvera, L. and Quintana, R. C. (2021). Audiovisual translation through nmt and subtitling in the netflix series 'cable girls'. *Proceedings of the Translation and Interpreting Technology Online Conference TRITON 2021*.

Cambedda, G., Nunzio, G. M. D., and Nosilia, V. (2021). A study on automatic machine translation tools: A comparative error analysis between deepl and yandex for russian-italian medical translation.

Chiorrini, A., Diamantini, C., Mircoli, A., and Potena, D. (2021). Emotion and sentiment analysis of tweets using bert. In *EDBT/ICDT Workshops*, 03.

Davani, A. M., Díaz, M., and Prabhakaran, V. (2022). Dealing with Disagreements: Looking Beyond the Majority Vote in Subjective Annotations. *Transactions of the Association for Computational Linguistics*, 10:92–110, 01.

Devlin, J., Chang, M.-W., Lee, K., and Toutanova, K. (2019). Bert: Pre-training of deep bidirectional transformers for language understanding. In *NAACL*.

Dudy, S., Bedrick, S., and Webber, B. (2021). Refocusing on relevance: Personalization in nlg. *EMNLP 2021 main conference*.

Fayek, H., Lech, M., and Cavedon, L. (2016). Modeling subjectiveness in emotion recognition with deep neural networks: Ensembles vs soft labels. In *2016 International Joint Conference on Neural Networks (IJCNN)*, pages 566–570, 07.

Ghosh, S. and Kumar, S. (2021). Cisco at SemEval-2021 task 5: What's toxic?: Leveraging transformers for multiple toxic span extraction from online comments. In *Proceedings of the 15th International Workshop on Semantic Evaluation (SemEval-2021)*, pages 249–257, Online, August. Association for Computational Linguistics.

He, X., Liao, L., Zhang, H., Nie, L., Hu, X., and Chua, T.-S. (2017). Neural collaborative filtering. *Proceedings of the 26th International Conference on World Wide Web*.

Hernandez, J., Lovejoy, J., McDuff, D., Suh, J., O'Brien, T., Sethumadhavan, A., Greene, G., Picard, R., and Czerwinski, M. (2021). Guidelines for assessing and minimizing risks of emotion recognition applications. *2021 9th International Conference on Affective Computing and Intelligent Interaction (ACII)*.

Hidalgo-Ternero, C. M. (2021). Google translate vs. deepl: analysing neural machine translation performance under the challenge of phraseological variation. *MonTI. Monographs in translation and interpreting*, pages 154–177.

Janz, A., Kocon, J., Piasecki, M., and Zasko-Zielinska, M. (2017). plWordNet as a basis for large emotive lexicons of Polish. *Proceedings of Human Language Technologies as a Challenge for Computer Science and Linguistics Poznan: Fundacja Uniwersytetu im. Adama Mickiewicza w Poznaniu*, pages 189–193.

Kamran, S., Zall, R., Kangavari, M. R., Hosseini, S., Rahmani, S., and Hua, W. (2021). Emodnn: Understanding emotions from short texts through a deep neural network ensemble.

Kanclerz, K., Figas, A., Gruza, M., Kajdanowicz, T., Kocon, J., Puchalska, D., and Kazienko, P. (2021). Controversy and conformity: from generalized to personalized aggressiveness detection. In *Proceedings of the 59th Annual Meeting of the Association for Computational Linguistics and the 11th International Joint Conference on Natural Language Processing (Volume 1: Long Papers)*, pages 5915–5926, Online, August. Association for Computational Linguistics.

Kocoń, J., Figas, A., Gruza, M., Puchalska, D., Kajdanowicz, T., and Kazienko, P. (2021a). Offensive, aggressive, and hate speech analysis: From data-centric to human-centered approach. *Information Processing & Management*, 58(5):102643.

Kocoń, J., Gruza, M., Bielaniewicz, J., Grimling, D., Kanclerz, K., Miłkowski, P., and Kazienko, P. (2021b). Learning personal human biases and representations for subjective tasks in natural language processing. In *2021 IEEE International Conference on Data Mining (ICDM)*, pages 1168–1173, 12.

Krommyda, M., Rigos, A., Bouklas, K., and Amditis, A. (2021). An experimental analysis of data annotation methodologies for emotion detection in short text posted on social media. *Informatics*, 8(1).

Lee, J.-H., Kim, H.-J., and Cheong, Y.-G. (2020). A multi-modal approach for emotion recognition of tv drama characters using image and text. In *2020 IEEE International Conference on Big Data and Smart Computing (BigComp)*, pages 420–424, 02.

Li, J.-L. and Lee, C.-C. (2019). Attentive to Individual: A Multimodal Emotion Recognition Network with Personalized Attention Profile. In *Proc. Interspeech 2019*, pages 211–215.

Li, W. and Xu, H. (2014). Text-based emotion classification using emotion cause extraction. *Expert Systems with Applications*, 41(4, Part 2):1742–1749.

Liu, Y., Ott, M., Goyal, N., Du, J., Joshi, M., Chen, D., Levy, O., Lewis, M., Zettlemoyer, L., and Stoyanov, V. (2019). Roberta: A robustly optimized bert pretraining approach. *ArXiv*, abs/1907.11692.

Miłkowski, P., Gruza, M., Kanclerz, K., Kazienko, P., Grimling, D., and Kocoń, J. (2021). Personal bias in prediction of emotions elicited by textual opinions. In *Proceedings of the 59th Annual Meeting of the Association for Computational Linguistics and the 11th International Joint Conference on Natural Language Processing: Student Research Workshop*, pages 248–259, 08.

Mohammad, S. M. and Bravo-Marquez, F. (2017). Emotion intensities in tweets. In *Proceedings of the sixth joint conference on lexical and computational semantics (*Sem)*, Vancouver, Canada.

Wang, X. and Tong, Y. (2021). Application of bert+attention model in emotion recognition of netizens during epidemic period. *Journal of Physics: Conference Series*, 1982(1):012102, jul.

Zaśko-Zielińska, M. and Piasecki, M. (2018). Towards emotive annotation in plWordNet 4.0. In *Proceedings of the 9th Global Wordnet Conference*, pages 153–162.

11. Language Resource References

Demszky, Dorottya and Movshovitz-Attias, Dana and Ko, Jeongwoo and Cowen, Alan and Nemade, Gaurav and Ravi, Sujith. (2020). *GoEmotions: A Dataset of Fine-Grained Emotions*. arXiv.

Kennedy, Chris J and Bacon, Geoff and Sahn, Alexander and von Vacano, Claudia. (2020). *Constructing interval variables via faceted Rasch measurement and multitask deep learning: a hate speech application*.

Kocoń, Jan and Miłkowski, Piotr and Kanclerz, Kamil. (2021). *MultiEmo: Multilingual, Multilevel, Multidomain Sentiment Analysis Corpus of Consumer Reviews*. Springer International Publishing.

Kocoń, Jan and Janz, Arkadiusz and Miłkowski, Piotr and Riegel, Monika and Wierzba, Małgorzata and Marchewka, Artur and Czoska, Agnieszka and Grimling, Damian and Konat, Barbara and Juszczyk, Konrad and Klessa, Katarzyna and Piasecki, Maciej. (2019). *Recognition of emotions, valence and arousal in large-scale multi-domain text reviews*.

Leonardelli, Elisa and. Menini, Stefano and Palmero Aprosio, Alessio and Guerini, Marco and Tonelli, Sara. (2021). *Agreeing to Disagree: Annotating Offensive Language Datasets with Annotators' Disagreement*. Association for Computational Linguistics.

Wierzba, Małgorzata and Riegel, Monika and Kocoń, Jan and Miłkowski, Piotr and Janz, Arkadiusz and Klessa, Katarzyna and Juszczyk, Konrad and Konat, Barbara and Grimling, Damian and Piasecki, Maciej and Marchewka, Artur. (2021). *Emotion norms for 6000 Polish word meanings with a direct mapping to the Polish wordnet*.

Proceedings of the 1st Workshop on Perspectivist Approaches to NLP @LREC2022, pages 56–65
Marseille, 20 June 2022

Annotator Response Distributions as a Sampling Frame

Christopher M. Homan, Tharindu Cyril Weerasooriya, Lora Aroyo, Chris Welty
Rochester Institute of Technology, Google
USA
cmh@cs.rit.edu, {cyriltcw, l.m.aroyo, cawelty}@gmail.com

Abstract

Annotator disagreement is often dismissed as noise or the result of poor annotation process quality. Others have argued that it can be meaningful. But lacking a rigorous statistical foundation, the analysis of disagreement patterns can resemble a high-tech form of tea-leaf-reading. We contribute a framework for analyzing the variation of per-item annotator response distributions to data for humans-in-the-loop machine learning. We provide visualizations for, and use the framework to analyze the variance in, a crowdsourced dataset of hard-to-classify examples of the OpenImages archive.

Keywords: preserving disagreement, statistical methods, empirical study

1. Introduction

With a market expected to hit $1.2 billion by 2023, human annotation accounts for 80% of the time spent building A.I. technology. (Metz, 2019). Whether obtained by a small team of experts, or an anonymous pool of crowdworkers, it is generally considered good practice to obtain responses from multiple annotators for each example in a dataset, for the reason that human annotators are unreliable and annotation tasks are ambiguous. And so disagreement is seen as a sign of something to be corrected. Put more formally, machine learning problems are probability distributions over a joint (example, response) space $\mathcal{X} \times \mathcal{Y}$ (Shalev-Shwartz and Ben-David, 2014). Usually, the distribution over $\mathcal{Y}$ has a Bayesian interpretation, where $\mathrm{P}(y \mid x)$ is seen as uncertainty over the response.

An alternate view is that disagreement is meaningful and may be the result of differences in annotator values, beliefs, or values that carries meaningful signals (Aroyo and Welty, 2015; Liu et al., 2019; Akhtar et al., 2019; Klenner et al., 2020; Weerasooriya et al., 2020; Davani et al., 2022; Basile, 2020). We are particularly interested in crowdsourced settings, where there are typically more annotators per example than with expert annotations. Taking a strictly frequentist approach, we interpret $\mathrm{P}(y \mid x)$ as the likelihood of drawing an annotator who responds to example x with y. We are thus interested in asking *How confident are we that* $\mathrm{P}(y \mid x)$ *represents the ground truth distribution of annotator responses?*.

We apply hypothesis tests via bootstrap sampling (Efron, 1992) to explore this question on a dataset that is particularly rich in annotatator disagreement. A major design decision in this case is which test statistic to use. If we were measuring machine performance, we could use any number of standard evaluation measures, such as accuracy or precision. But here, we need a statistic that can measure the difference in two probability distributions. Many exist, such as KL-divergence and Wasserstein distance. However, these measures do not take into account that our distributions are merely samples. We argue that the likelihood function of the hypothesized sampling frame is the best test statistic in this case.

In this paper, we contribute a framework for analyzing the variance of annotator responses in machine learning training data when the goal is to preserve diversity in annotator responses by treating them as a sample from an underlying pool of respondents. We introduce two variants of bootstrap sampling tailored to this setting that are more efficient and/or less sensitive to sparse data than true bootstrapping. We explore the use of the log-likelihood as a statistic for hypothesis testing in exploratory analyses of response distribution data. And we apply this framework to an empirical study of a data set rich in annotator disagreement.

2. Related Work

Although not as commonly used as in other scientific fields, hypothesis tests has a long history in machine learning (Mitchell, 1997).

Dietterich (Dietterich, 1998) provides a taxonomy of use cases for hypothesis testing on machine learning problems. He focuses on one particular case: that of choosing between two learning algorithms A and B with a small amount ($n \approx 300$) of data. He defines the p-value to be the probability that A's error is less than B's by at least the observed error difference $\delta(\mathbf{x})$, where $\mathbf{x}$ is a sample from the test population. assuming as the null hypothesis H_0 that A and B have equal error rates in the population from which $\mathbf{x}$ was sampled. Formally, this is denoted $p(\delta(\mathbf{x}^*) > \delta(\mathbf{x})|H_0)$, where $\mathbf{x}^*$ is a population sample of size n drawn according to H_0. Thus, in contrast to our paper, he is interested in paired hypothesis tests, as is frequently the case in machine learning.

He compares five different approximations of the p-value on experiments where A and B are simulated and by design have the same error rate, though their responses differ on specific items. He repeats these experiments using two actual (i.e., nonsimulated) machine learning algorithms, where one is "hobbled" to have exactly the same error rate as the other. In this setting he tests the approximations' resistance to Type I errors, as well as their statistical power in the event that the two algorithms do have different error rates.

Berg-Kirkpatrick et al. (Berg-Kirkpatrick et al., 2012) perform an empirical investigation of hypothesis testing across a seven natural language processing (NLP) problems. They survey prior work on these problems where the systems were available for evaluation, and study the relationship between metric gain, $\delta(\mathbf{x})$, statistical significance, and p-values. They argue that the best approach is to bootstrap from the input sample and then consider $p(\delta(\mathbf{x}^*) > 2\delta(\mathbf{x})|H_0)$. Søgaard et al. (Søgaard et al., 2014) study the practical impact of various estimators on p-values.

Reidsma and Carletta (Reidsma and Carletta, 2008) explore the relationship between interrater reliability and machine learning performance. They show that high reliability scores ($> .8$) predict good machine learning performance *as long as noise is unbiased.* If noise is biased, the machine learning algorithm may learn the bias pattern and overfit.

Szymański and Gorman (Szymański and Gorman, 2020) apply a Bayesian framework due to (Corani et al., 2017) to evaluate the performance of English part-of-speech taggers. Rather than p-values based on H_0, their framework estimates the likelihood that system A outperforms system B, using k-fold cross evaluation (across multiple datasets). Zhang et al. (Zhang et al., 2004) use bootstrapping to construct confidence intervals for BLEU scores.

Welty et al. (Welty et al., 2019) study the problem of measuring AI systems from the perspective of *metrology*, the science of measurement and its application. They demonstrate these principles on WordSim (WS353),[1] a crowd-powered dataset for word similarity. They show that the dataset can be *instrumentalized* by describing procedures for (1) collecting the human or crowd data (2) using this data to evaluate the performance of an AI system. The introduce a number of key concepts in metrology and show how they apply in this context. For instance, the *principle of measurement* translates into understanding the limits and opportunities of the measurement frame and how the measurement procedure works, and *indication* translates into the itemwise statistics gathered from asking multiple annotators about the same question. A crucial element of metrology is the recognition that ground truth is fundamentally unknowable, and that one must test and assess the accuracy of any instrument used to measure performance.

[1]https://aclweb.org/aclwiki/WS353ilarity-353_Test_Collection_(State_of_theart)

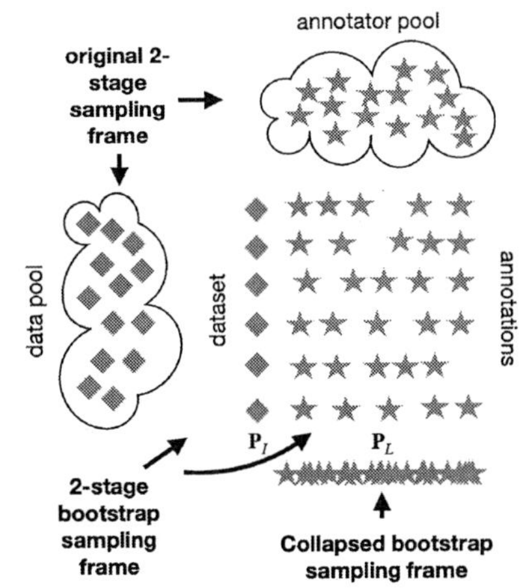

Figure 1: Bootstrapping is a stochastic method for analyzing variance in samples. It treats the sample as an estimate of the underlying (original) sampling frame, and then repeatedly samples with replacement from the empirical sample, obtaining a sample of samples. Annotator sampling is itself a two-stage process, where the empirical sample consists of first drawing from a set of data items (in our case image/label pairs from the Open Images Dataset) and, for each item, sampling from a pool of annotators. However, when the space of annotator responses is relatively simple, we can marginalize over the data items to create a collapsed, one-stage bootstrap sampling frame.

3. Annotator sampling

Here, we describe three variants of bootstrapping that we explore in this paper. We adapt notation from (Efron, 1992). Suppose we have a set of m data items $\mathrm{x} = (x_1, \ldots, x_m)$, sampled from some domain F_I. For each item i, we also have a sample y_i of r annotator responses, where each response comes from a discrete domain of q options, indexed by l. There are multiple ways to represent $\hat{y}_i$. For each response l, we can count the number of annotators what respond with l, which we denote $\hat{y}_{i,l}$. Or we can indicate the response that annotator j provides, which we denote $y_{i,j}$. Note that we use y with and without the $\hat{}$ in part to distinguish these two representations, but also to stress that $\hat{y}_{i,l}$ is not necessarily representative of the underlying population's value for the number of l responses (assuming the underlying population of annotators is much larger than the number of responses in y_i, it is most certainly a much larger number), where $y_{i,j}$ is in fact annotator j's response to item i. We can extend this latter representation to the set of all annotations as a matrix, where the data examples are aligned along the vertical axis and the responses along the horizontal. See Figure 1.

Finally, we can represent y_i as a distribution $\hat{F}_{y_i}$.

Bootstrapping (Efron, 1992) is a stochastic method for estimating the variance of a *test statistic* ϕ from any *empirical sample* $\mathbf{x}$. It constructs a sample of B samples $\mathbf{x}^{*1}, \mathbf{x}^{*2}, \ldots, \mathbf{x}^{*B}$, where each of these latter samples is the same size as the empirical sample and is drawn with replacement from the empirical sample, effectively using the empirical sample as an estimate $\hat{F}_I$ of the original sampling frame F_I. Thus, in our setting, each bootstrap sample $\mathrm{x}^{*j} = (x_1^{*j}, x_2^{*j}, \ldots, x_m^{*j})$ consists of m items sampled with replacement from $\mathrm{x} = (x_1, \ldots, x_m)$. In this way it can account for the impact of sample size on the variance of any test statistic, though if the empirical sample is too small to be representative of the original sampling frame the method can be ineffective.

In the past, when bootstrapping was used to analyze variance in machine learning datasets (Mitchell, 1997; Dietterich, 1998; Zhang et al., 2004; Berg-Kirkpatrick et al., 2012; Søgaard et al., 2014), it was performed over the items only, i.e., in the vertical direction only according to the matrix-style representation shown in Figure 1. In the parlance of our notation, each item x_i^{*j} in each bootstrap sample x^{*j} is associated with the same label y_i^{*j} as its corresponding empirical item. Of course, in most past settings, y_i represented a single response value, as all annotator disagreement was typically resolved before the data was used, and so this vertical-only approach made perfect sense.

As a baseline, we adapt this strategy to our case, i.e., we associate each item x_i^{*j} in each bootstrap sample $\mathbf{x}^{*j}$ with the empirical distribution y_i^{*j} associated with the corresponding empirical item. We call this vertical-only baseline process a *naive bootstrap*.

However, in case of annotator modeling, where we care about the ground truth distribution of annotator responses, the empirical sample is really the result of two-stage process. See Figure 1. First, choose a data item i in the vertical direction, then choose r annotators in the horizontal direction to annotate it.[2]

In many datasets the number of annotators r varies from item to item. But (as in the case of the data we analyze here) if r is the same for each item, then the number of possible response distributions is $\binom{q+r-1}{r-1}$, and when this number is sufficiently small we can simplify boostrapping over this two-stage process by pre-computing the horizontal bootstrap and marginalizing over the examples i. Thus, we construct a distribution $\hat{F}_{q,r}$ over all annotator response distributions y^* of size

[2]This is a simplification of how annotation works in practice. Typically, annotators are not chosen independently for each item, as we assume here. However, for large datasets, as long as the number of items any one annotator sees is small—as is often the case for crowdsourced annotations—we do not believe dependencies between annotators have a significant impact on the analysis described here, although this is certainly a topic worthy of future research.

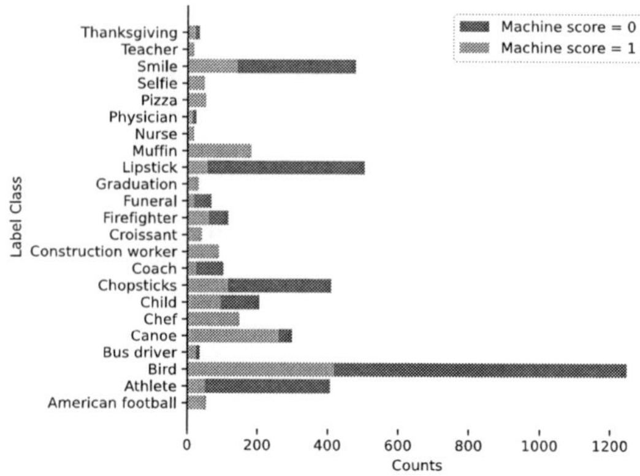

Figure 2: Counts of image/label pairs by machine score.

r:

$$\hat{F}_{q,r}(y^*) = \sum_{i=1}^{m} \hat{F}_{y_i,r}(y^*)\hat{F}_I(x_i) = \frac{1}{m}\sum_{i=1}^{m} \hat{F}_{y_i,r}(y^*), \quad (1)$$

where $\hat{F}_I(x_i) = \frac{1}{m}$ per the rules of bootstrap sampling, and $\hat{F}_{y_i,r}(y^*)$ is the likelihood of drawing the distribution y^* by drawing (with replacement) a sample of size r from $\hat{F}_{y_i}$. We call this approach *collapsed bootstrapping*. Collapsing can greatly speed up the sampling process by eliminating one stage of sampling. Moreover, it removes some of the stochasticity from the process. This, in turn, means that a smaller bootstrap sample is needed.

Finally, many of the annotator response distributions themselves may have no mass on some of the responses (e.g., cases where all five annotators agree on a single response). Therefore, it may make sense to add smoothing to the collapsed distribution. We use Laplace smoothing, with $\alpha = 1$, which assumes a uniform prior over all choices, and we apply this to both stages (i.e., to each $\hat{F}_{y_i,r}$ and to $\hat{F}_{q,r}$ in Equation 1). We call this *smoothed bootstrapping*.

Beyond the sampling process itself, bootstrapping is often used for *hypothesis testing*. This involves choosing test statistics and hypotheses. The mean of some quantity of interest is by far the most common test statistic used. But when the data under consideration (representing the sampling frame) is categorical, or if we are interested qualitatively in the shape of the distribution, KL-divergence or Wasserstein distance might be more appropriate choices. The best statistic and hypotheses to use depends what one is trying to learn from the test. So let us first introduce the dataset we are analyzing, and some of the questions we seek to answer, before considering this question further.

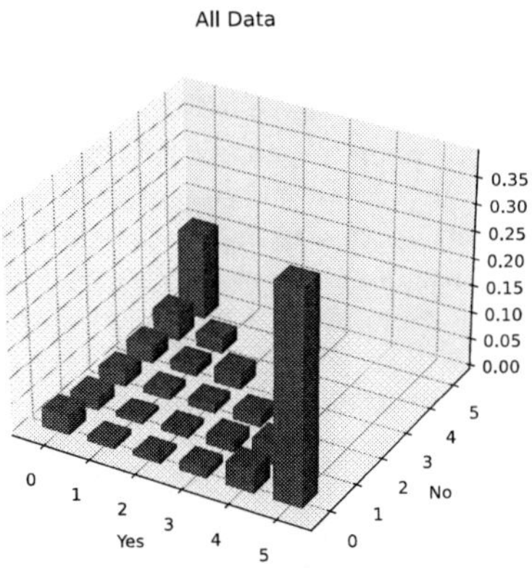

(a) Entire dataset.

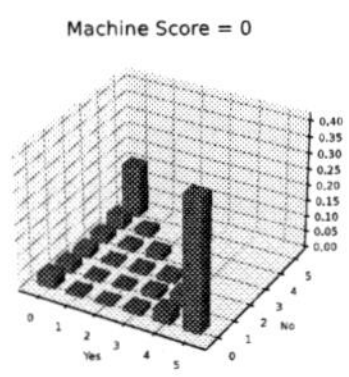

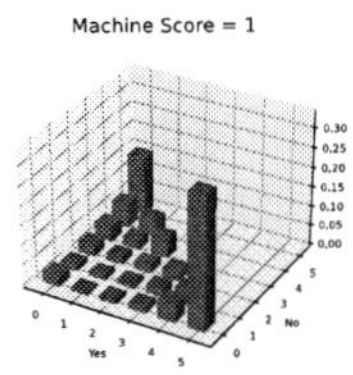

(b) Only item-annotator pairs with $Machine_i = 0$

(c) Only item-annotator pairs with $Machine_i = 1$

Figure 3: Histograms of annotator response distributions. Each image/label is indicated by the number of *Yes* and *No* annotator responses. The number of *Don't know* responses can be calculated from the number of *Yes* and *No* annotator responses and so is not shown. For instance, the $(0, 0)$ corner represents the number of images where all five responses were *Don't know*. The two large peaks in the corners are the item-label pairs on which all annotators agreed on *No* (respectively, *Yes*). The much smaller peak in the left-hand corner are the item-label pairs on which all annotators agreed on the *Don't know*. Note that there appears to be more disagreement among the image/pairs with $Machine_i = 1$.

4. Data

The CATS4ML (Crowdsourcing Adverse Test Sets for Machine Learning) Data Challenge[3] asked participants to find machine learning *blind spots*, i.e., data instances that humans can easily classify, but on which machine learning algorithms fail.

The data consists of $6,393$ examples of image/label pairs from the Open Images Dataset (OID). The labels in these image/label pairs were selected from among 23 label classes, which were sampled from 30K classes available in the OID. Note that "label" often refers to the annotator responses y_i. Here and throughout this paper, we use "label" only to refer to the label class,

[3] https://github.com/google-research-datasets/cats4ml-2021-dataset. See also https://cats4ml.humancomputation.com/.

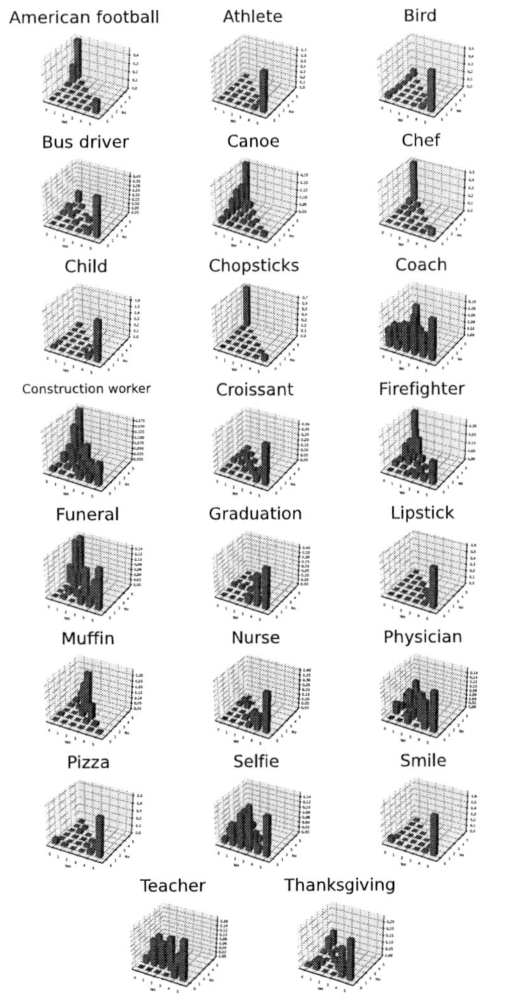

Figure 4: Annotator response distributions by label class.

which is part of the input, and not the annotator responses.

As for the responses, for each image in each image/label pair, five annotators were asked whether the label matched the image. Each image/label pair i has a distribution F_{y_i} over $q = 3$ annotator response choices: *Yes*, *No*, $\neg Know$, which indicate the number of annotators who respond *Yes*, *No*, or *Don't know*, respectively. There is also $\text{Machine}_i \in \{0, 1\}$, a machine response, chosen by randomly sampling the output from two machine-based classifiers (variants of the InceptionV2-based classification that are internal to Google). These human and machine responses were used to adjudicate the submissions to the contest. Figure 2 shows the distribution of images/pairs in the dataset by machine score.

Since there are only three possible label responses, the space of *annotator response distributions* forms a 2-simplex (or triangle), where, since each image/label

Annotator rating		Machine rating 0	1	total
Plurality	Yes	2552	1024	3576
	No	1578	853	2431
Majority	Yes	2423	964	3387
	No	1284	729	2013
≥ 4	Yes	2171	840	3011
	No	998	502	1500
Unanimous	Yes	1820	667	2487
	No	708	298	1000

(a) Distribution of *Yes* and *No* annotator responses based on various disagreement resolution/exclusion policies: only those where the number of yes (respectively, no) responses exceeds no (respectively, yes), those with a majority of yes vs. no votes, those with at least four votes in agreement, and those with unanimous agreement.

Annotator rating		Machine rating 0	1	total
Plurality	Yes	2479	1119	3599
	No	1640	740	2380
Majority	Yes	2341	1057	3398
	No	1391	628	2018
≥ 4	Yes	2094	945	3040
	No	1096	495	1591
Unanimous	Yes	1855	837	2692
	No	836	377	1213

(b) Estimated number of data items by user and machine response according to the collapsed boostrap frame.

Annotator rating		Machine rating 0	1	total
Plurality	Yes	2490	1124	3614
	No	1636	739	2375
Majority	Yes	2307	1042	3349
	No	1357	613	1970
≥ 4	Yes	1968	888	2856
	No	1012	457	1469
Unanimous	Yes	1287	581	1868
	No	584	264	848

(c) Estimated number of data items by user and machine response according to smoothed ($\alpha = 1$) bootstrap frame.

Table 1: According to various bootstrap methods, the distribution of *Yes* and *No* annotator responses based on various disagreement resolution/exclusion policies: only those where the number of yes (respectively, no) responses exceeds no (respectively, yes), those with a majority of yes vs. no votes, those with at least four votes in agreement, and those with unanimous agreement.

pair i has exactly five annotator responses, i.e., $y_{i,\,Yes} + y_{i,No} + y_{i,\neg Know} = 5$, the vertices of the triangle represent unanimous responses (i.e., EITHER $y_{i,\,Yes} = 5$ OR $y_{i,No} = 5$ OR $y_{i,\neg Know} = 5$, and the remaining response choices equal to zero), and the edges and interior space represent responses that have at least some level of annotator disagreement. It is a discrete space of cardinality 21 and so it is easy to precompute the bootstrapping, as shown in Equation (1).

The three-option response schema used in this dataset lends itself very well to visualization. Figure 3 shows histograms in this triangle-like structure of annotator response distributions over, respectively, the entire dataset, just those image/label pairs with $\text{Machine}_i = 0$, and just those with $\text{Machine}_i = 1$, respectively. The differences between the three are very small, though there appears to be slightly more disagreement among the pairs with machine score 1, suggesting that the CATS4ML contestants had mixed (though reasonable given the sparsity of blind spot data) success against the reference machine responses.

Figure 4 shows these same distributions by label class. Here, in contrast to Figure 3, there appear to be significant patterns. For instance, in the *Muffin* label class there is substantial annotator disagreement among annotators between *Yes* and *No*, with very few annotators responding *Don't Know*. This may be because muffins are only well-known in the US, Canada, and Great Britain, and in the US and Canada they are sweet snacks resembling cupcakes, but in Great Britain they are flat, savory rounds of bread (known as 'English Muffins' in the US and Canada). And so in this case disagreement is not the result of a poorly formed question, and it is not even "ambiguous" in the sense that a single annotator would necessarily recognize that there are multiple interpretations.

In short, there are two obvious ways to partition the data: by the machine score used to adjudicate the CATS4ML contest, and by the label classes. The hypothesis tests we consider in this paper will help us determine whether the patterns of annotator responses seen in Figures 3 and 4 are significant.

But before we get to hypothesis testing, one reason why annotator disagreement is sometimes questioned as a useful signal is because the tasks for which machine classifiers are trained often require discrete decisions (Gordon et al., 2022). But even then, the presence of disagreement requires some sort of resolution process, and the choice of a particular resolution strategy can lead to bias.

Table 1a shows how several common strategies for resolving annotator disagreement affects the distribution of the responses over examples, after resolution over the empirical annotator response distributions. Table 1b (respectively, Table 1c) shows what happens when we use collapsed (respectively, smoothed) bootstrapped frames instead (and taking the expected counts of the image/label pairs, rounded to the nearest whole number, given the sample sample size as the original dataset). The differences between the three sets are very small when the plurality response is used. This is in keeping with conventional wisdom that the number of annotators need not be very large if plurality is used to resolve disagreement (Snow et al., 2008).

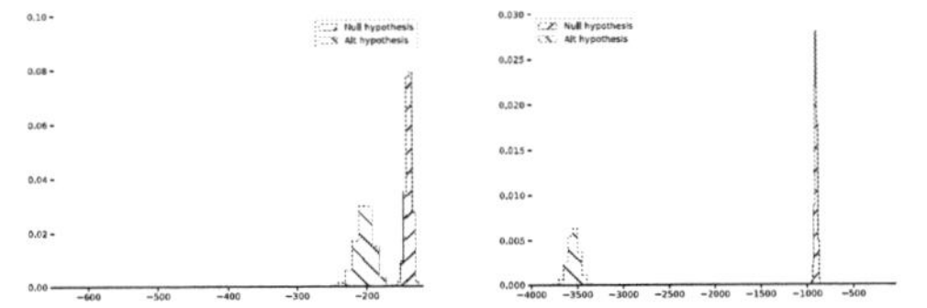

(a) Naive bootstrap ($p = 3 \times 10^{-5}$). (e) Naive bootstrap ($p < 10^{-5}$).

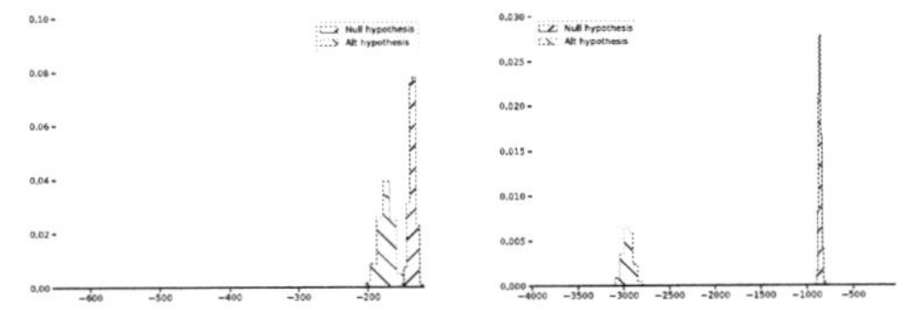

(b) Collapsed bootstrap ($p = .003$). (f) Collapsed bootstrap ($p < 10^{-5}$).

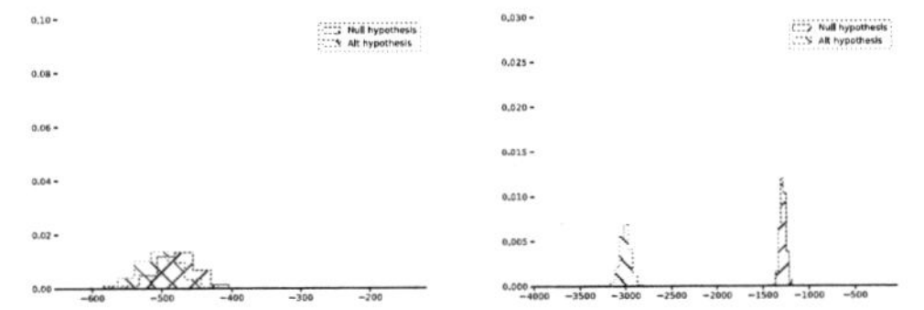

(c) Smoothed bootstrap ($p = .3$). (g) Smoothed bootstrap ($p < 10^{-5}$).

(d) The alternative hypothesis is that the data associated with each **machine score** was generated from a distinct distribution. (h) The alternative hypothesis is that the data associated with each **label class** came from a distinct distribution.

Figure 5: Bootstrap samples where the test statistic is *the log-likelihood of annotator response distributions under the null hypothesis*, with the null hypothesis is that the data was generated from a single distribution and the alternative hypothesis that the data associated with each **machine score** (left) **label class** (right) was generated from a distinct distribution.

However, the differences between the samples became increasingly stark as the aggregation methods become stricter.

5. Tests

We now construct tests for whether the differences observed in annotator response distributions between the data with machine scores of zero versus one, as shown in Figure 3, or with different label classes, as shown in Figure 4, are significant. For any partitioning of the dataset $D = D_1 \cup \cdots \cup D_s$ (where the partitioning might represent the different machine scores or the various label classes), let the *null hypothesis* be that the annotator response distributions y_i were sampled from the same underlying distribution F_D, as estimated by the bootstrap sampling frame over all the label distributions D. In our dataset, for naive bootstrapping this is the distribution shown in Figure 3a.

This is a very strong null hypothesis. It is much more common to define the null hypothesis in terms of a test statistic and not worry about the underlying distributions. This is because, when the null hypothesis is rejected, such weaker hypotheses tend to confer a more positive view of the test statistic, and often it is the test statistic that is of primary interest, because it is a measure of performance. But our motivation here is not to evaluate performance; rather, it is exploratory in nature. And so we are simply interested in whether the differences in the distributions we observed are meaningful. The downside to this approach is that if we reject the null hypothesis, we can only conclude that the differences observed are significant; we cannot reasonably conclude anything positive about the nature of the distributions.

As our test statistic, we use the log-likelihood of the null hypothesis:

$$\log F_D(D_1^*) + \log F_D(D_2^*) + \cdots + \log F_D(D_s^*) \tag{2}$$

Where $D_1^*, \ldots, D_s^*$ are samples of each partition under the null hypotheses, i.e., they are samples of the bootstrap frame F_D.

As for computing the p-value, we could, for each bootstrap sample, compare the value of Equation (2) to the log-likelihood of the original sample $\log F_D(D_1) + \log F_D(D_2) + \cdots + \log F_D(D_s)$. However, this does not take into account that there is sample variance in the *alternative hypothesis* i.e., that each $D_1, D_2, \ldots, D_s$ was drawn from a unique distribution, $F_{D_1}, F_{D_2}, \cdots, F_{D_s}$, respectively, that is estimated by sampling with replacement only from the response distributions in each partition.

And so we compute a second bootstrap, using the alternative hypothesis as the sampling frame, sampling each $D_1^*, D_2^*, \ldots, D_s^*$ directly from the bootstrapping frame associated with its partition's original sample $F_{D_1}, F_{D_2}, \cdots, F_{D_s}$ and for each sample compute its log-likelihood $\log F_D(D_1^*) + \log F_D(D_2^*) + \cdots + \log F_D(D_s^*)$ under the null hypothesis.

We then take the p-value to be the point at which the the observed test statistic is more likely under the alternative hypothesis than the null hypothesis, according to the bootstrap samples.

In each of the subfigures in of Figures 5d and 5h, the orange (leftmost) distributions are the values of the test statistic under the alternative hypothesis and the blue (rightmost) distributions are same values under the null hypothesis. The p-value is the area under the blue distribution's curve to the left of where the two curves intersect (when they intersect).

6. Experiments

Figures 5d and 5h show the results of these tests for partitioning by machine score and label class, respectively, along with the p-values associated with each test. The size of each bootstrap sample was $100K$.

	Smoothed	Collapsed	Naive	KL	Wasserstein
Precision	9/9	9/9	8/9	6/9	5/9
1	Muffin	Muffin	Muffin	Muffin	Teacher
2	Canoe	Canoe	Canoe	Canoe	Athlete
3	Chopsticks	Chopsticks	Chopsticks	Teacher	Physician
4	Chef	Chef	Chef	Graduation	Chopsticks
5	Athlete	Athlete	Athlete	Chopsticks	Coach
6	Lipstick	Coach	Coach	Chef	Funeral
7	Smile	Lipstick	Lipstick	Athlete	Smile
8	Coach	Smile	Selfie	American football	Selfie
9	Child	Child	Smile	Coach	Child
10	Selfie	Bird	Child	Lipstick	Graduation
11	Firefighter	Selfie	Firefighter	Nurse	Construction worker
12	American football	Firefighter	Bird	Selfie	American football
13	Construction worker	American football	American football	Smile	Lipstick
14	Teacher	Construction worker	Construction worker	Construction worker	Thanksgiving
15	Bird	Teacher	Funeral	Child	Firefighter
16	Funeral	Funeral	Teacher	Firefighter	Canoe
17	Physician	Physician	Physician	Physician	Bird
18	Pizza	Pizza	Pizza	Pizza	Nurse
19	Graduation	Croissant	Croissant	Funeral	Pizza
20	Croissant	Graduation	Graduation	Croissant	Muffin
21	Nurse	Nurse	Thanksgiving	Thanksgiving	Chef
22	Thanksgiving	Thanksgiving	Nurse	Bus driver	Croissant
23	Bus driver	Bus driver	Bus driver	Bird	Bus driver

Table 2: Label classes ranked by most-to-least distant from the null hypothesis distribution, according to p-value by bootstrap strategy (smoothed, naive, collapsed), KL-divergence, or Wasserstein distance. In the smoothed test, all items above line 9 reject the null hypothesis at the $p = .05$ level, with Bonferroni correction. Note that the first seven results in the first column (and more in the second and third columns) all have a p-values of less than 10^{-5}, which is beyond the precision of the bootstrap to handle. And so we used the order of the items in the KL column to settle ties in those cases.

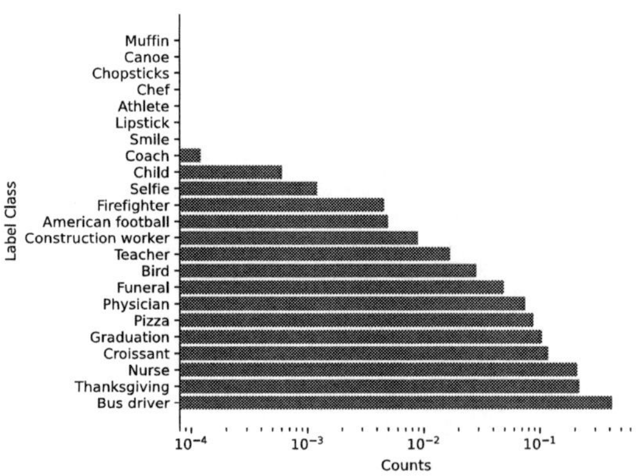

Figure 6: p-values from smoothed bootstrap samples where the test statistic is *the log-likelihood of annotator response distributions under the null hypothesis, for each class independently*, with the null hypothesis that the data was generated from a single distribution and the alternative hypothesis that data associated with each **label class** was generated from a distinct distribution. Values with no bar have estimated p-values $< 10^{-5}$. The nine classes above "Selfie" are significant at the .05 level after Bonferroni correction for 69 (3×23) tests.

As we expect, as we move from naive to collapsed to smoothed bootstrapping, the variance in each bootstrap sample increases and the null and alternative distributions move closer together. In the case of label class partitioning (Figure 5h), these trends are too small to have a measurable impact on the p-values, which were too small to measure anyway. But Figure 5d shows that for machine score the choice of bootstrap strategy makes a big difference. There, both the naive and collapsed bootstraps yield very low p-values ($p = 3 \times 10^{-5}$ and $p = .003$, respectively) and so reject the null hypothesis at very low levels, whereas the p-value for the smoothed bootstrap ($p = .3$) is too high to reject the null hypothesis at any conventional level. However, recall that we used a smoothing parameter $\alpha = 1$ that is higher than what is typically used, and smaller values can significantly decrease the p-value. For instance for $\alpha = .5$ the p-value was .18. So prior knowledge about what constitutes meaningful smoothing can be important here.

We can take these tests further and use them to discover label classes that are particularly unlikely under the null hypothesis, i.e., they are label classes that seem to invoke particularly anomalous annotator responses. Figure 6 shows the p-values for hypothesis tests using the same null and alternate hypotheses and statistical test as above, but applied one label class at a time only to the subset of the data associated with that label.

Table 2 ranks the label classes by p-value in ascending order. For comparison to standard probability distance measures, we also show the ranked (in descending order) KL-divergence and Wasserstein distance between the class distributions (i.e., the alternative hypothesis) and the null hypothesis.

These results show that the null hypothesis distribution of all annotator distributions from all label classes combined does not represent the distributions from individual label classes. Thus it makes sense to compare label classes directly to each other. That is, we can repeat the above experiments with two label classes, where one class plays the role of the null hypothesis, the other plays the alternative hypothesis, and we use the likelihood under null hypothesis as the test statistic. In this way, p-values can be used as a similarity measure between classes. Figure 7 shows the p-values between each these pairwise tests, for smoothed bootstrapping and, for comparison purposes, KL-divergence and Wasserstein distance.

The likelihood tests above are effective for showing that conditioning on certain variables leads to meaningful distinctions in annotator response distributions. However, they tell us little about the quality of those distinctions. So, turning now on the label class condition only, we use the entropy of the annotator response distributions in each class, averaged over all of the classes.

Figure 8 shows the results of these experiments. One might expect that, as one moves from naive to collapsed to smoothed that the entropy of both the null and alternate distributions would be higher and the two distributions would move closer together. But instead, somewhat unexpected things occur. First, the entropy distributions decrease slightly between the naive ($p < 10^{-5}$) and collapsed ($p < .16$) bootstraps. And then, when smoothing ($p = .0095$) is added, the entropies both increase and the distributions separate. We believe this is due to the presence in the collapsed sample of annotator distributions with no mass on certain responses (e.g., $[y_{Yes}, y_{No}, y_{\neg Know}] = [5, 0, 0]$. With no smoothing, such distributions cannot during bootstrapping generate all distributions (for instance, bootstrapping over $[5, 0, 0]$ will only ever generate $[5, 0, 0]$, whereas bootstrapping on $[1, 2, 2]$ can potentially generate any 5-annotator response). This creates biases toward these distributions, which also happen to be where most of the annotator distribution mass is located in the first stage. And so bootstrap sampling from them tends to drive entropy down. Smoothing seems to correct this, even when less smoothing is present. For instance smoothing with $\alpha = .5$ yields a p-value of $.0074$, which is still acceptably low by most standards.

7. Discussion

As a rule of thumb, the stronger the null hypothesis, the weaker the test. Our null hypothesis was that the an-

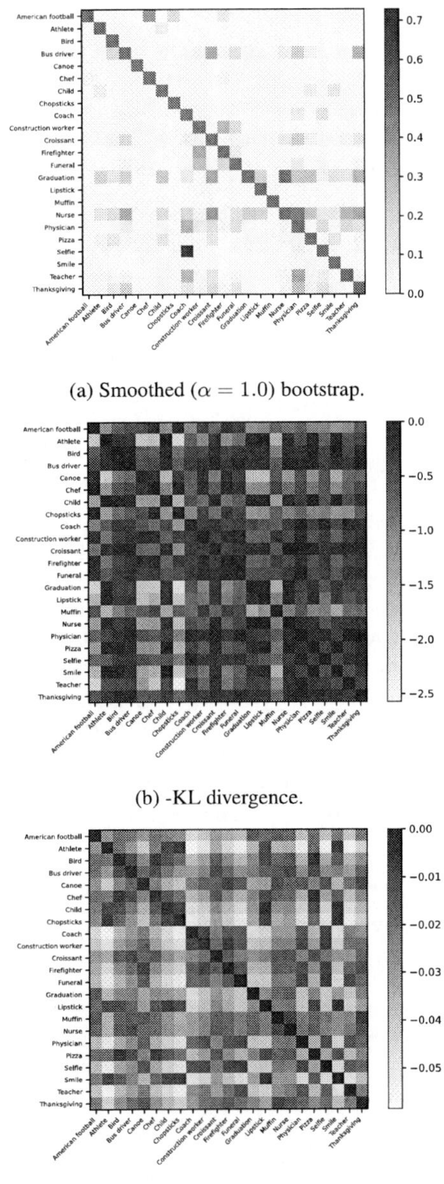

(a) Smoothed ($\alpha = 1.0$) bootstrap.

(b) -KL divergence.

(c) -Wasserstein distance.

Figure 7: Similarities between the distributions of annotator response distribution between each pair of label classes, according to p-value by smoothed bootstrapping, KL-divergence, and Wasserstein distance, respectively. For the p-value results, we zeroed out all pairs whose p-values were less than .05 after Bonferroni correction. This is because, for the purpose of hypothesis testing at the .05 level, such results are indistinguishable from those whose p-values were less than our bootstrap's precision 10^{-5}. We apply smoothing to the KL divergence results to avoid infinity results, and we take the negative of KL-divergence and Wasserstein distance.

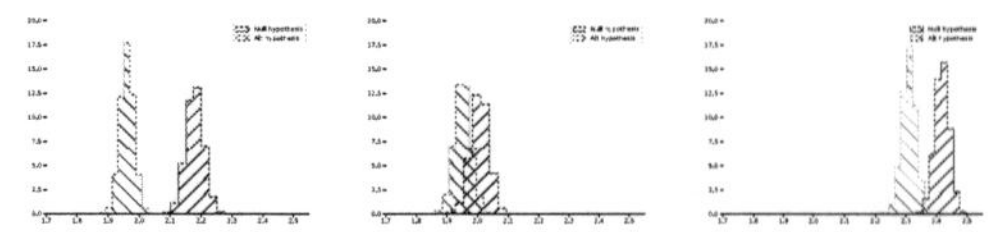

(a) Naive bootstrap ($p < 10^{-5}$). (b) Collapsed bootstrap ($p = .16$). (c) Smoothed bootstrap ($p = .0095$).

Figure 8: Bootstrap samples where the test statistic is *the mean entropy (over all label classes) of the distribution of annotator response distributions*, with the null hypothesis that the data was generated from a single distribution and the alternative hypothesis that data associated with each *label class* was generated from a distinct distribution.

notator distributions observed in key partitions of the CATS4ML dataset were are all drawn from the same distribution. We showed that when the partitions are based on machine label alone, we may not be able to reject this hypothesis, depending on how we model variance. However, when the partitions are based on label class, differences in the annotator distributions *are* significant across multiple variants of bootstrapping.

We were able to use bootstrap-based hypothesis tests to discover annotator classes that were particularly unlikely to have been sampled from the null hypothesis, even after Bonferroni correction. We showed that the classes discovered differ slightly based on the variant of bootstrap sampling used, and differed even more from other measures of distribution similarity, including KL-divergence and Wasserstein distance.

As for how we see these methods used in the future, we found the p-values based on the log-likelihood under the null hypothesis to be useful for quantifying how different various subsamples were from each other, *in light of sampling error.* We could see it being used as an alternative to other distance or similarity measures, one that has the advantage of taking sample size into account. Often, when pairwise comparing large amounts of data, it is necessary to sparsify feature relationships, i.e., eliminate all but the most closely related pairs. Figure 7 suggests that p-values could provide a principled way to sparsify data.

This study had a number of limitations. It focused solely on differences in subsets of the dataset, which is useful for understanding the quality of data used for training and test AI systems. We would like to use similar methods to compare the performance of different AI systems on the same dataset. Such comparisons require paired hypothesis testing, which has its own complications. Hypothesis testing over items (but not annotators has long been a part of AI research (Mitchell, 1997; Dietterich, 1998; Zhang et al., 2004; Berg-Kirkpatrick et al., 2012; Søgaard et al., 2014) even if it is not as common as perhaps it should be. It is not entirely clear how much of what we learned here would apply. For instance, it would not be as easy to collapse the sampling frames in a paired setting.

We have yet to explore whether the bootstrapping methods explored here are consistent, in the sense that the expected estimates they provide approach the actual population statistics as the sample size approaches the population size. Bootstrapping, for instance fails, to have this property with respect to many statistics over long-tailed distributions.

8. Conclusion

We explore annotator responses as a sampling frame. Using the CATS4ML dataset, we show that annotator response distributions form patterns related to specific input features (*labels classes* in our case) that cannot be explained by chance, as witness by our hypothesis tests. We show that hypothesis testing can be used to identifying particularly anomalous distributional patterns and to measure the similarity between different samples in a way that accounts for sample size. We propose the log-likelihood of a sample under the null hypothesis as a used test statistic for exploration in this space. Future work will seek to extend these methods to A/B testing of AI systems that predict annotator response distributions.

Akhtar, S., Basile, V., and Patti, V. (2019). A new measure of polarization in the annotation of hate speech. In *International Conference of the Italian Association for Artificial Intelligence*, pages 588–603. Springer.

Aroyo, L. and Welty, C. (2015). Truth is a lie: Crowd truth and the seven myths of human annotation. *AI Magazine*, 36(1):15–24.

Basile, V. (2020). It's the end of the gold standard as we know it. on the impact of pre-aggregation on the evaluation of highly subjective tasks. In *2020 AIxIA Discussion Papers Workshop, AIxIA 2020 DP*, volume 2776, pages 31–40. CEUR-WS.

Berg-Kirkpatrick, T., Burkett, D., and Klein, D. (2012). An empirical investigation of statistical significance in nlp. In *Proceedings of the 2012 Joint Conference on Empirical Methods in Natural Language Processing and Computational Natural Language Learning*, pages 995–1005.

Corani, G., Benavoli, A., Demšar, J., Mangili, F., and Zaffalon, M. (2017). Statistical comparison of classifiers through bayesian hierarchical modelling. *Machine Learning*, 106(11):1817–1837.

Davani, A. M., Díaz, M., and Prabhakaran, V. (2022). Dealing with disagreements: Looking beyond the majority vote in subjective annotations. *Transactions of the Association for Computational Linguistics*, 10:92–110.

Dietterich, T. G. (1998). Approximate statistical tests for comparing supervised classification learning algorithms. *Neural computation*, 10(7):1895–1923.

Efron, B. (1992). Bootstrap methods: another look at the jackknife. In *Breakthroughs in statistics*, pages 569–593. Springer.

Gordon, M. L., Lam, M. S., Park, J. S., Patel, K., Hancock, J. T., Hashimoto, T., and Bernstein, M. S. (2022). Jury learning: Integrating dissenting voices into machine learning models. *arXiv preprint arXiv:2202.02950.*

Klenner, M., Göhring, A., Amsler, M., Ebling, S., Tuggener, D., Hürlimann, M., and Volk, M. (2020). Harmonization sometimes harms.

Liu, T., Venkatachalam, A., Sanjay Bongale, P., and Homan, C. (2019). Learning to predict population-level label distributions. In *Companion Proceedings of The 2019 World Wide Web Conference*, pages 1111–1120.

Metz, C. (2019). A.I. is learning from humans. many humans. *New York Times*, August 16. `https://www.nytimes.com/2019/08/16/technology/ai-humans.html`, retrieved 5/21/2021.

Mitchell, T. M. (1997). *Machine learning, International Edition.* McGraw-Hill Series in Computer Science. McGraw-Hill.

Reidsma, D. and Carletta, J. (2008). Reliability measurement without limits. *Computational Linguistics*, 34(3):319–326.

Shalev-Shwartz, S. and Ben-David, S. (2014). *Understanding machine learning: From theory to algorithms.* Cambridge university press.

Snow, R., O'connor, B., Jurafsky, D., and Ng, A. Y. (2008). Cheap and fast–but is it good? evaluating non-expert annotations for natural language tasks. In *Proceedings of the 2008 conference on empirical methods in natural language processing*, pages 254–263.

Søgaard, A., Johannsen, A., Plank, B., Hovy, D., and Alonso, H. M. (2014). What's in a p-value in NLP? In *Proceedings of the eighteenth conference on computational natural language learning*, pages 1–10.

Szymański, P. and Gorman, K. (2020). Is the best better? bayesian statistical model comparison for natural language processing. *arXiv preprint arXiv:2010.03088.*

Weerasooriya, T. C., Liu, T., and Homan, C. M. (2020). Neighborhood-based pooling for population-level label distribution learning. In *ECAI 2020*, pages 490–497. IOS Press.

Welty, C., Paritosh, P., and Aroyo, L. (2019). Metrology for AI: From benchmarks to instruments. *arXiv preprint arXiv:1911.01875.*

Zhang, Y., Vogel, S., and Waibel, A. (2004). Interpreting bleu/nist scores: How much improvement do we need to have a better system? *Proc. LREC, Lisbon, Portugal, 2004*, pages 2051–2054.

Proceedings of the 1st Workshop on Perspectivist Approaches to NLP @LREC2022, pages 66–72
Marseille, 20 June 2022

Variation in the Expression and Annotation of Emotions: a Wizard of Oz Pilot Study

Sofie Labat[◇], **Naomi Ackaert**[◇], **Thomas Demeester**[♣] **and Véronique Hoste**[◇]
[◇]LT3, Language and Translation Technology Team, Ghent University, Belgium
[♣]T2K, Text-to-Knowledge Research Group, IDLab, Ghent University - imec, Belgium
{sofie.labat, naomi.ackaert, thomas.demeester, veronique.hoste}@ugent.be

Abstract

This pilot study employs the Wizard of Oz technique to collect a corpus of written human-computer conversations in the domain of customer service. The resulting dataset contains 192 conversations and is used to test three hypotheses related to the expression and annotation of emotions. First, we hypothesize that there is a discrepancy between the emotion annotations of the participant (the experiencer) and the annotations of our external annotator (the observer). Furthermore, we hypothesize that the personality of the participants has an influence on the emotions they expressed, and on the way they evaluated (annotated) these emotions. We found that for an external, trained annotator, not all emotion labels were equally easy to work with. We also noticed that the trained annotator had a tendency to opt for emotion labels that were more centered in the *valence-arousal* space, while participants made more 'extreme' annotations. For the second hypothesis, we discovered a positive correlation between the personality trait *extraversion* and the emotion dimensions *valence* and *dominance* in our sample. Finally, for the third premise, we observed a positive correlation between the internal-external agreement on emotion labels and the personality traits *conscientiousness* and *extraversion*. Our insights and findings will be used in future research to conduct a larger Wizard of Oz experiment.

Keywords: emotion analysis, Wizard of Oz study, conversational data collection, customer profiling, customer service

1. Introduction

Customer service (CS) delivery models are transforming due to recent technological advances (Deloitte Digital, 2021). Besides assisting human operators in their tasks, NLP techniques are increasingly implemented in autonomous conversational agents that can engage with clients on a 24/7 basis. To improve the quality of conversation, novel resources and methodologies are introduced to make human-computer interactions more personalized and empathic.

In this paper, we investigate variation in the expression and annotation of emotions during human-computer conversations. Insights in these types of variation will not only be helpful to craft more representative annotation frameworks, but they can also be used in the design of emotion detection systems. We present a pilot Wizard of Oz (WOZ) experiment that was conducted to study these variations. In a WOZ experiment, a *wizard* (the experimenter) pretends to be an autonomous conversational agent that interacts with the participants. Our experimental setup involved 16 voluntary participants that each had 12 successive conversations with the wizard. Each conversation was grounded in an event associated with a commercial sector (e-commerce, tourism, telecommunication) and was linked to a predefined sentiment trajectory along which the wizard tried to steer the conversation (e.g., *negative → positive*). The events and sentiment trajectories were kept consistent across participants, while we also tried to restrict the variation in responses of the wizard to a minimal. The conversations were afterwards annotated for emotions by both the participant and a trained annotator. Finally, we collected profiling information (age, gender, personality) on the participants.

The resulting dataset is also used to tentatively investigate three hypotheses. First, the annotation and subsequent prediction of emotions are notoriously difficult tasks due to the high degree of ambiguity that is involved. The fact that it is hard to obtain acceptable scores of inter-annotator agreement (IAA) on emotion annotations underscores this point (Schuff et al., 2017; De Bruyne et al., 2020; Troiano et al., 2021). **We thus hypothesize that not all emotions are equally easy to annotate by external annotators, as some might simply be expressed too implicitly**. Second, we regard emotions as dynamic attributes of the customer that can shift at each utterance in the conversation. Even though dialogue participants remain often in the same emotional state while exchanging turns, this can change if external stimuli are introduced (Poria et al., 2019). Emotions are therefore closely linked to (i) the event that happened prior to the conversation, and (ii) the response strategies the wizard applied. **We hypothesize that the effect of external stimuli on emotions differs across individuals depending on their personality.** We combine the two previous hypotheses in our final premise **by postulating that a participant's personality influences the annotator agreement he/she obtains with the external annotator.**

The remainder of this paper is structured as follows. Section 2 introduces the related research on emotion annotations and the Wizard of Oz technique. Section 3 describes the experimental setup of our study, while the resulting dataset is analyzed along three hypotheses in Section 4. Finally, Section 5 concludes this study with our main findings and suggestions for future research.

2. Related Research

Section 2.1 gives a concise overview of the different models used to capture emotions. It also focuses on IAA studies conducted for emotion annotation tasks, and links these studies to research on the possible causes of annotation disagreement. Section 2.2 introduces the WOZ technique and describes other studies that applied this technique.

2.1. Emotion Models and IAA

Emotions can be captured in two types of frameworks: categorical and dimensional models. Ekman (1992) introduced the most popular categorical model that consists of six emotions based on universal facial expressions: *anger*, *disgust*, *fear*, *joy*, *sadness*, *surprise*. This model was extended by Plutchik (1980) who added the primary emotions *anticipation* and *trust*. In recent years, researchers have realized that our ability to express and interpret emotions goes beyond a small set of basic emotions (Skerry and Saxe, 2015), which resulted in new datasets annotated along large taxonomies of categorical labels (Cowen and Keltner, 2017; Rashkin et al., 2019; Demszky et al., 2020).

Dimensional emotion models are less frequently used, even though, in contrast to categorical frameworks, they are not limited in the number of emotions they can capture (Canales and Martínez-Barco, 2014). Moreover, they can more easily be compared across different domains (Buechel and Hahn, 2016). Dimensional emotion annotations are made along two or three independent axes. The first dimension *valence* represents emotions on a displeasure-pleasure continuum; the second dimension *arousal* depicts the intensity of emotions on a passive-active continuum; the third (often omitted) dimension *dominance* portrays the degree of control over the affective state on a submissive-dominant scale (Mehrabian and Russell, 1974).

As emotion annotations are linked to a high degree of subjectivity and ambiguity, both categorical and dimensional models struggle to reach acceptable levels of inter-annotator agreement (Wood et al., 2018; De Bruyne et al., 2020). Moreover, the more fine-grained the annotation framework is, the lower the agreement amongst annotators becomes (Labat et al., under review). Some researchers have recently started to look at factors that potentially cause disagreement between annotators (Troiano et al., 2021). Our current study contributes to this line of work.

2.2. Wizard of Oz Study

The Wizard of Oz technique is mainly used to mimic human-robot interactions and to test hypotheses in that setting. Participants of a WOZ experiment interact with a wizard that pretends to be an autonomous computer system, but that in reality is partially/fully controlled by a human operator (Riek, 2012). Some WOZ studies involve prior knowledge of the participant, other studies apply a low level of deceit to elicit more natural responses. Since its introduction in the mid-80s, the technique is frequently used in interdisciplinary research on a variety of topics, such as the effect of politeness on learning outcomes (Wang et al., 2008), analysis of customer experiences (Wei and Le, 2018), diagnosis of mental health problems (Gratch et al., 2014), the successfulness of persuasion strategies (Adler et al., 2016), and the creation of data-driven dialogue systems (Budzianowski et al., 2018).

3. Experimental Design

To collect written conversational data, we designed an online interface in which participants acted in the role of customers and chatted with a wizard about events that occurred in a customer service setting. Our participants did not know that the so-called computer system they interacted with was actually fully controlled by the experimenter. As we collected profiling information, the experimental setup was submitted to and approved by the Ethics Committee of the faculty of Arts and Philosophy at Ghent University.[1]

3.1. Events and Sentiment Trajectories

All participants had 12 successive conversations with our wizard. Each of these conversations was grounded in a predefined event description. Descriptions are linked to a company that is active in Flanders, the Dutch-speaking community in Belgium, and that represents one of three economic sectors: Bol.com (e-commerce), Airbnb (tourism), and Telenet (telecom).

The events are further associated with one of four predefined sentiment trajectories: *positive* → *negative*, *negative* → *positive*, *neutral* → *negative*, *neutral* → *positive*. The sentiment trajectories were only visible to the experimenter who had to steer the conversation towards a given end sentiment. We decided to work with sentiment trajectories instead of emotion trajectories (e.g., *anger* → *admiration*) to give more conversational freedom to both the participant and the wizard.

In the Appendix, Figure 5 contains an example conversation, while Table 2 offers a detailed overview of the 12 event descriptions in which the conversations were grounded. Even though we worked with these 12 event descriptions for all participants, the order in which they were presented to the participants differed to avoid undesired sequential effects.

3.2. Response Strategies

The wizard tried to direct each conversation along a fixed sentiment trajectory. For example, positive emo-

[1] Participants could withdraw their participation up to 5 days after the experiment. The data records were anonymized in order to assure the privacy of the participants.

tions could be evoked by being helpful or showing empathy, while negative emotions were induced by being impolite, introducing repetitions, or answering beside the point. To remain as consistent as possible across different participants, we worked with standardized replies for eight response strategies that are typical in the domain of customer service: (i) *apology*, (ii) *cheerfulness*, (iii) *empathy*, (iv) *gratitude*, (v) *explanation*, (vi) *help offline*, (vii) *request information*, and (viii) *other* (Labat et al., 2020). We must, however, acknowledge that one can never fully control the participant's conversational output. As the wizard must reply at all times, its responses can slightly differ across participants. Nevertheless, responses are always in line with the given sentiment trajectory.

3.3. Emotion Annotations

Once all conversations were collected, both the participant and the external, trained annotator (the experimenter) proceeded to annotate emotions. Both parties were given a set of 15 emotions to label utterances: *admiration*, *amusement*, *anger*, *annoyance*, *approval*, *confusion*, *desire*, *disappointment*, *disapproval*, *disgust*, *fear*, *gratitude*, *joy*, *love*, *sadness*. An additional *neutral* category was introduced to label objective utterances. We composed the emotion taxonomy by combining a concise set of five emotions used for cross-domain comparisons (De Bruyne et al., 2020) with emotion labels that are frequent in the domain of customer service (Labat et al., under review). Besides categorical annotations, the experimenter also made dimensional annotations for *valence-arousal-dominance* (VAD) on three 5-point scales. While annotators were not restricted in the number of emotion labels they could assign to a given utterance, only one score per utterance could be made for each VAD dimension.

3.4. Participants and Profiling Information

This pilot study was conducted with 16 participants. Participants had to be older than 18 years, have a stable internet connection, and speak Dutch as a mother tongue. Given the small scale of our experiment, participants were recruited through word-of-mouth advertising and participated on a voluntary basis without remuneration. The experiments were conducted from mid-March to mid-April 2021.

After the WOZ session, participants were asked to fill out their customer profile. We collected three types of profiling information: year of birth, biological gender, and personality. To collect personality types, participants filled in a Dutch version of the IPIP-NEO-120 test (Johnson, 2014). The test measures personality across five dimensions: *neuroticism*, *extraversion*, *openness*, *agreeableness*, and *conscientiousness*. For each dimension, 24 questions are answered with one of five possible answers ranging from *very inaccurate* to *very accurate*.

4. Corpus Analysis along Hypotheses

The resulting dataset of our experiment consists of 192 conversations that contain 3,089 utterances in total. 1,684 of these utterances are written by the wizard, while the remaining 1,405 are written by the participants and have been annotated for emotions. In Section 4.1, we introduce the proposed hypotheses with respect to the variables of our corpus, and their interrelationship. Afterwards, we analyze our three hypotheses in chronological order in Sections 4.2, 4.3, and 4.4.

4.1. Hypotheses

We are interested in three hypotheses:

- **H1**: Not all emotions are equally easy to annotate by external annotators. Some experienced emotions might simply be expressed too implicitly.
- **H2**: The effect of external stimuli (such as event and responses) differs across individuals, depending on their personality.
- **H3**: A participant's personality influences the level of agreement he/she achieves on emotion annotations with the external annotator.

To better explain these hypotheses in the context of our dataset, we created an interrelationship digraph in Figure 1. In this digraph and our hypotheses, we distinguish internal annotations A_i (made by the person who experienced an affective state) from external annotations A_e (made by a trained annotator who has only access to the written utterance). For the first hypothesis, we will look at the agreement between internal and external annotations to investigate which emotion labels cause disagreement when the point of view of the annotator shifts. The second hypothesis focuses on the relationship between personality (part of the customer profile P) and emotion annotations A_e. Finally, the third hypothesis studies the relationship between personality (part of P) and the internal-external annotator agreement (A_i-A_e).

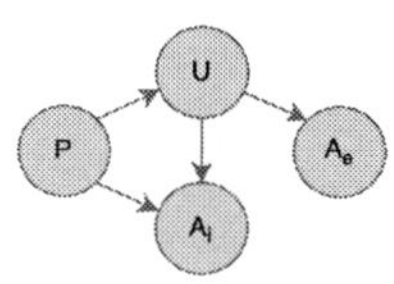

Figure 1: Interrelationship digraph of the variables customer profile (P), expressed utterances (U), internal annotations (A_i), and external annotations (A_e).

4.2. Internal versus External Annotations

For H1, we explore the extent to which the participants and the external annotator agree on the task of emotion labelling. Since we are especially interested in the agreement on each emotion label, we calculate Cohen's κ for individual labels. We also take into account the frequencies with which labels were assigned to utterances, as lower levels of agreement will usually be obtained for more infrequent labels. The results of this analysis are shown in Table 1. From this table, we extract five emotion labels that occur frequently, but that still have relatively low κ scores: *confusion*, *desire*, *anger*, *disapproval*, and *approval*. These five emotions are examined in more detail in Figure 2.

Emotion	C(A_i)	C(A_e)	**Cohen's κ**
Gratitude	184	215	0.565
Neutral	487	502	0.480
Joy	66	47	0.401
Annoyance	281	324	0.384
Disappoint.	72	38	0.340
Confusion	102	38	0.182
Admiration	16	6	0.177
Desire	58	139	0.165
Anger	60	10	0.161
Disapproval	97	153	0.126
Amusement	17	5	0.086
Disgust	23	6	0.063
Approval	48	67	0.013
Sadness	6	2	-0.002
Fear	9	0	NA
Love	0	0	NA

Table 1: The table shows the number of internal annotations (C(A_i)), the number of external annotations (C(A_e)), and the IAA of internal and external annotators (Cohen's κ) for each emotion.

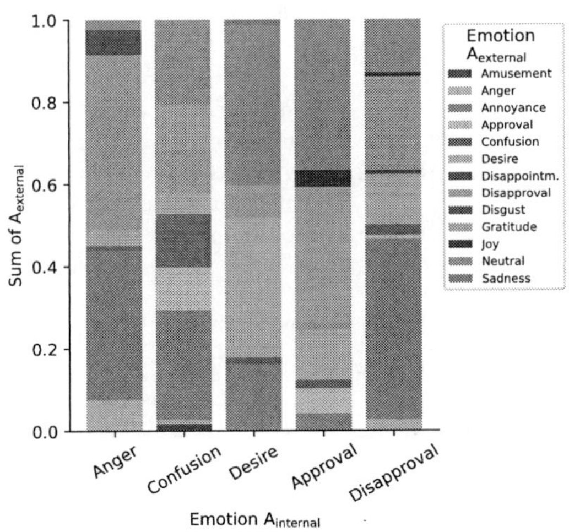

Figure 2: For all internal annotations ($A_{internal}$) with a given emotion category, this figure plots the emotions that the external annotator ($A_{external}$) picked to label the same instances.

Figure 2 investigates the extent to which the external annotator agreed with the internal annotators. If disagreement occurred, we explore which other emotion labels the external annotator selected. Although labels selected by the external annotator do not always correspond to the internal annotations, we find that the two groups of annotations are often semantically related. For the more extreme emotion *anger*, we see that the external annotator prefers similar labels that are, however, more centered in the *valence-arousal* (VA) space (see Labat et al. (under review) for a detailed overview). Similarly, internal annotations with more 'moderate' labels (e.g., *approval*, *confusion*, *desire*) are often confused with *neutral*. Finally, the internal emotion *confusion* seems particularly daunting to label, as it is often labelled with both negative and positive emotions by the external annotator.

4.3. Personality and Emotion Expressions

For our second hypothesis, we explore how variation in expressed emotions A_e can be linked to personality (part of P). As our study was conducted with a small group of 16 participants, we only aim to tentatively investigate whether some correlations can be found. We decided to work with the external annotations A_e for this hypothesis, as (i) they are consistently made by the same annotator across different experimental trials, and (ii) they contain VAD scores.

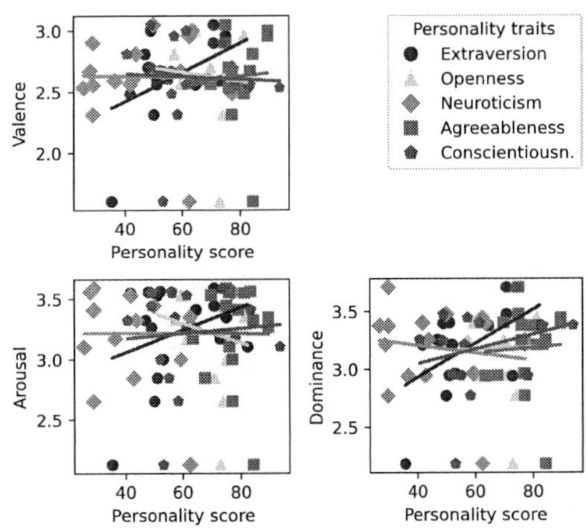

Figure 3: Three scatterplots with regression lines that plot the correlations between each personality dimension and the variables *valence*, *arousal*, *dominance*.

We plotted three scatterplots in Figure 3. Each plot shows the relation between the independent variable personality and one of the VAD dimensions. Since personality traits were captured on five dimensions, the colour and form of the markers distinguish between these five traits. For each personality dimension, we plotted one point per participant. To this end, we used a single score per VAD dimension, which was obtained by averaging all scores for a given dimension across the different utterances of a participant. For each personality dimension, we also plotted a linear regression line to better visualize possible correlations. In most cases, there seems to be no correlation between personality and emotional dimensions. There are, however, two exceptions to this trend, as the personality trait *extraversion* correlates positively with valence (Pearson's correlation coefficient r-value = 0.480, p-value = 0.060) and dominance (r-value = 0.551, p-value = 0.027^{*}). This implies that in our small sample, extraverted participants were more positive and dominant in the emotions they expressed than their introverted counterparts.

4.4. Personality and Emotion Annotations

The third and final hypothesis states that participants' personality (part of P) not only influences the emotions they express, but also the way in which they evaluate their own emotional states through annotations. To study variation in annotations across participants, we looked at the level of agreement between their emotion annotations (A_i) and the annotations of our external, trained annotator (A_e), since the latter made consistent annotations across the different participants. We used Krippendorff's α (Krippendorff, 2004) with Jaccard distance to calculate internal-external annotator agreement on the emotion labelling task.

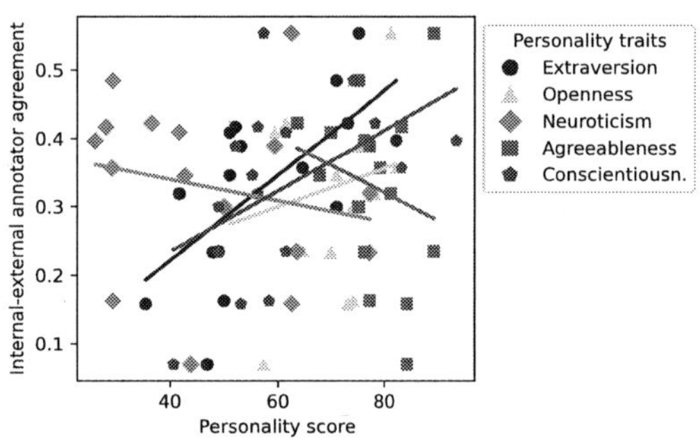

Figure 4: Scatterplot with regression lines showing the correlation between each personality dimension and the internal-external annotator agreement.

Figure 4 plots the relation between the independent variables personality traits and the dependent variable internal-external annotator agreement. As in Figure 3, the colour and form of the markers represent the different personality traits. For each personality trait, we also plotted a linear regression line to visualize possible correlations. We find that there exists a strong positive correlation between the personality trait *extraversion* and the annotator agreement (r-value = 0.655, p-value = 0.006^{**}). Moreover, we notice a moderate positive correlation between the personality trait *conscientiousness* and the annotator agreement (r-value = 0.484, p-value = 0.058). This means that in our sample, participants who are more outgoing or conscientious achieve higher agreement with the standard emotion annotations of our external annotator. We are unknown to the exact causes of this correlation, as multiple other variables may also play a role. The positive effect on annotator agreement could, for example, also be caused by the fact that (i) these participants lexicalize their emotions more strongly, or that (ii) their personality corresponds better to the personality of our external annotator. More research is needed to see whether these findings hold for a larger sample size and for other external annotators with different personalities.

5. Conclusion

In this paper, we presented a WOZ experiment that was conducted to investigate variation in both the annotation and expression of emotions during human-machine conversations in the domain of customer service. We found that some emotion classes are more easy to label in written chat conversations than others. Moreover, in contrast to the internal annotations, our external annotator often opted for emotion labels that were less extreme in their *valence* and *arousal*. This finding is interesting for the design of annotation guidelines in the domain of CS, as it is crucial to detect negative emotions in time before they become too extreme. For the link between personality and the expression of emotions, we discovered that the personality trait *extraversion* correlated positively with both *valence* and *dominance* in our sample. Finally, as for the relation between personality and internal-external annotator agreement, we observed that the personality traits *extraversion* and *conscientiousness* correlated positively with annotator agreement. Given the promising results of this study, we will apply our insights and findings to conduct a similar Wizard of Oz experiment on a larger group of participants.

6. Acknowledgements

This research received funding from the Flemish Government under the Research Program Artificial Intelligence (174U01222) and from the Research Foundation Flanders (FWO-Vlaanderen) with grant number 1S96322N. We would also like to thank the anonymous reviewers for their valuable and constructive feedback.

7. Bibliographical References

Adler, R. F., Iacobelli, F., and Gutstein, Y. (2016). Are you convinced? A Wizard of Oz study to test emotional vs. rational persuasion strategies in dialogues. *Computers in Human Behavior*, 57:75–81.

Budzianowski, P., Wen, T.-H., Tseng, B.-H., Casanueva, I., Ultes, S., Ramadan, O., and Gašić, M. (2018). MultiWOZ - A Large-Scale Multi-Domain Wizard-of-Oz Dataset for Task-Oriented Dialogue Modelling. In *Proceedings of the 2018 Conference on Empirical Methods in Natural Language Processing*, pages 5016–5026. Association for Computational Linguistics.

Buechel, S. and Hahn, U. (2016). Emotion Analysis as a Regression Problem — Dimensional Models and Their Implications on Emotion Representation and

Metrical Evaluation. In *Proceedings of the Twenty-Second European Conference on Artificial Intelligence*, ECAI'16, page 1114–1122, NLD. IOS Press.

Canales, L. and Martínez-Barco, P. (2014). Emotion Detection from text: A Survey. In *Proceedings of the Workshop on Natural Language Processing in the 5th Information Systems Research Working Days (JISIC)*, pages 37–43. Association for Computational Linguistics.

Cowen, A. S. and Keltner, D. (2017). Self-report captures 27 distinct categories of emotion bridged by continuous gradients. *Proceedings of the National Academy of Sciences*, 114(38):E7900–E7909.

De Bruyne, L., De Clercq, O., and Hoste, V. (2020). An Emotional Mess! Deciding on a Framework for Building a Dutch Emotion-Annotated Corpus. In *Proceedings of the 12th Language Resources and Evaluation Conference*, pages 1643–1651. European Language Resources Association.

Deloitte Digital. (2021). From cost center to experience hub. Tapping the potential of customer service to help drive business growth.

Demszky, D., Movshovitz-Attias, D., Ko, J., Cowen, A., Nemade, G., and Ravi, S. (2020). GoEmotions: A Dataset of Fine-Grained Emotions. In *Proceedings of the 58th Annual Meeting of the Association for Computational Linguistics*, pages 4040–4054. Association for Computational Linguistics.

Ekman, P. (1992). An argument for basic emotions. *Cognition and Emotion*, 6(3-4):169–200.

Gratch, J., Artstein, R., Lucas, G., Stratou, G., Scherer, S., Nazarian, A., Wood, R., Boberg, J., DeVault, D., Marsella, S., Traum, D., Rizzo, S., and Morency, L.-P. (2014). The Distress Analysis Interview Corpus of human and computer interviews. In *Proceedings of the Ninth International Conference on Language Resources and Evaluation (LREC'14)*, pages 3123–3128. European Language Resources Association (ELRA).

Johnson, J. A. (2014). Measuring thirty facets of the Five Factor Model with a 120-item public domain inventory: Development of the IPIP-NEO-120. *Journal of Research in Personality*, 51:78–89.

Krippendorff, K. (2004). *Content Analysis: An Introduction to Its Methodology*. SAGE Publications, 2nd edition.

Labat, S., Demeester, T., and Hoste, V. (2020). Guidelines for annotating fine-grained emotion trajectories in customer service dialogues (version 1.0). Technical report, Ghent University.

Labat, S., Demeester, T., and Hoste, V. (under review). EmoTwiCS: a corpus for modelling emotion trajectories in Dutch customer service dialogues on Twitter. *Language Resources and Evaluation*.

Mehrabian, A. and Russell, J. A. (1974). *An Approach to Environmental Psychology*. The MIT Press.

Plutchik, R. (1980). A general psychoevolutionary theory of emotion. In Robert Plutchik et al., editors, *Theories of Emotion*, pages 3–33. Academic Press.

Poria, S., Majumder, N., Mihalcea, R., and Hovy, E. (2019). Emotion Recognition in Conversation: Research Challenges, Datasets, and Recent Advances. *IEEE Access*, 7:100943–100953.

Rashkin, H., Smith, E. M., Li, M., and Boureau, Y.-L. (2019). Towards Empathetic Open-domain Conversation Models: A New Benchmark and Dataset. In *Proceedings of the 57th Annual Meeting of the Association for Computational Linguistics*, pages 5370–5381. Association for Computational Linguistics.

Riek, L. D. (2012). Wizard of Oz Studies in HRI: A Systematic Review and New Reporting Guidelines. *J. Hum.-Robot Interact.*, 1(1):119–136, jul.

Schuff, H., Barnes, J., Mohme, J., Padó, S., and Klinger, R. (2017). Annotation, Modelling and Analysis of Fine-Grained Emotions on a Stance and Sentiment Detection Corpus. In *Proceedings of the 8th Workshop on Computational Approaches to Subjectivity, Sentiment and Social Media Analysis*, pages 13–23. Association for Computational Linguistics.

Skerry, A. E. and Saxe, R. (2015). Neural Representations of Emotion Are Organized around Abstract Event Features. *Current Biology*, 25(15):1945–1954.

Troiano, E., Padó, S., and Klinger, R. (2021). Emotion Ratings: How Intensity, Annotation Confidence and Agreements are Entangled. In *Proceedings of the Eleventh Workshop on Computational Approaches to Subjectivity, Sentiment and Social Media Analysis*, pages 40–49. Association for Computational Linguistics.

Wang, N., Johnson, W. L., Mayer, R. E., Rizzo, P., Shaw, E., and Collins, H. (2008). The politeness effect: Pedagogical agents and learning outcomes. *International Journal of Human-Computer Studies*, 66(2):98–112.

Wei, Y. and Le, T. (2018). Using the Wizard-of-Oz Method for Exploring Deep Customer Experience Preferences. In *2018 IEEE International Conference on Engineering, Technology and Innovation (ICE/ITMC)*, pages 1–8.

Wood, I., McCrae, J. P., Andryushechkin, V., and Buitelaar, P. (2018). A Comparison Of Emotion Annotation Schemes And A New Annotated Data Set. In *Proceedings of the Eleventh International Conference on Language Resources and Evaluation (LREC 2018)*, pages 1197–1202. European Language Resources Association (ELRA).

Appendix

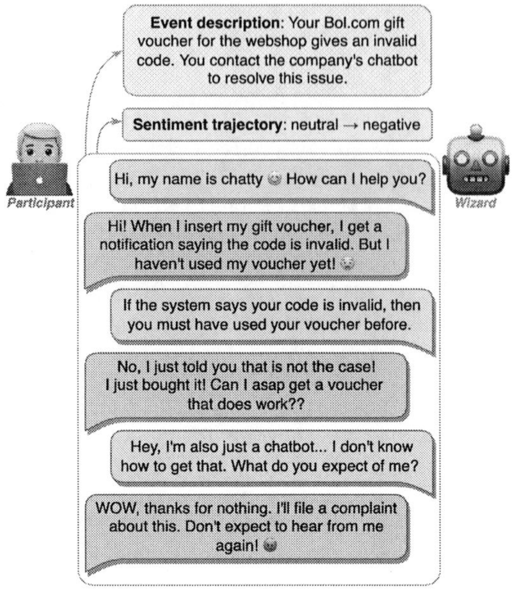

Figure 5: Example conversation to illustrate our experimental setup. Although the conversations in our dataset are in Dutch, this example is in English so that non-native Dutch speakers can also understand it.

	positive → negative	*negative → positive*	*neutral → negative*	*neutral → positive*
Bol.com	C thanks B for speedy package delivery.	C complains about undelivered product and bad service.	Gift voucher gives an invalid code.	C wants to return headphones that arrived damaged.
Airbnb	C thanks B for great service.	Host cancelled stay, C asks for sanctions.	C forgot phone charger in the accommodation.	C needs to cancel stay due to quarantine.
Telenet	C thanks B for listening to suggestion.	C missed promotion due to bad client service.	Digicorder records wrong show.	C wants to change subscription due to lack of mobile data.

Table 2: Event descriptions and corresponding sentiment trajectories in which the 12 conversations are grounded. *C* stands for customer, while *B* stands for the (chat)bot that is in reality operated by a human experimenter.

Proceedings of the 1st Workshop on Perspectivist Approaches to NLP @LREC2022, pages 73–82
Marseille, 20 June 2022

Beyond Explanation: A Case for Exploratory Text Visualizations of Non-Aggregated, Annotated Datasets

Lucy Havens[†] **Benjamin Bach**[†] **Melissa Terras**[‡] **Beatrice Alex**[†§]
[†]School of Informatics, [‡]College of Arts, Humanities and Social Sciences,
[§]Edinburgh Futures Institute, [§]School of Literatures, Languages and Cultures
University of Edinburgh
lucy.havens@ed.ac.uk, bbach@inf.ed.ac.uk, m.terras@ed.ac.uk, balex@ed.ac.uk

Abstract

This paper presents an overview of text visualization techniques relevant for data perspectivism, aiming to facilitate analysis of annotated datasets for the datasets' creators and stakeholders. Data perspectivism advocates for publishing non-aggregated, annotated text data, recognizing that for highly subjective tasks, such as bias detection and hate speech detection, disagreements among annotators may indicate conflicting yet equally valid interpretations of a text. While the publication of non-aggregated, annotated data makes different interpretations of text corpora available, barriers still exist to investigating patterns and outliers in annotations of the text. Techniques from text visualization can overcome these barriers, facilitating intuitive data analysis for NLP researchers and practitioners, as well as stakeholders in NLP systems, who may not have data science or computing skills. In this paper we discuss challenges with current dataset creation practices and annotation platforms, followed by a discussion of text visualization techniques that enable open-ended, multi-faceted, and iterative analysis of annotated data.

Keywords: annotation, dataset, visualization, data analysis, exploratory search, inter-annotator agreement, perspectivism

1. Introduction

In response to growing evidence of biases in machine learning models, such as classification (Dinan et al., 2020; Diaz et al., 2018), topic modeling (Morstatter et al., 2018), N-grams (Nobata et al., 2016), coreference resolution (Rudinger et al., 2018), machine translation (Nekoto et al., 2020), word embeddings (Caliskan et al., 2017; Bolukbasi et al., 2016), search engines and information retrieval (Noble, 2018; Sweeney, 2013), and computer vision (Prabhu and Birhane, 2021), efforts to uncover the source of such biases have found biased training datasets to be a contributing factor (Prabhu and Birhane, 2021; Cao and Daumé III, 2020; Perez, 2019). The machine learning community has moved towards ever-larger datasets, based on the assumption that more data means more representative datasets (Frické, 2015). In reality, the bigger the dataset, the more difficult it is to ensure the data do not contain harmful representations of people (Bender et al., 2021; Prabhu and Birhane, 2021). The size of a dataset does not correlate to how representative its data are because data must be collected with instruments, and instruments are imperfect (Bender et al., 2021; Welty et al., 2019; Frické, 2015). Choices made regarding what data to collect and how to collect them influence how well a dataset represents the population it is meant to represent (D'Ignazio and Klein, 2020; Perez, 2019; Frické, 2015). Hutchinson et al. (2021), Jo and Gebru (2020), Bender and Friedman (2018), and Gebru et al. (2018) encourage new documentation practices to contextualize datasets and facilitate critical reflection on the implications of their use in models. Documentation alone, however, cannot mitigate datasets' biases and resulting harms.

While documentation of a dataset provides valuable contextual information about why data were collected, how the data are structured, and what the intended use of the data are, documentation cannot replace analysis for understanding the perspectives represented in a dataset. Methods for studying which perspectives are and are not included in a dataset have yet to be established. While methods such as jury learning (Gordon et al., 2022) and perspective-aware modeling (Akhtar et al., 2021) aim to incorporate more than one annotator's perspective in model development, they can only incorporate perspectives that have been represented in the annotation process.

For communities of people not involved in a dataset's creation or annotation, existing approaches to creating and analyzing datasets continue to exclude their perspectives. In this paper, we encourage collaboration across the natural language processing (NLP) and text visualization communities to diversify the perspectives considered during dataset creation. Building on data perspectivism, which advocates for the publication of non-aggregated, annotated datasets (Basile, 2022; Basile et al., 2021), we propose exploratory text visualization techniques as a method for analyzing the different perspectives represented in *and missing from* annotated data.

Though existing text annotation platforms incorporate data visualizations, these platforms assume the aim of the annotation process will be to reconcile disagreements to create a single version of a dataset, or gold standard. This paper presents exploratory text visualization techniques as a complement to data perspectivism, aiming to improve the quality of datasets for model training through analysis of perspectives that are and are not represented in annotations. We begin by defining three key terms used throughout this paper (§2). Next, we summarize current practices for creating annotated datasets and their associated challenges (§3). We then present techniques from the text visualization community that can address these challenges and advance data perspectivism in NLP (§5). Lastly, we conclude with a summary of the paper and envisioned future work for analysis of non-aggregated, annotated text corpora (§6).

2. Definitions

Data Perspectivism We use *data perspectivism* as Basile et al. (2021) define the term: "the adoption of methods that integrate opinions and perspectives of human subjects involved in the knowledge representation step of ML [machine learning] processes" (1). The Perspectivist Data Manifesto expands on this definition with action points for executing data perspectivism in NLP research: publishing non-aggregated, annotated datasets and avoiding training models on aggregated annotated datasets, often referred to as gold standards (Basile, 2022).

Exploratory Search Drawing on information retrieval and human-computer interaction literature, we use the term *exploratory search* to refer to an information seeking process in which the information seeker's task cannot be reduced to a single question and answer. Exploratory search is distinct from look up or querying search tasks (Athukorala et al., 2015; Marchionini, 2006). During exploratory search, the information seeker refines their questions as they become more familiar with a topic. The answer to an initial question often reveals new questions for the seeker to research. Information retrieval and human-computer interaction literature characterizes exploratory search as multi-faceted, iterative, and open-ended (White and Roth, 2009), involving mental processes of synthesis and evaluation to learn something new (Athukorala et al., 2015; Marchionini, 2006).

Stakeholders We refer to *stakeholders* of datasets, and by extension machine learning models trained on those datasets, as people who influence or are influenced by the datasets. Drawing on the definition of stakeholders in NLP research from Havens et al. (2020), we include "(1) the researcher(s), (2) producers of the data, (3) institutions providing access to the data, (4) people represented in the data, and (5) people who use the data" (110) in our use of the term. Furthermore, as Bender and Friedman (2018) note, we emphasize that a dataset's stakeholders may or may not directly interact with the dataset; people may be influenced by a dataset even if they did not participate in its creation. Stakeholders may experience these influences positively, if they are given power or advantage over others, or negatively, if they are oppressed or discriminated against (D'Ignazio and Klein, 2020).[1] For extensive discussion of how stakeholders experience positive and negative impacts from data, please refer to the books by Perez (2019), Noble (2018), and O'Neil (2017).

3. Related Work

Existing annotation platforms assume the aim of the annotation process will be reconciling disagreements to create a single version of a dataset, or gold standard. Many annotation platforms focus on supporting the actual annotation work: loading a text corpus, applying labels, and adding notes explaining the labels (Pérez-Pérez et al., 2015). Among the platforms that allow for annotation workflow management more broadly, such as GATE Teamware (Bontcheva et al., 2013), Argo (Batista-Navarro et al., 2016), and Marky (Pérez-Pérez et al., 2015), the focus is on the management of multiple annotators, facilitating annotation corrections and reconciliation. The underlying assumption of these platforms is that annotator disagreement should be minimized and one version of a dataset will be created. These platforms thus have limited support for a perspectivist approach, where researchers investigate annotators' disagreements and publish non-aggregated, annotated data.

Though existing annotation platforms do provide helpful data visualizations, the visualizations are explanatory rather than exploratory. For example, GATE Teamware uses a flow diagram for visualizing the annotation workflow and a pie chart for visualizing annotation progress (Bontcheva et al., 2013), and Marky uses a bar chart to visualize F scores across rounds of annotation (Pérez-Pérez et al., 2015). As explanatory visualizations, these diagrams and charts are effective in their aim of explaining the annotation workflow, process, and agreement measures. However, they cannot facilitate analysis of patterns and outliers in annotators' distinct approaches to labeling text. Such analysis requires navigation between overviews and detailed views of annotated text corpora, and comparative views of different annotators' labels to the same text. Existing annotation platforms provide no way to study the inconsistencies in an annotator's labels, which could indicate uncertainty in the text that cannot be represented with a single label; nor do they provide a way to study outliers in annotators' labels, which could indicate perspectives that are underrepresented in the data. Instead, existing annotation platforms support practices that minimize inconsistencies and outliers.

For tasks that yield high variability among annotators, there is value in maintaining annotators' disagreeing labels (Davani et al., 2022; Sang and Stanton, 2022; Basile et al., 2021). Basile et al. (2021) propose "data perspectivism" as particularly valuable for these annotation tasks, such as detecting hate speech (Sang and Stanton, 2022), social biases (Sap et al., 2020), or gender biases (Havens et al., 2022). Data perspectivism incorporates multiple perspectives in datasets intended for model training, keeping all annotators' representations of knowledge through the publication of non-aggregated versions of the annotated text data. Representing multiple perspectives in data is important because interpretation of language changes across contexts, such as different geographic locations and cultures (Sambasivan et al., 2021), racialized ethnicities (Crenshaw, 1991), domains (Basta et al., 2020), time periods (Shopland, 2020; Spencer, 2000), and people (Denton et al., 2021).

Data perspectivism aligns with "data feminism" (D'Ignazio and Klein, 2020) which views data as situated and partial. Data feminism draws on feminist theories' rejection of universal knowledge in favor of multiple, different, and equally valid perspectives (Harding, 1995; Haraway, 1988). The process of labeling text and documents, whether

[1] For example, Sweeney (2013) demonstrated how Google Ads discriminated against people whose names are predominant in black communities relative to names predominant in white communities in the United States. This positively impacts job applicants with stereotypically white names and negatively impacts job applicants with stereotypically black names.

with human annotators or classification models, inevitably records, and thus gives power to, particular people's perspectives while excluding others' perspectives (D'Ignazio and Klein, 2020; Bowker and Star, 1999). Though writing for the information sciences, the caution of Bowker and Star (1999) remains relevant to NLP dataset creation and model development: "each category valorizes some point of view and silences another. This is not inherently a bad thing–indeed it is inescapable. But it *is* an ethical choice, and as such it is dangerous" (5). Publishing non-aggregated, annotated data is the first step towards addressing the dangers of classification, making the data available. That being said, the availability of data does not ensure its accessibility (Mons et al., 2017).

4. Why Data Perspectivism Needs Exploratory Visualization

Due to annotated text data's (1) **large size**, (2) **complexity**, and (3) **variability**, publishing non-aggregated, annotated data does not ensure the data's accessibility. Firstly, the amount of annotations and text needed to train NLP models results in annotated datasets of such large size that they cannot be reasonably expected to be manually reviewed. Consequently, analyzing annotated text data requires skills with particular data formats and programming languages, excluding stakeholders in NLP systems who do not have these skills from the data analysis process. Secondly, annotation taxonomies are not standardized. Even for the same task, multiple taxonomies may exist. For example, Dinan et al. (2020) and Hitti et al. (2019) propose two different taxonomies for the same task, classifying gender biased language, that do not have a single category in common.

Thirdly, data formats for annotated text corpora vary. For example, existing annotation platforms may output annotated data as Plaintext (Stenetorp et al., 2012), CSV (Chew et al., 2019), or JSON (Nakayama et al., 2018). The organization of annotated data within these file formats varies according to each annotation platform's design and each project's annotation taxonomy. As a result, anyone wishing to review an annotated dataset must first learn how the annotations and original text are represented in particular file formats. Though Plaintext, CSV, and JSON are not unusual data formats, for stakeholders of a dataset without data science or computing experience, these file format's organization of data may not be intuitive. Moreover, while documentation such as data statements (Bender and Friedman, 2018) provides valuable overviews of annotated datasets, if a person aims to understand the perspectives that different annotations communicate across a text corpus, data analysis remains necessary. To complement the overview that documentation such as data statements provide, we encourage NLP dataset creators to utilize text visualization techniques when publishing non-aggregated, annotated data.

Within the data visualization community, numerous techniques exist to explore text. For a comprehensive survey of text visualizations, please refer to the survey of surveys by Alharbi and Laramee (2019) or, for an interactive exploration, the Text Visualization Browser of Kucher and Kerren (2015). Focusing specifically on opportunities between text visualization and text mining, Liu et al. (2019) survey 4,609 papers and identify classification as underrepresented in text visualization papers relative to text mining papers. The authors note an opportunity in text visualization research to better study how to interactively visualize the complexities of text classification processes. With many publications of visualization techniques repeatedly using the same selection of datasets that do not reflect the complexities of more widely relevant or important datasets (Kosara, 2018), we identify a mutually beneficial collaboration opportunity between the NLP and data visualization communities. This collaboration could lead to "new techniques for AI explainability" (Basile et al., 2021, 2-3), contributing to the NLP and wider machine learning community, while also beginning to address the "ethical challenge in visualization...to visualize the provenance of data and decision-making" (Correll, 2018, 7), contributing to the data visualization community. The next section describes specific techniques from text visualization relevant to analyzing non-aggregated, annotated data.

5. Exploratory Text Visualization Techniques for Data Perspectivism

Recognizing the need to facilitate exploratory search of non-aggregated, annotated data, we see an opportunity for the NLP community to collaborate with the text visualization community. As defined in §2, *exploratory search* refers to an open-ended information seeking process in which the questions guiding an information seeker are multi-faceted, and the answers to those questions are put together iteratively (Athukorala et al., 2015; White and Roth, 2009; Marchionini, 2006). Exploratory search requires collaboration between computers and humans, as an information retrieval system responds to the information seeker's interactions with it, and the seeker refines and tailors their interactions with the system based on the information presented to them (White and Roth, 2009). Interactive data visualization facilitates such collaboration between computers and humans (Hammer et al., 2013; Keim, 2002).

Interactive data visualization, specifically text visualization for text data, provide techniques for visually representing and interrogating non-aggregated, annotated text data:

(1) **Large Size** Exploring data visually makes use of humans' "perceptual abilities" (Keim, 2002). For a person exploring non-aggregated, annotated text datasets, visual design cues such as color, transparency, and position draw on the strength of human vision (Hutmacher, 2019) to communicate patterns and outliers in the annotations when presented at a high level, or zoomed out, overview.

(2) **Complexity** Providing manual interaction mechanisms facilitates self-guided, iterative analysis. For a person exploring non-aggregated, annotated text data, interactions with high- and low-level views of the data would facilitate learning and comprehension of how different annotators interpreted an annotation taxonomy. Notably, this learning and comprehension would be based on the actual application of the taxonomy's labels to text, rather than an abstract representation of text, for example, in vector space (which Goldfarb-Tarrant et al. (2021) have demonstrated the limitations of regarding offensive language in text).

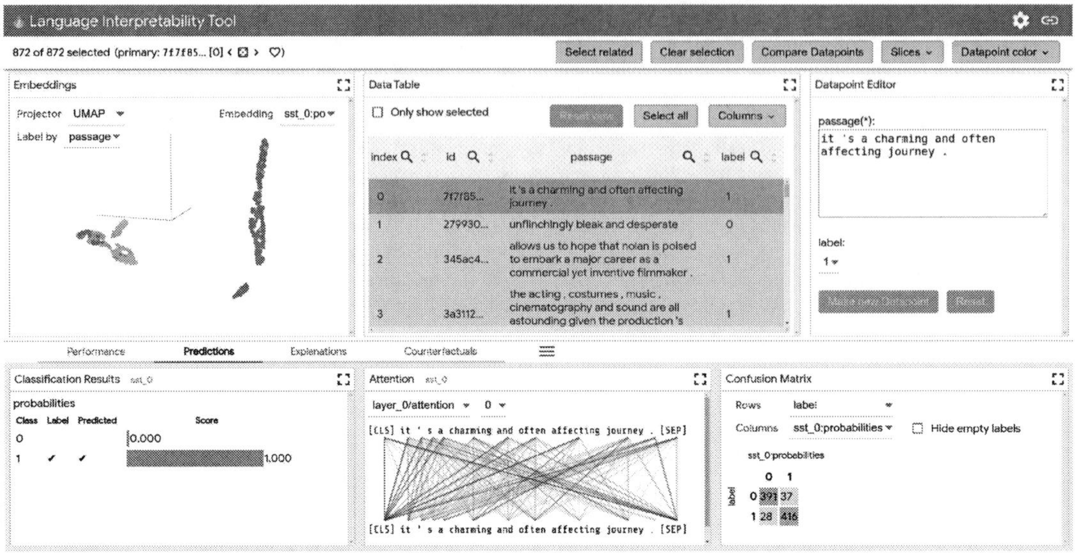

Figure 1: The Language Interpretability Tool by Tenney and Wexler et al. (2020) uses multiple coordinated views for exploratory analysis of a model's performance: "The top half shows a selection toolbar, and, left-to-right: the embedding projector, the data table, and the datapoint editor. Tabs present different modules in the bottom half; the view above shows classifier predictions, an attention visualization, and a confusion matrix." (108). *Figure reproduced with author permission.*

(3) **Variability** Representing annotated text data visually relies on human intuition rather than knowledge of mathematical or statistical concepts, or skills with a particular data format or programming language (Keim, 2002). For a person exploring non-aggregated, annotated text datasets, a text visualization interface would facilitate efficient search and analysis without requiring any prior knowledge or skills in data science or computing. As a result, a more diverse group of stakeholders in an NLP system could participate in the analysis of annotated text corpora.

From among the many text visualization techniques (Cao and Cui, 2016; Puretskiy et al., 2010) that exist, we highlight two techniques particularly relevant to data perspectivism: multiple coordinated views and interconnected terms. Multiple coordinated views combine multiple visual representations of a text corpus at different levels of detail, where interaction with one representation leads to corresponding changes in the other representations (Cao and Cui, 2016). The Language Interpretability Tool (LIT)[2] of Tenney and Wexler et al. (2020), displayed in Figure 1, uses multiple coordinated views to analyze a language model's performance. The visualization supports the three characteristics of exploratory search:

- **Multi-faceted** A person can analyze multiple aspects of a model's performance at multiple levels of detail, including the application of labels in the "Classification Results" view, the attention of the model to specific terms in the "Attention" view, and the data on which to study a model's performance in the "Data Table" and "Datapoint Editor" views.
- **Iterative** A person can iteratively refine their analysis by selecting different subsets of data in the "Data Table" view, or editing datapoints with the "Datapoint Editor" view.
- **Open-Ended** A person is not guided toward a particular answer to a question; rather, a person can ask many questions, each of which can have several answers.

Tenney and Wexler et al. (2020) state that the questions guiding LIT's design was: "What kind of examples does my model perform poorly on? Why did my model make this prediction? And critically, does my model behave consistently if I change things like textual style, verb tense, or pronoun gender?" (107). To answer these questions, people can try numerous approaches, such as applying counterfactual methods to change their data or iterating between analysis tasks at different levels of detail, such as a selected subset of passages in the "Data Table" view or higher-level aggregate views of the model's performance in the "Embeddings" view. The authors' guiding questions are thus exploratory in nature, suitable for an exploratory visualization. For more examples of multiple coordinated views, please refer to the work of Kim et al. (2021), Liu et al. (2015), Isaacs et al. (2014), and Shutt et al. (2009).

Network, or node-link, graphs have been used to visualize interconnected terms. NEREx, displayed in Figure 2, visualizes named entities in a text corpus using a network graph,[3] where nodes represent entities and links represent the distance between the pair of entities they connect (El-

[2] pair-code.github.io/lit/

[3] NERE x also contains five other visualizations.

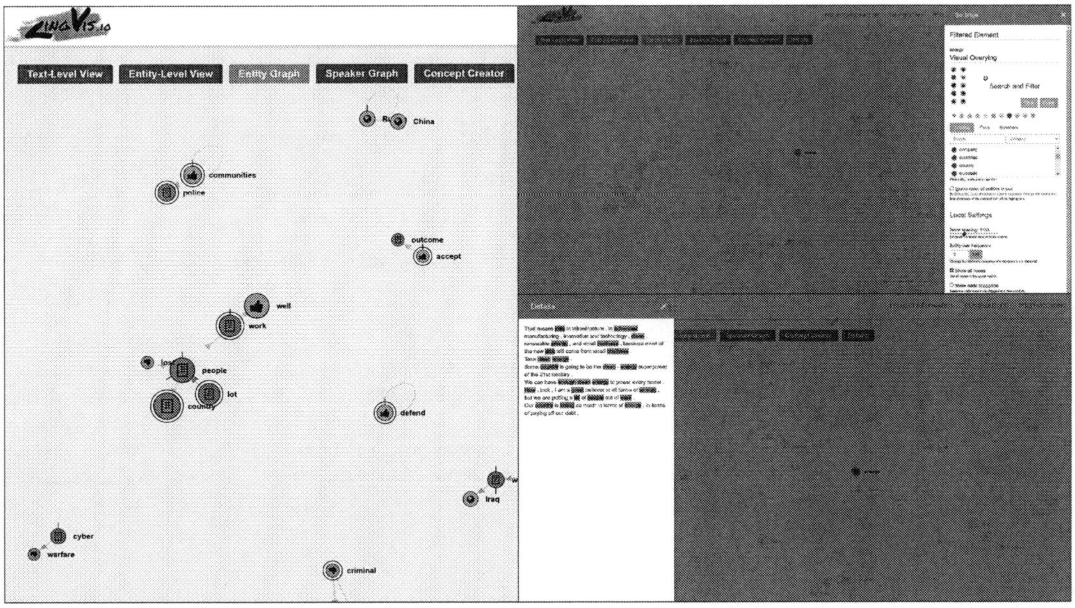

Figure 2: NERExx (El-Assady et al., 2017) uses a network graph, called the "Entity Graph," to provide an overview of text data in a corpus, displaying named identities as nodes and their relationships as links. People can interact with the graph and adjust the data it displays using the "Settings" pane displayed in the top right image. People can view the original text with the "Detail" pane displayed in the bottom left image, which overlays color-coded highlights onto the text to indicate associated words in the text and nodes in the graph. *Figure reproduced with author permission.*

Assady et al., 2017). The network of named entities supports the three characteristics of exploratory search:

- **Multi-faceted** A person can choose to study multiple types of named entities, represented in Figure 2 by color and icon, and study the relationship between the entities, represented by the links between the nodes. Longer links indicate greater distance between the entities as they appear in the text corpus.

- **Iterative** A person can refine their search by filtering the visualization using the "Settings" pane (Figure 2, top right), selecting particular entities, entity pairs, or speakers; or a person can iterate between a detailed view of the text using the "Detail" pane (Figure 2, bottom right) and a distant view of the text as the network graph (Figure 2, left).

- **Open-Ended** A person is not directed toward a particular question and answer. Instead, a person can ask many questions and obtain many answers, such as getting an overview of relationships between named entities, studying the influence of particular people, and analyzing the frequency of and relationships between topics.

For analyzing non-aggregated, annotated text data, connections between terms in network graphs could be based on labels annotators applied to the terms, where a link's length corresponds to the distance between two annotated terms. Location clouds and lattice graphs also provide approaches to visualizing interconnected terms in text visualization. The Trading Consequences platform of Hinrichs et al. (2015) includes a location cloud (Figure 3) to display relationships between commodities and country names over time. Adapting this visualization to exploring non-aggregated, annotated data, an annotation label could be searched instead of a commodity, and the decade columns could be replaced with columns for each annotator of a corpus, displaying the text spans to which each annotator applied the searched label. The lattice graph proposed for machine translation and automated speech recognition systems (Figure 4) by Collins et al. (2007) provides another example of visualizing interconnected terms. Adapting this visualization to exploring non-aggregated, annotated data, different annotators' labels of a particular sentence or document could be displayed above the sentence or document running along the bottom of the visualization, instead of alternative translations.

Though collaboration with the text visualization community in support of data perspectivism may be new, examples of other interdisciplinary collaborations with the visualization community exist as guides. `Lingvis.io` contains a repository of projects focused on data visualization for linguistics and machine learning. Interdisciplinary work between the humanities and visualization communities demonstrates the value of collaboratively creating visualizations, in addition to using the visualizations for analysis (Hinrichs et al., 2018; Jänicke et al., 2017). That

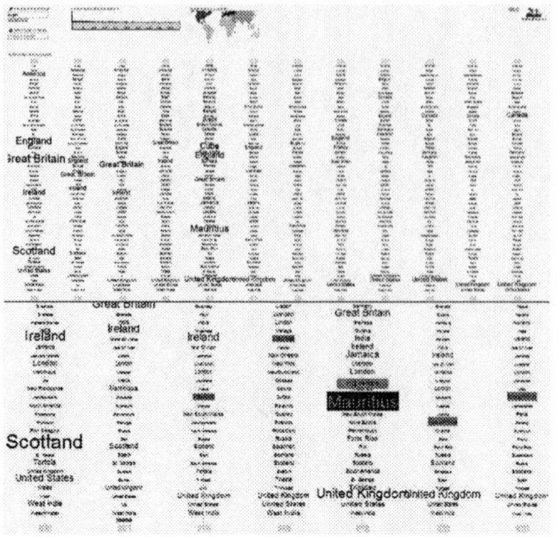

Figure 3: In the location cloud by Hinrichs et al. (2015), country names that appear in the text corpus in relation to a commodity ("sugar" above) are visualized. The size of a country's name indicates the frequency of that country in documents from the corresponding column's decade. When a country name is hovered over ("Mauritius" above), that name is highlighted where it appears in all decades, facilitating easy comparison of how frequently it is mentioned in relation to the searched commodity in the corpus. *Figure reproduced with author permission.*

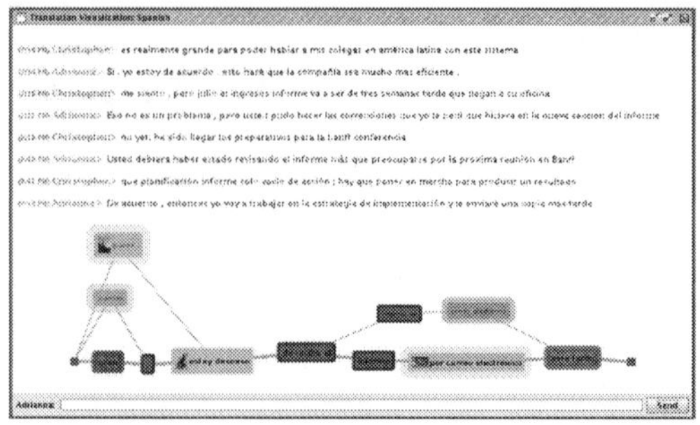

Figure 4: Collins et al. (2007) demonstrate how visualizing a machine translation system's output as a lattice graph facilitates communication between people who speak different languages. The transparency of each word's rectangle and the position of the words correspond to a model's score of its likelihood of being an accurate translation. *Figure reproduced with author permission.*

being said, interdisciplinary collaboration presents challenges due to different vocabularies, working practices, and project timelines across disciplines. Hinrichs et al. (2017) encourage critical reflection on the process of collaboration when undertaking interdisciplinary projects, providing questions that can serve as a guide for such reflection to support effective communication between people in different disciplines. For a broader summary of the benefits and challenges to working across disciplines to collaboratively create data visualizations, please refer to the survey of Jänicke et al. (2017).

6. Conclusion and Future Work

We have described how collaboration between the NLP and visualization communities could facilitate exploratory analysis of non-aggregated, annotated datasets. Exploratory analysis of these datasets would lead to better understandings of the perspectives they represent, improving the transparency of datasets' documentation. Furthermore, by using exploratory analysis to identify perspectives that are not represented in an annotated dataset, along with the perspectives that are represented, dataset creators will be able to determine how to collect additional data that make their dataset more representative of its stakeholders. Due to the underlying motivation of existing annotation platforms (to support the development of one aggregated dataset), the platforms do not provide the exploratory search capabilities necessary for such analysis.

The process of creating a dataset for NLP models inevitably involves curation (Rogers, 2021). We encourage the NLP community's collaboration with the text visualization community to facilitate critical analysis of who and what are included and excluded during dataset creation in support of data perspectivism (Basile et al., 2021), as well as data-centric AI (Press, 2021) and data feminism (D'Ignazio and Klein, 2020). As approaches to incorporating more diverse perspectives in datasets develop, the NLP community could look beyond the text visualization community for collaboration opportunities. Jo and Gebru (2020) recommend looking towards the archival sciences for guidance on data collection and curation. More broadly, the gallery, library, archive, and museum (GLAM) sector has extensive experience creating datasets and enabling their interoperability across systems with metadata standards and supporting infrastructures (RDA Steering Committee, 2022; Library of Congress, 2021; Dunsire and Willer, 2014). Interdisciplinary collaboration would lend value to datasets published under the data perspectivism paradigm, facilitating access to data for stakeholders outside the NLP and wider machine learning communities.

We encourage the development of new platforms with interactive, exploratory text visualizations, in which data analysis becomes an intuitive process relying on human vision, rather than a person's data science or computing skills. Such platforms could lead to new insights about annotations and empower of a more diverse group of stakeholders to participate in data analysis. In future work we will create an exploratory visualization for data published under the data perspectivist paradigm, providing a use case for multi-faceted, iterative, and open-ended analysis of non-aggregated, annotated text data.

7. Acknowledgements

Thank you to the reviewers for their thoughtful comments on this paper. Additional thanks go to the School of Informatics Graduate School and Edinburgh Futures Institute at the University of Edinburgh, and the UK's Engineering and Physical Sciences Research Council for funding our research. We are also grateful to the text visualization creators who permitted us to include images of their work in this paper, Mennatallah El-Assady, Rita Sevastjanova, James Wexler, Uta Hinrichs, and Christopher Collins.

8. Bibliographical References

Akhtar, S., Basile, V., and Patti, V. (2021). Whose Opinions Matter? Perspective-aware Models to Identify Opinions of Hate Speech Victims in Abusive Language Detection. *CoRR*, abs/2106.15896.

Alharbi, M. and Laramee, R. S. (2019). SoS TextVis: An Extended Survey of Surveys on Text Visualization. *Computers*, 8(1).

Athukorala, K., Glowacka, D., Jacucci, G., Oulasvirta, A., and Vreeken, J. (2015). Is exploratory search different? A comparison of information search behavior for exploratory and lookup tasks. *Journal of the Association for Information Science and Technology*, 67(11):2635–2651, October. DOI: 10.1002/asi.23617.

Basile, V., Cabitza, F., Campagner, A., and Fell, M. (2021). Toward a Perspectivist Turn in Ground Truthing for Predictive Computing. *CoRR*, abs/2109.04270.

Basile, V. (2022). The Perspectivist Data Manifesto. [Online; accessed March 21, 2022].

Basta, C., Costa-jussà, M. R., and Casas, N. (2020). Extensive Study on the Underlying Gender Bias in Contextualized Word Embeddings. *Neural Computing & Applications*, 33(8):3371–3384.

Bender, E. M. and Friedman, B. (2018). Data Statements for Natural Language Processing: Toward Mitigating System Bias and Enabling Better Science. *Transactions of the Association for Computational Linguistics*, 6:587–604, December. DOI: 10.1162/tacl_a_00041.

Bender, E. M., Gebru, T., McMillan-Major, A., and Shmitchell, S. (2021). On the Dangers of Stochastic Parrots: Can Language Models Be Too Big? In *Proceedings of the 2021 ACM Conference on Fairness, Accountability, and Transparency*, FAccT '21, page 610–623, New York, NY, USA. Association for Computing Machinery. DOI: 10.1145/3442188.3445922.

Bolukbasi, T., Chang, K.-W., Zou, J., Saligrama, V., and Kalai, A. (2016). Man is to Computer Programmer as Woman is to Homemaker? Debiasing Word Embeddings. In *Proceedings of the 30th International Conference on Neural Information Processing Systems*, pages 4356–4364. DOI: 10.18653/v1/2020.acl-main.485.

Bowker, G. C. and Star, S. L. (1999). *Sorting Things Out: Classification and Its Consequences*. Inside technology. MIT Press, Cambridge, USA.

Caliskan, A., Bryson, J. J., and Narayanan, A. (2017). Semantics derived automatically from language corpora contain human-like biases. *Science*, 356(6334):183–186, April. DOI: 10.1126/science.aal4230.

Cao, N. and Cui, W. (2016). *Overview Text Visualization Techniques*. Atlantis Briefs in Artificial Intelligence ; 1. Atlantis Press, Paris, 1st ed. 2016. edition.

Cao, Y. T. and Daumé III, H. (2020). Toward Gender-Inclusive Coreference Resolution. *Proceedings of the 58th Annual Meeting of the Association for Computational Linguistics*. DOI: 10.18653/v1/2020.acl-main.418.

Collins, C., Carpendale, S., and Penn, G. (2007). Visualization of Uncertainty in Lattices to Support Decision-Making. In *Proceedings of Eurographics/IEEE VGTC Symposium on Visualization (EuroVis)*, pages 51–58, Norrköping, Sweden, May. Eurographics. DOI: 10.2312/VisSym/EuroVis07/051-058.

Correll, M. (2018). Ethical Dimensions of Visualization Research. *CoRR*, abs/1811.07271.

Crenshaw, K. (1991). Mapping the Margins: Intersectionality, Identity Politics, and Violence against Women of Color. *Stanford Law Review*, 43(6):1241–1299. DOI: 10.2307/1229039.

Davani, A. M., Díaz, M., and Prabhakaran, V. (2022). Dealing with Disagreements: Looking Beyond the Majority Vote in Subjective Annotations. *Transactions of the Association for Computational Linguistics*, 10:92–110.

Denton, E., Díaz, M., Kivlichan, I., Prabhakaran, V., and Rosen, R. (2021). Whose Ground Truth? Accounting for Individual and Collective Identities Underlying Dataset Annotation. *CoRR*, abs/2112.04554.

Diaz, M., Johnson, I., Lazar, A., Piper, A. M., and Gergle, D. (2018). Addressing Age-Related Bias in Sentiment Analysis. In *Proceedings of the 2018 CHI Conference on Human Factors in Computing Systems - CHI '18*, pages 1–14, Montréal, CA. ACM Press. DOI: 10.1145/3173574.3173986.

D'Ignazio, C. and Klein, L. F. (2020). *Data Feminism*. Strong ideas series. The MIT Press, Cambridge, MA, USA.

Dinan, E., Fan, A., Wu, L., Weston, J., Kiela, D., and Williams, A. (2020). Multi-Dimensional Gender Bias Classification. In *Proceedings of the 2020 Conference on Empirical Methods in Natural Language Processing (EMNLP)*, pages 314–331, Online, November. Association for Computational Linguistics.

Dunsire, G. and Willer, M. (2014). The local in the global: universal bibliographic control from the bottom up. In *80th IFLA General Conference And Assembly*, Lyon, FR. International Federation of Library Associations.

El-Assady, M., Sevastjanova, R., Gipp, B., Keim, D., and Collins, C. (2017). NEREx: Named-Entity Relationship Exploration in Multi-Party Conversations. *Computer Graphics Forum*, 36(3):213 – 225.

Frické, M. (2015). Big data and its epistemology. *Journal of the Association for Information Science and Technology*, 66(4):651–661. DOI: 10.1002/asi.23212.

Gebru, T., Morgenstern, J., Vecchione, B., Vaughan, J. W., Wallach, H. M., III, H. D., and Crawford, K. (2018). Datasheets for Datasets. *Computing Research Repository*, arXiv:1803.09010.

Goldfarb-Tarrant, S., Marchant, R., Muñoz Sánchez, R., Pandya, M., and Lopez, A. (2021). Intrinsic Bias Metrics Do Not Correlate with Application Bias. In *Proceedings of the 59th Annual Meeting of the Association for Computational Linguistics and the 11th International Joint Conference on Natural Language Processing (Vol-*

ume 1: Long Papers), pages 1926–1940, Online, August. Association for Computational Linguistics. DOI: 10.18653/v1/2021.acl-long.150.

Gordon, M. L., Lam, M. S., Park, J. S., Patel, K., Hancock, J. T., Hashimoto, T., and Bernstein, M. S. (2022). Jury Learning: Integrating Dissenting Voices into Machine Learning Models. *CoRR*, abs/2202.02950.

Hammer, B., Keim, D., Lawrence, N., and Lebanon, G. (2013). Preface: Intelligent interactive data visualization. *Data Mining and Knowledge Discovery*, pages 1–3. DOI: 10.1007/s10618-013-0309-y.

Haraway, D. (1988). Situated Knowledges: The Science Question in Feminism and the Privilege of Partial Perspective. *Feminist Studies*, 14(3):575. DOI: 10.2307/3178066.

Harding, S. (1995). "Strong objectivity": A response to the new objectivity question. *Synthese*, 104(3), September. DOI: 10.1007/BF01064504.

Havens, L., Terras, M., Bach, B., and Alex, B. (2020). Situated Data, Situated Systems: A Methodology to Engage with Power Relations in Natural Language Processing Research. In *Proceedings of the Second Workshop on Gender Bias in Natural Language Processing*, pages 107–124, Barcelona, Spain (Online), December. Association for Computational Linguistics.

Havens, L., Terras, M., Bach, B., and Alex, B. (2022). Uncertainty and Inclusivity in Gender Bias Annotation: An Annotation Taxonomy and Annotated Datasets of British English Text. In *Proceedings of the Fourth Workshop on Gender Bias in Natural Language Processing*, Seattle, WA, USA, July. Association for Computational Linguistics. [Forthcoming].

Hinrichs, U., Alex, B., Clifford, J., Watson, A., Quigley, A., Klein, E., and Coates, C. M. (2015). Trading Consequences: A Case Study of Combining Text Mining and Visualization to Facilitate Document Exploration. *Digital Scholarship in the Humanities*, 30(Supplement 1):i50–i75, 10. DOI: 10.1093/llc/fqv046.

Hinrichs, U., El-Assady, M., Bradely, A. J., Forlini, S., and Collins, C. (2017). Risk the drift! Stretching disciplinary boundaries through critical collaborations between the humanities and visualization. *Second Workshop on Visualization for the Digital Humanities*.

Hinrichs, U., Forlini, S., and Moynihan, B. (2018). In defense of sandcastles: Research thinking through visualization in digital humanities. *Digital Scholarship in the Humanities*, 34(Supplement 1):i80–i99, 10. DOI: 10.1093/llc/fqy051.

Hitti, Y., Jang, E., Moreno, I., and Pelletier, C. (2019). Proposed Taxonomy for Gender Bias in Text; A Filtering Methodology for the Gender Generalization Subtype. In *Proceedings of the First Workshop on Gender Bias in Natural Language Processing*, pages 8–17, Florence, IT. Association for Computational Linguistics. DOI: 10.18653/v1/W19-3802.

Hutchinson, B., Smart, A., Hanna, A., Denton, E., Greer, C., Kjartansson, O., Barnes, P., and Mitchell, M. (2021). Towards Accountability for Machine Learning Datasets: Practices from Software Engineering and Infrastructure. In *Proceedings of the 2021 ACM Conference on Fairness, Accountability, and Transparency*, FAccT '21, page 560–575, New York, NY, USA. Association for Computing Machinery. DOI: 10.1145/3442188.3445918.

Hutmacher, F. (2019). Why Is There So Much More Research on Vision Than on Any Other Sensory Modality? *Frontiers in Psychology*, 10(2246). DOI: 10.3389/fpsyg.2019.02246.

Isaacs, E., Damico, K., Ahern, S., Bart, E., and Singhal, M. (2014). Footprints: A Visual Search Tool that Supports Discovery and Coverage Tracking. *IEEE Transactions on Visualization and Computer Graphics*, 20(12):1793–1802. DOI: 10.1109/TVCG.2014.2346743.

Jänicke, S., Franzini, G., Cheema, M. F., and Scheuermann, G. (2017). Visual Text Analysis in Digital Humanities. *Computer Graphics Forum*, 36(6):226–250.

Jo, E. S. and Gebru, T. (2020). Lessons from Archives: Strategies for Collecting Sociocultural Data in Machine Learning. In *Proceedings of the 2020 Conference on Fairness, Accountability, and Transparency*, FAT* '20, page 306–316, New York, NY, USA. Association for Computing Machinery. DOI: 10.1145/3351095.3372829.

Keim, D. A. (2002). Information visualization and visual data mining. *IEEE Transactions on Visualization and Computer Graphics*, 8(1):1–8. DOI: 10.1109/2945.981847.

Kim, C., Lin, X., Collins, C., Taylor, G. W., and Amer, M. R. (2021). Learn, Generate, Rank, Explain: A Case Study of Visual Explanation by Generative Machine Learning. *ACM Trans. Interact. Intell. Syst.*, 11(3–4), August. DOI: 10.1145/3465407.

Kosara, R. (2018). How to Get Excited About Standard Datasets.

Kucher, K. and Kerren, A. (2015). Text visualization techniques: Taxonomy, visual survey, and community insights. In *2015 IEEE Pacific Visualization Symposium (PacificVis)*, pages 117–121. DOI: 10.1109/PACIFICVIS.2015.7156366.

Library of Congress. (2021). Library of Congress Subject Headings PDF Files.

Liu, S., Chen, Y., Wei, H., Yang, J., Zhou, K., and Drucker, S. M. (2015). Exploring Topical Lead-Lag across Corpora. *IEEE Transactions on Knowledge and Data Engineering*, 27(1):115–129. DOI: 10.1109/TKDE.2014.2324581.

Liu, S., Wang, X., Collins, C., Dou, W., Ouyang, F., El-Assady, M., Jiang, L., and Keim, D. A. (2019). Bridging Text Visualization and Mining: A Task-Driven Survey. *IEEE Transactions on Visualization and Computer Graphics*, 25(7):2482–2504. DOI: 10.1109/TVCG.2018.2834341.

Marchionini, G. (2006). Exploratory Search: From Finding to Understanding. *Commun. ACM*, 49(4):41–46, apr. DOI: 10.1145/1121949.1121979.

Mons, B., Neylon, C., Velter, J., Dumontier, M., da Silva Santos, L. O. B., and Wilkinson, M. D. (2017). Cloudy, increasingly FAIR; revisiting the FAIR

Data guiding principles for the European Open Science Cloud. *Information Services & Use*, 37(1):49–56. DOI: 10.3233/ISU-170824.

Morstatter, F., Wu, L., Yavanoglu, U., Corman, S. R., and Liu, H. (2018). Identifying Framing Bias in Online News. *ACM Transactions on Social Computing*, 1(2):1–18, 6. DOI: 10.1145/3204948.

Nekoto, W., Marivate, V., Matsila, T., Fasubaa, T., Kolawole, T., Fagbohungbe, T., Akinola, S. O., Muhammad, S. H., Kabongo, S., Osei, S., Freshia, S., Niyongabo, R. A., Macharm, R., Ogayo, P., Ahia, O., Meressa, M., Adeyemi, M., Mokgesi-Selinga, M., Okegbemi, L., Martinus, L. J., Tajudeen, K., Degila, K., Ogueji, K., Siminyu, K., Kreutzer, J., Webster, J., Ali, J. T., Abbott, J., Orife, I., Ezeani, I., Dangana, I. A., Kamper, H., Elsahar, H., Duru, G., Kioko, G., Murhabazi, E., van Biljon, E., Whitenack, D., Onyefuluchi, C., Emezue, C., Dossou, B., Sibanda, B., Bassey, B. I., Olabiyi, A., Ramkilowan, A., Öktem, A., Akinfaderin, A., and Bashir, A. (2020). Participatory Research for Low-resourced Machine Translation: A Case Study in African Languages. *Findings of the Association for Computational Linguistics: EMNLP 2020*.

Nobata, C., Tetreault, J., Thomas, A., Mehdad, Y., and Chang, Y. (2016). Abusive Language Detection in Online User Content. In *Proceedings of the 25th International Conference on World Wide Web - WWW '16*, pages 145–153, Montréal, QC, CA. ACM Press. DOI: 10.1145/2872427.2883062.

Noble, S. U. (2018). *Algorithms of Oppression: How Search Engines Reinforce Racism*. New York University Press, New York, USA.

O'Neil, C. (2017). *Weapons of Math Destruction: How Big Data Increases Inequality and Threatens Democracy*. Broadway Books, New York, NY, USA, first paperback edition. edition.

Perez, C. C. (2019). *Invisible Women: Exposing Data Bias in a World Designed for Men*. Vintage, London, GB.

Prabhu, V. U. and Birhane, A. (2021). Large image datasets: A pyrrhic win for computer vision? *2021 IEEE Winter Conference on Applications of Computer Vision (WACV)*, pages 1536–1546.

Press, G. (2021). Andrew Ng Launches A Campaign For Data-Centric AI. *Forbes*.

Puretskiy, A. A., Shutt, G. L., and Berry, M. W., (2010). *Survey of Text Visualization Techniques*, chapter 6, pages 105–127. John Wiley & Sons, Ltd. DOI: 10.1002/9780470689646.ch6.

RDA Steering Committee. (2022). About RDA.

Rogers, A. (2021). Changing the World by Changing the Data. In *Proceedings of the 59th Annual Meeting of the Association for Computational Linguistics and the 11th International Joint Conference on Natural Language Processing (Volume 1: Long Papers)*, pages 2182–2194, Online, August. Association for Computational Linguistics. DOI: 10.18653/v1/2021.acl-long.170.

Rudinger, R., Naradowsky, J., Leonard, B., and Van Durme, B. (2018). Gender Bias in Coreference Resolution. *Proceedings of the 2018 Conference of the North American Chapter of the Association for Computational Linguistics: Human Language Technologies, Volume 2 (Short Papers)*. DOI: 10.18653/v1/N18-2002.

Sambasivan, N., Arnesen, E., Hutchinson, B., Doshi, T., and Prabhakaran, V. (2021). Re-Imagining Algorithmic Fairness in India and Beyond. In *Proceedings of the 2021 ACM Conference on Fairness, Accountability, and Transparency*, FAccT '21, page 315–328, New York, NY, USA. Association for Computing Machinery. DOI: 10.1145/3442188.3445896.

Sang, Y. and Stanton, J. (2022). The Origin and Value of Disagreement Among Data Labelers: A Case Study of Individual Differences in Hate Speech Annotation. In *Information for a Better World: Shaping the Global Future*, Lecture Notes in Computer Science, pages 425–444. Springer International Publishing, Cham.

Sap, M., Gabriel, S., Qin, L., Jurafsky, D., Smith, N. A., and Choi, Y. (2020). Social Bias Frames: Reasoning about Social and Power Implications of Language. In *Proceedings of the 58th Annual Meeting of the Association for Computational Linguistics*, pages 5477–5490, Online, July. Association for Computational Linguistics. DOI: 10.18653/v1/2020.acl-main.486.

Shopland, N. (2020). *A Practical Guide to Searching LGBTQIA Historical Records*. Taylor & Francis Group, Milton. DOI: 10.4324/9781003006787.

Shutt, G. L., Puretskiy, A. A., and Berry, M. W. (2009). FutureLens: Software for Text Visualization and Tracking. In *Proceedings of the Ninth SIAM International Conference on Data Mining*, Sparks, NV, USA.

Spencer, D. (2000). Language and reality: Who made the world? (1980). In Lucy Burke, et al., editors, *The Routledge language and cultural theory reader*. Routledge, London, UK.

Sweeney, L. (2013). Discrimination in online ad delivery. *Communications of the ACM*, 56(5):44–54, May. DOI: 10.1145/2447976.2447990.

Tenney, I., Wexler, J., Bastings, J., Bolukbasi, T., Coenen, A., Gehrmann, S., Jiang, E., Pushkarna, M., Radebaugh, C., Reif, E., and Yuan, A. (2020). The Language Interpretability Tool: Extensible, Interactive Visualizations and Analysis for NLP Models. In *Proceedings of the 2020 Conference on Empirical Methods in Natural Language Processing: System Demonstrations*, Online, October.

Welty, C., Paritosh, P. K., and Aroyo, L. (2019). Metrology for AI: From Benchmarks to Instruments. *CoRR*, abs/1911.01875.

White, R. W. and Roth, R. A. (2009). *Exploratory search: beyond the query-response paradigm*. Synthesis lectures on information concepts, retrieval, and services ; # 3. Morgan & Claypool Publishers, San Rafael, CA, USA.

9. Language Resource References

Batista-Navarro, R., Carter, J., and Ananiadou, S. (2016). Argo: enabling the development of bespoke workflows and services for disease annotation. *Database*, 2016, 05.

Kalina Bontcheva and Hamish Cunningham and Ian Roberts and Angus Roberts and Valentin Tablan and

Niraj Aswani and Genevieve Gorrell. (2013). *GATE Teamware: a web-based, collaborative text annotation framework*. Springer.

Chew, Rob and Wenger, Michael and Kery, Caroline and Nance, Jason and Richards, Keith and Hadley, Emily and Baumgartner, Peter. (2019). *SMART: An Open Source Data Labeling Platform for Supervised Learning*. JMLR.org.

Hiroki Nakayama and Takahiro Kubo and Junya Kamura and Yasufumi Taniguchi and Xu Liang. (2018). *doccano: Text Annotation Tool for Human*.

Martín Pérez-Pérez and Daniel Glez-Peña and Florentino Fdez-Riverola and Anália Lourenço. (2015). *Marky: A tool supporting annotation consistency in multi-user and iterative document annotation projects*.

Pontus Stenetorp and Sampo Pyysalo and Goran Topić and Tomoko Ohta, Sophia Ananiadou and Jun'ichi Tsujii. (2012). Proceedings of the Demonstrations Session at EACL 2012, v1.3 Crunchy Frog (2012-11-08).

Proceedings of the 1st Workshop on Perspectivist Approaches to NLP @LREC2022, pages 83–94
Marseille, 20 June 2022

The *Measuring Hate Speech* Corpus: Leveraging Rasch Measurement Theory for Data Perspectivism

Pratik S. Sachdeva[1], Renata Barreto[1,2], Geoff Bacon[3], Alexander Sahn[4], Claudia von Vacano[1], Chris J. Kennedy[5]
[1]D-Lab, University of California Berkeley
[2]School of Law, University of California, Berkeley
[3]Google
[4]Center for the Study of Democratic Politics, Princeton University
[5]Center for Precision Psychiatry, Harvard Medical School
pratik.sachdeva@berkeley.edu

Abstract

We introduce the *Measuring Hate Speech* corpus, a dataset created to measure hate speech while adjusting for annotators' perspectives. It consists of 50,070 social media comments spanning YouTube, Reddit, and Twitter, labeled by 11,143 annotators recruited from Amazon Mechanical Turk. Each observation includes 10 ordinal labels: sentiment, disrespect, insult, attacking/defending, humiliation, inferior/superior status, dehumanization, violence, genocide, and a 3-valued hate speech benchmark label. The labels are aggregated using faceted Rasch measurement theory (RMT) into a continuous score that measures each comment's location on a hate speech spectrum. The annotation experimental design assigned comments to multiple annotators in order to yield a linked network, allowing annotator disagreement (perspective) to be statistically summarized. Annotators' labeling strictness was estimated during the RMT scaling, projecting their perspective onto a linear measure that was adjusted for the hate speech score. Models that incorporate this annotator perspective parameter as an auxiliary input can generate label- and score-level predictions conditional on annotator perspective. The corpus includes the identity group targets of each comment (8 groups, 42 subgroups) and annotator demographics (6 groups, 40 subgroups), facilitating analyses of interactions between annotator- and comment-level identities, i.e. identity-related annotator perspective.

Keywords: hate speech, item response theory, Rasch measurement theory, measurement, annotator identity

1. Introduction

The application of machine learning on increasingly diverse and difficult tasks has required the curation and annotation of new, large-scale datasets (Bender and Friedman, 2018). These tasks, particularly in natural language processing (NLP), can exhibit low *intersubjectivity*, in which observer variability may be high: annotators may assign different labels to a data sample (Basile et al., 2021b; Basile et al., 2021a). Such disagreement may stem from differences in how annotators interpret the task, their knowledge and understanding of the data sample, or their subjective opinion on the label to assign. Typically, annotator agreement metrics (Krippendorff, 2018) are used to assess the "quality" of *gold labels*, in which a single label is assigned to a data sample based on the input of one or more annotators. At the same time, these tasks are often constructed around binary or ordinal labels which may be limited in their ability to capture complex phenomena.

Data perspectivism (Basile et al., 2021a) argues that annotator disagreement is an informative feature of the data, rather than noise that must be tamped down. Thus, disaggregated datasets, containing the labels provided by all annotators to each sample, are preferable. Data perspectivism, however, requires the development of new methods to facilitate the analysis and training of models on disaggregated datasets.

Measurement theory, a framework in which latent attributes of observed data are estimated, is well suited to the data perspectivist paradigm. In particular, Rasch measurement theory provides a framework to construct a measurement scale to a problem, develop annotation tasks appropriate for that measurement scale, and fit a probabilistic model whose parameters detail important contributions to the scale (Engelhard and Wind, 2017; Hambleton et al., 1991; Rasch, 1968). Specifically, *faceted* Rasch measurement (Linacre, 1994) allows one to capture multiple features ("facets") that influence the generation of a label, including content of the data sample, the annotator's perspective, and the task at hand. The features are measured on a continuous scale, providing more information than binary or ordinal labels generally encountered in NLP corpora. Rasch measurement theory, therefore, motivates not just the development of disaggregated datasets suitable for perspectivist analysis, but those suitable for *measurement*.

In this work, we introduce the *Measuring Hate Speech* (MHS) corpus, a dataset created to measure hatefulness in social media comments. Hate speech detection, particularly in social media comments, has become an increasingly studied and prevalent problem. We chose to study hate speech due to its importance as both a computational social science and human rights problem. Furthermore, hate speech is a complex linguistic phenomena, with no unified definition, which limits

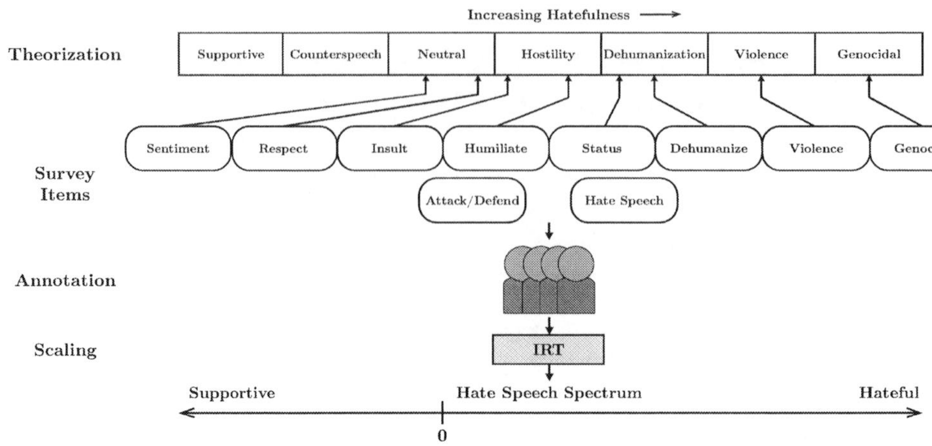

Figure 1: **Measuring hate speech requires the theorization of a construct, development of survey items, annotation, and scaling.** The major steps in developing a measurement scale consist of theorization, developing survey items, annotation, and scaling. **Theorization.** Seven theorized levels of hatefulness, ranging from supportive to genocidal speech. These levels increase in hatefulness from left to right. **Survey Items.** Survey items, or labeling tasks for annotators, consisted of 10 questions that interrogated the data samples at various points along the construct. **Annotators.** Each annotator provided labels on the 10 survey items for some subset of the comments. **Scaling.** Annotator responses are passed as input to an *item response theory* model, resulting in parameter estimates capturing, for example, the hatefulness of each comment, the annotator bias, and the level of hatefulness captured by each survey item. These parameter estimates formulate a hate speech spectrum, centered around 0.

the use of classical gold-label corpora while motivating data perspectivist approaches (Sellars, 2016).

This paper is organized as follows. First, in Section 2, we discuss related work in hate speech detection/measurement and data perspectivism. We introduce the *Measuring Hate Speech* corpus in Section 3, providing a details on the data collection, annotation, and a discussion on Rasch measurement theory. We provide exploratory analyses on the MHS corpus in Section 4. We conclude with a discussion in Section 5.

2. Related Work

Scholars in the emerging field of data perspectivism have identified a number of assumptions about the data generation process, such as the idea that there is only one truth resulting in the creation of gold standard ground-truth datasets and that disagreements among annotators "should be avoided or reduced" (Aroyo and Welty, 2015). Beginning in computational linguistics and spreading in other ML applications, empirical analyses operationalizing data perspectivism theories have found that annotator disagreements are not statistical noise, but rather indicative of ambiguities (Plank et al., 2014) and driven by background and lived experiences (Akhtar et al., 2019). Researchers have found that for annotations of highly subjective tasks, namely offensive language, labelers' different decisions should all be considered correct (Basile et al., 2021b).

The literature in particular acknowledges that disagreement is more likely to occur in tasks such as "detecting affect, aggression, and hate speech" (Davani et al., 2022)–in other words, in tasks modulated by social factors that are "highly polarizing" (Akhtar et al., 2019). In a novel, mixed-methods study, Sang and Stanton (2022) carried out interviews with 170 annotators in a hate speech task to understand where these differences come from. They found that "age and personality differences were connected with the dimensional evaluation of hate speech". To handle these disagreements, researchers have developed methods that incorporate this signal into their models. Akhtar et al. (2019) create a metric of polarization at the individual comment level, which is used to weight samples during training. Other methods have used multi-task or multi-label models to capture annotator differences (Davani et al., 2022). Our work builds on the recognition that annotator disagreements are useful at the data, model, and audit level.

Several existing corpora similarly capture multiple aspects of hate speech beyond a binary label (Waseem and Hovy, 2016; Zampieri et al., 2019; Cercas Curry et al., 2021) and label multiple identity targets (Kennedy et al., 2022; Röttger et al., 2021). However, to our knowledge, the MHS corpus is the only corpus created for hate speech measurement.

3. The *Measuring Hate Speech* Corpus

The *Measuring Hate Speech (MHS)* corpus, created by Kennedy et al. (2020), consists of annotations on social media comments designed to construct a measurement scale for hate speech. In contrast to traditional hate speech corpora, the MHS corpus contains multiple hate-informative labels for each annotator's review of a comment. These labels reflect a theoretical construct of hate speech, which captures degrees of "hatefulness" on a continuous spectrum rather than a yes/no dichotomy (Fig. 1).

We organize this section to first broadly introduce Rasch measurement theory, the motivating theory behind the MHS corpus (Section 3.1), followed by a summary of the data collection and preprocessing (Section 3.2). We then roughly follow the outline shown in Figure 1, discussing key components of the datasets in the context of Rasch measurement theory, including construct theorization, survey items, data annotation, and scaling procedure. While we highlight many of the components of data collection, annotation, and preprocessing, we refer the reader to Kennedy et al. (2020) for additional details.

The MHS dataset is publicly available on HuggingFace[1]. Additionally, the code used to conduct the analyses and create the figures shown in this paper is publicly available on GitHub[2].

3.1. Rasch Measurement Theory

The goal of measurement theory is to measure a latent attribute of a particular unit, such as a social media comment. Measurement frameworks allow one to transform observations–such as examination responses, or in this context, annotations–into variables that reflect an underlying scale. Rasch measurement theory is a measurement framework capable of assessing multiple contributions to the observed labels via the development of a measurement scale, coupled with a multilevel probabilistic model that explicitly captures separate contributions to the ratings in its parameters (Engelhard and Wind, 2017; Hambleton et al., 1991; Rasch, 1968). It simultaneously places the fitted parameters on a common, continuous scale that represents the task at hand.

Critically, Rasch measurement theory requires one to obtain data (in this case, annotations on comments) that fits a proposed model, rather than proposing a model to suit the data. To be clear, one must first develop a theorization for the measurement scale, as well as a labeling instrument (i.e., survey items) that allow one to measure along the theorized scale. Annotations must be obtained *given* this theorization, to which a measurement scale can be obtained (Fig. 1).

3.2. Data Collection and Preprocessing

We sourced comments from three major platforms–YouTube, Twitter, and Reddit–performing collection between March and August 2019. We only considered comments that were written primarily in English and were between 4 and 600 characters. Additionally, we aimed to source 40% of the corpus from Reddit, 40% from Twitter, and 20% from YouTube. We used fewer comments from YouTube for two reasons: first, scraping from YouTube was comparatively more difficult, resulting in a smaller comment pool, and second, YouTube comments tended to be shorter and simpler, with less complex language.

To build the corpus, we leveraged each platform's public API to download comments posted on each site. On Reddit, we collected all comments from posts on the real-time stream of `/r/all`, which contains all public posts on the site. For Twitter, we collected tweets from Twitter's streaming API, which is a random sample of all tweets on Twitter. For YouTube, we first searched for videos within proximity of the top 300 most populated U.S. cities, which were most likely to contain English comments with U.S.-based authors. We then downloaded all comments and responses on these videos. Once we scraped comments, we applied a simple preprocessing pipeline, removing URLs, phone numbers, and contiguous whitespace and accents.

In order to account for the fact that hate speech is relatively rare, we subsampled the scraped comments to create the final corpus. We used two predictive algorithms (multilayer perceptron and a random forest: see Kennedy et al. (2020) for more details) to bin comments into five groups: (i) irrelevant, (ii) relevant but not hateful, (iii) moderately hateful, (iv) very hateful, and (v) extremely hateful. We stratified sampling from each bin, heavily oversampling bins (ii), (iv), and (v), resulting in the comment set.

3.3. Construct Theorization

Developing a measurement scale for a problem requires the theorization of a *construct* that represents the underlying scale (Wilson, 2004). The construct represents an effort to make an underlying scale for a phenomenon explicit. In the context, this amounts to theorizing levels of comments: what are the character of comments that are increasingly hateful, culminating in the most hateful content? Developing a construct requires a rigorous qualitative evaluation of example hate speech comment.

We theorized a construct as follows. From a manual review of social media comments, we curated a *reference set*, a small corpus of example text for each conceptual level. We selected 10 comments to serve as examples of each of the theoretical levels, totalling 70 comments. In concert with construct development using existing literature, we manually reviewed thousands of comments from our corpus. We also selected reference set comments for each level that yielded a diversity of target groups, text length, and linguistic styles. Iteratively, we selected comments that we felt best exemplified levels of hate speech, and when we found ambiguities, used the comments to refine the definitions of each level.

The theorized levels we constructed are shown at the top of Figure 1. The levels build off a *Neutral* level,

[1]`https://huggingface.co/datasets/ucberkeley-dlab/measuring-hate-speech`

[2]`https://github.com/dlab-projects/hate_measure_data`

or speech not evidently positive or negative, in opposite directions. The levels toward the right on the scale designate hate speech of increasing severity: *Hostility*, *Dehumanization*, *Violence*, and *Genocidal*. We placed speech supporting genocide, the systematic killing of a specific group, as the most severe form of hate speech (ADL, 2016; Stanton, 2013). We constructed the remaining levels as pathways to genocide, with special attention to threats of violence and dehumanization that may justify violence. On the other side of neutral speech are two levels denoting speech positive in nature: *Counterspeech*, or speech that explicitly seeks to counter hateful content, and *Supportive* speech.

3.4. Labels and Data Annotation

With the theorized levels of the construct in place, we then developed a *labeling instrument*. The labeling instrument contained three components: (i) a set of 10 *survey items* that allowed the annotator to interrogate the comment along several distinguishing features of hate speech, (ii) specification of any identity groups targeted by the comments, and (iii) questions about the annotator's demographic information. The data annotation process was approved by the University of California, Berkeley Institutional Review Board. Annotators were allowed to omit any demographic information, and all data samples were anonymized to protect annotator privacy.

We recruited annotators from Amazon Mechanical Turk to complete the labeling instrument. We used each worker's IP address to ensure that we only recruited annotators within the United States. Each annotator was provided 26 comments, of which 6 were reference set comments. Thus, the reference set comments generally received the most annotations. The median time to complete the survey was 49 minutes. We compensated participants \$7, yielding a median pay rate of \$8.57 per hour, which is above the minimum wage in the United States. We provided annotators the opportunity to provide feedback on the labeling process. A manual review of their feedback revealed high satisfaction with the compensation for the task, and appreciation that the results would contribute to an understanding of social media conversations.

Annotators provided ratings on five-level Likert-style scales for 10 different survey items, capturing the following aspects of hate speech: sentiment, respect, insult, humiliation, dehumanization, violence, genocide, attacking/defending, inferior/superior status, and a binary hate speech classification. These survey items were designed to roughly span the hate speech construct (Fig. 1: survey items). In each case, a higher rating on the item aligned with "more hatefulness". For example, on survey item "respect", a higher rating implies that the annotator feels the comment expresses a greater degree of disrespect (with disrespect being aligned with more hatefulness).

We examined the quality of each annotator's labels with an *infit mean-squared statistic*, a rater fit diagnostic that is calculated during the Rasch scaling. This statistic ranges from 0 to infinity, with an expected value of 1. Annotators whose infit mean-squared statistic was greater than 1 had more randomness or noise in their responses than expected by an IRT model, with values of 2 or greater seen as degrading the measurement system. Those with a statistic less than 1 had less randomness than expected, suggesting that they may have favored certain response options. We chose to exclude raters whose infit mean-squared statistic fell outside $[0.37, 1.9]$. This range corresponded to the previously mentioned heuristics and excluded a cluster of annotators whose infit mean-squared statistic was too low (see the Appendix of Kennedy et al. (2020) for more details). We additionally removed annotators with extreme severity parameters, completed the task too quickly, or whose IP addresses were either geolocated to outside the United States, linked to known proxy services, or associated with more than 4 annotation tasks. Lastly, we excluded raters who did not tag a sufficient number of targeted identity groups, specifically on samples known to contain a targeted identity group. Application of these criteria left 8,472 annotators, with 39,565 accompanying comments.

3.5. Item Response Theory

The labels for each survey item constitute a set of ordinal responses aimed to interrogate each comment for their placement on the hate speech construct. The goal of item response theory (IRT) is to utilize these ordinal responses to devise the continuous scale corresponding to the construct. This is done via a multilevel probabilistic model that maps the labels onto latent parameters which set the scale. There are a variety of possible IRT models one can use depending on the use case.

We detail a *faceted partial credit model*, as it is the most appropriate IRT model for the MHS corpus. This model captures the decision of opting for rating k (say, "strongly agree") versus rating $k-1$ ("agree"). Specifically, let p_{nijk} be the probability that for rater j assigns comment n a rating k on survey item i. Similarly define $p_{nij(k-1)}$, but for rating $k-1$. The model defines an *odds ratio* as a function of several parameters to be learned from the data:

$$\log\left[\frac{p_{nijk}}{p_{nijk-1}}\right] = \theta_n - \delta_i - \alpha_j - \tau_k. \qquad (1)$$

We reiterate that survey items are aligned in their numerical code ordering. Thus, "increasing" a rating (going from $k-1$ to k) *always* corresponds to a higher degree of hatefulness. A larger odds ratio implies that the annotator is more likely to rate a particular comment as possessing some aspect of hate speech. Intuitively, the odds ratio should depend on the following *facets*:

- θ_n, or the **hate speech score** of comment n. Higher values of θ_n indicate a more inherently hateful comment.

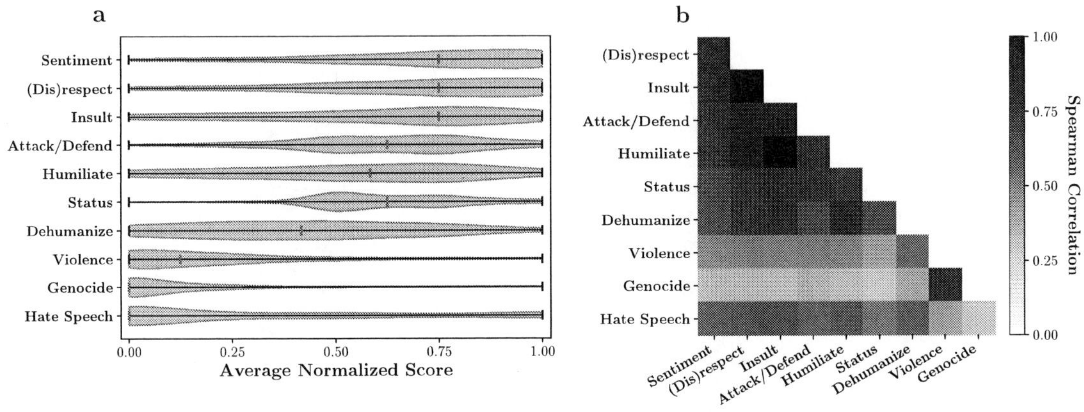

Figure 2: **Survey items allow annotators to evaluate comments at different degrees of hatefulness. a.** The distribution of the survey item ratings, across comments, averaged across annotators for each comment. Each score is normalized to the maximum rating allowed on the Likert scale (4 for all items except "hate speech", which had a maximum of 2). A higher normalized score implies a greater degree of hatefulness. Red lines denote median across comments. **b.** The distribution of Spearman correlations, calculated across comments, between the average ratings of each pair of survey items.

- δ_i, or the **difficulty** of survey item i. The difficulty sets the scale on the hatefulness spectrum. We should expect survey items that probe the higher end of the hatefulness spectrum, such as genocide, to have higher difficulties. In this sense, it is more "difficult" for a comment to exhibit aspects of genocide due to it corresponding to a higher level on the construct.

- α_j, or the **severity** of rater j. We can interpret this quantify as directly quantifying annotator perspective. Specifically, annotators with higher severity are less likely to label comments as possessing features of hate speech: their threshold for "hatefulness" tends to be higher.

- τ_k is also referred to as the **difficulty** of response k. In contrast to the difficulty of the survey item, τ_k is an indicator of the rarity of the ordinal response k relative to $k-1$. This term allows the distances between each response option to vary by item, rather than, for example, "strongly agree" being at the same location on the scale for every item.

The faceted partial credit model separates the content of the comment from any modulation stemming from the annotators or survey items, allowing the examination of each facet separately. The distribution of the parameters forms a *hate speech spectrum* (Fig. 1: bottom). The strength of this approach is that comments, survey items, and annotators simultaneously lie on a common scale, allowing one to interpret the model parameters in the context of the construct.

4. Exploratory Analysis of MHS Corpus

We provide exploratory analyses on the annotations and features available in the MHS corpus. Specifically, we show analyses of survey item annotations, target identity annotations, and annotator demographics. Overall, we aim to quantify the intersubjectivity of each set of features, while suggesting potential future analyses on the data. We refer the reader to Kennedy et al. (2020) for an IRT analysis of the data.

4.1. Survey items capture the spectrum of hatefulness

The ten survey items labeled by annotators were designed to align the measurement scale to the theorization proposed in Figure 1. The item responses are chosen such that a higher "value" always aligns with more hatefulness. Survey item responses on different Likert scales, then, can be compared by dividing annotator responses by the maximum possible response, resulting in a *normalized score*. A comment can be summarized in aggregated fashion by taking the mean of normalized scores across annotators, resulting in an *average normalized score*.

To better understand the the behavior of the survey item responses along the theorized construct, we examined the distribution of averaged normalized scores across comments in the corpus (Fig. 2a). We found that, generally, the average normalized scores decreased on survey items that probed for increasingly hateful content (Fig. 2a: top to bottom). This implies that, within the MHS corpus, fewer comments tend to exhibit the most hateful content (e.g., violence and genocide), which we may expect as a reasonable prior on the distribution of hateful content on social media.

Since the survey items probe points along the theorized hatefulness spectrum, we should expect item responses closer to each other to correlate more strongly. Thus, we computed the Spearman correlations between averaged normalized scores for each pair of survey items, across comments (Fig. 2b). We found that nearby survey items exhibit strong correlations with each other (Fig. 2b: diagonal). Importantly, pairs of survey item further away on the hatefulness spectrum have markedly lower correlations with each other. For example, "violence" and "genocide" are weakly correlated with the remaining survey items, but exhibit strong correlations with each other. Furthermore, the hate speech survey item showed moderate correlations with all other survey items, indicating that each survey item is capturing some component of hate speech (Fig. 2b: bottom row). Together, these results demonstrate that the chosen survey items adequately probe the theorized hatefulness spectrum.

4.2. Annotators exhibit low agreement on survey item responses

In traditional corpora, labels are aggregated across annotators to assign a "gold label" to each sample (Basile et al., 2021a; Ide and Pustejovsky, 2017). In order to assess the reliability of the gold label, annotator agreement metrics such as Cohen's kappa or Krippendorff's alpha are generally computed (Krippendorff, 2018; Waseem and Hovy, 2016). However, in NLP datasets, these metrics are often low, indicating that annotators do not tend to strongly agree on the label for each data sample (Poletto et al., 2021) This holds particularly true for hate speech corpora: hate speech can be difficult to define, may require intimate knowledge of in-group language or slurs, and generally exhibits low intersubjectivity (Sellars, 2016). In the MHS corpus, we might expect that annotator agreement to be low, given that annotators likely have different interpretations of the survey instrument (e.g., "sentiment" may be interpreted differently by annotators) and they may exhibit subjectivity in assigning different Likert scale ratings (i.e., annotators have different internalized thresholds for each response).

We evaluated the annotator agreement on the responses to each survey item using Krippendorff's alpha. We found that annotators generally exhibited weak agreement on all survey items, with Krippendroff's alphas of less than 0.5 (Fig. 3: light grey bars). Some survey items–such as "attack/defend" and "status"–exhibited markedly lower agreement, indicating that these items are prone to more subjective responses. Meanwhile, the hate speech survey item received a higher Krippendorff's alpha than the remaining survey items. This implies that, while annotators may agree more often on whether a comment is hate speech, they agree less often on the *components* of that hate speech. Thus, the additional survey items allow finer examination on how the levels of the construct contribute to an annotator's

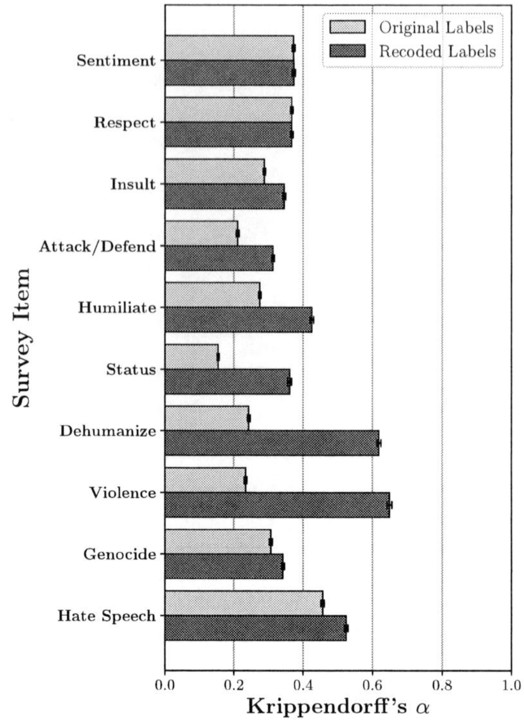

Figure 3: **Annotators exhibit low agreement on survey items, demonstrating the subjectivity of the task.** Annotator agreement on each survey item, as quantified by Krippendorff's α. Error bars denote 95% confidence intervals. Light grey bars denote agreement calculated on the original labels, while dark grey bars denoted agreement calculated on recoded labels, which were coarsened fom the original labels. The cardinalities of each label (before/after) recoding were as follows: sentiment (5/5), respect (5/5), insult (5/4), attack/defend (5/4), humiliate (5/3), status (5/2), dehumanize (5/2), violence (5/2), genocide (5/2).

perception of hate speech.

We found that a 5-level item may not be necessary for survey items aligned on the higher end of the hatefulness spectrum. For example, the item responses for "sentiment" (Appendix A) may naturally be suited to increased label granularity due to its lower intersubjectivity. However, a concept such as "genocide" may align more neatly to a lower level Likert item (or simply a binary item), since "genocide" may exhibit higher annotator intersubjectivity. Thus, we considered a recoding scheme in which annotator responses were mapped onto a lower level Likert items. We chose the recodings in order to improve the IRT modeling statistics (Kennedy et al. (2020)). Specifically, we retained the sentiment and respect survey items as is, but recoded insult ($5 \rightarrow 4$ levels), attack/defend ($5 \rightarrow 4$ levels), humiliate ($5 \rightarrow 3$ levels), status ($5 \rightarrow 2$ levels), de-

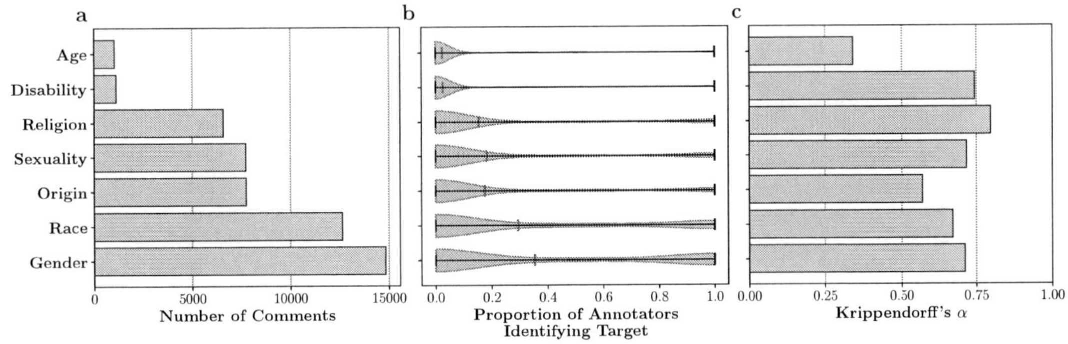

Figure 4: **Annotators recorded identity targets of comments, expressing stronger agreement than the survey items.** For each comment, annotators recorded a binary response specifying whether a particular identity group was targeted by the comment. **a.** The number of comments targeting each identity group, according to a 0.5 annotator agreement threshold. That is, if 50% or more annotators indicated a comment targeted a specific identity group, that comment was assigned a positive label for that group for purposes of the subplot. **b.** The distribution of "annotator agreements" across comments, for each identity group. Annotator agreements were calculated as proportions by averaging annotators' binary responses to whether an identity group was targeted. Red lines denote the mean proportion. **c.** Annotator agreement on each target identity group, quantified by Krippendorff's α.

humanize ($5 \rightarrow 2$ levels), violence ($5 \rightarrow 2$ levels), genocide ($5 \rightarrow 2$ levels), and hate speech ($3 \rightarrow 2$ levels). We found that, under the recoding, Krippendorff's alpha increased for each survey item (Fig. 3: dark gray bars). In particular, we found large increases for the "status", "dehumanize", and "violence" survey items. Thus, recoding schemes can reduce observer variability when the survey item tend to exhibit lower degrees of intersubjectivity.

The low annotator agreement observed in the MHS corpus further motivates the usage of methods better suited to handle disaggregated data. Specifically, item response theory models such as the faceted partial credit model discussed in Section 3.5 are particularly relevant, as they explicitly model the multiple components that may contribute to the results seen in Figure 3.

4.3. Annotation of identity group targets

Hate speech differs from other kinds of toxic or offensive speech in that it specifically targets an identity group(s) (Sellars, 2016; Poletto et al., 2021). Thus, identification of the targeted identity groups is a vital component of a hate speech corpus. Past studies have specified various characterizations of "targeting", such as explicit and implicit rhetoric (Kennedy et al., 2022) or individual and group targeting (Zampieri et al., 2019). While the notion of targeting can be captured by additional labels or possibly a measurement scale, we restricted labeling to the binary identification of pre-specified identity group and sub-groups targeted by a comment, as has been done in previous corpora (Röttger et al., 2021; Kennedy et al., 2022).

Annotators were asked *"Is the [comment] directed at or about any individuals or groups based on..."*, with the option to select among the following eight identity groups: race/ethnicity, religion, national origin or citizenship status, gender, sexual orientation, age, disability status, political identity; along with the option to select "none of the above" (options listed in order presented on the survey). Annotators were further asked to specify identity sub-groups targeted by the comment (see Appendix B). Annotators could select more than one option among these identity groups and sub-groups. Thus, the target identity annotations can be viewed as a multi-label binary variable indicating whether each identity sub-group was targeted or not.

Specification of target identities is a task that exhibits higher rater intersubjectivity than hate speech measurement, because comments often make clear which identity group is targeted. However, hateful content can subtly indicate its target, sometimes using specific vernacular, dog whistles, or vague language that may not be understood or difficult to notice by some annotators (Sellars, 2016). Thus, annotators still express disagreement on identity group targets.

We first examined the number of comments targeting each identity group. As a cursory analysis, we used majority voting across annotators to assign each comment a single binary label specifying whether it targeted any of the 8 identity groups. We found that most comments targeted based on gender and race (Fig. 4a), with the least number of comments targeting age and disability. This distribution likely reflects the true distribution of comments on social media. It also is likely influenced by the sampling procedure, as it is easier to identify hateful comments targeting groups that have larger available hate lexica, such as for race and gender.

We then computed the proportion of annotators labeling each identity group as the target of a comment. If this proportion is 1, all annotators agree that the comment targets the identity group. If the proportion is

0, all annotators agree that the comment does not target the identity group. Values between 0 and 1 indicate some measure of disagreement on the target. We examined the distribution of these proportions across comments for each target identity group (Fig. 2b). We found that, across identity groups, the density of proportions exhibited modes at 0 and 1, indicating that annotators generally agreed on the targets of comments. However, some density spanned between 0 and 1, indicating a sizeable amount of disagreement.

Lastly, we computed Krippendorff's alpha in order to quantify annotator agreement for each target identity group. We found that Krippendorff's alpha was greater than 0.60 for every identity group except for age, with religion and disability exhibiting the highest agreement. On the whole, these values are larger than those of the hate speech survey items, indicating that identifying targets of hate speech likely exhibits higher intersubjectivity than the hate speech survey items. Thus, these labels are more amenable for weak perspectivist direct prediction tasks, such as a model that aims to predict the target of the identity group.

4.4. Annotator demographics

A critical aspect of data perspectivism relies on the relationship between an annotator's perspective and the labels they assign to text on a task. Specifically, the various groups that an annotator may identify with can shape their perspective, thereby influencing their interpretation of subjective labeling tasks. Annotator demographics, therefore, are a necessary consideration in taking on a data perspectivist lens on NLP datasets.

The *MHS* dataset contains demographic information about the annotators for several identity groups. Annotators were asked to voluntarily specify their racial identity, gender identity, sexual orientation, religious affiliation, educational level, income, age, and political affiliation. The specific sub-groups annotators were asked to identify within these broad identity groups are specified in Appendix B. Within the race, gender, sexual orientation, and religion identity groups, annotators could select more than one sub-group.

We examined the distribution of annotator identities by calculating the proportion of annotators identifying as each sub-group (Fig. 5). We found that, while many racial identities were represented among the annotators, the vast majority identified as White (over 80% of the entire annotator pool). Among these annotators, roughly 90% identified solely as White (i.e., did not identify as multiracial). With respect to gender, most annotators identified as women (56%), followed by men (43%), with less than 1% of annotators identifying as non-binary. Additionally, nearly all (99%) annotators identified as cisgender. With respect to sexual orientation, most annotators identified as straight (85%). An array of religious affiliations were represented, with a plurality of annotators identifying as Christian (42%) followed by atheist annotators (21%).

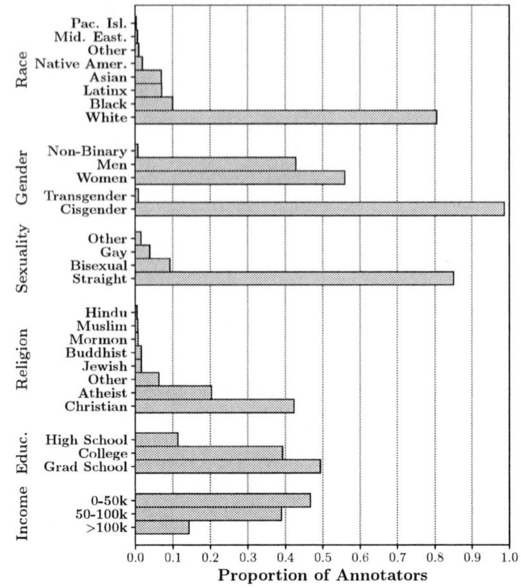

Figure 5: **Annotator demographic specifications span multiple identity group and sub-groups.** The proportion of annotators that identified as specific identity sub-groups. The sub-groups fall in larger identity groups, including race, gender, sexuality, religion, education, and income (y-axis labels). For race, sexuality, and religion identity groups, annotators could select multiple identity sub-groups. The gender identity group consisted of two separate questions, asking for gender identity (man, woman, non-binary) and annotator identification as transgender. Some sub-groups are coarsened from finer sub-group options (e.g., "High School" education constitutes annotators identifying their educational background as "Some High School" or "Completed High School"). For race, gender, sexuality, and religion, identity sub-groups are sorted in order of increasing proportion.

Nearly half of annotators had some level of graduate school education, including a master's degree, professional degree, or doctorate degree. Lastly, the majority of annotators stated that their income was less than $100,000 per year.

5. Discussion

We presented the *Measuring Hate Speech* corpus, a dataset created following Rasch measurement theory to measure hate speech. The 10 component labels, identity target labels, and annotator demographics available in the dataset can support a wide range of subsequent analyses that incorporate knowledge of annotator perspective in studies on hate speech.

The MHS dataset follows data perspectivism by providing the means to capture an annotator's perspective via the severity parameters. Usage of these parameters allow one to sidestep the need to consider annotator agreement, as an annotator's own strictness is explicitly captured in an IRT model. They are also useful in secondary analyses examining whether an annotator's labeling patterns exhibit identity-level interactions. For example, several studies have documented the relationship between an annotator's identity and the labels they assign to comments in hate speech classification tasks (Sap et al., 2021; Geva et al., 2019; Larimore et al., 2021). Item response theory offers avenues to perform similar analyses. For example, Sachdeva et al. (2022) used these techniques in the MHS corpus, finding that annotators were more likely to rate speech targeting groups they identify with as possessing elements of hate speech. Therefore, datasets structured with a measurement scale in mind can be flexibly analyzed to quantify annotator perspective. The ability to conduct such analyses is becoming increasingly important as perspectivist datasets are used in training downstream machine learning algorithms.

The outputs of the IRT model can be used for the development of machine learning algorithms that measure hate speech. For example, Kennedy et al. (2020) developed neural networks to predict the continuous hate speech score for each comment. These networks can be extended to incorporate annotator severity as an additional input. This modification can improve performance, as models can be trained on a fully disaggregated datasets in an annotator-aware fashion. Furthermore, fully trained networks can produce output scores dependent on a desired perspective, with the annotator severity input indicating the network's leniency or strictness in measuring the speech.

Future hate speech datasets, and others, can improve on the construct and labeling instrument of the MHS corpus. For example, the theorized construct can undergo further qualitative review and cognitive interviewing, resulting in more precise measurement. Ordinal responses to survey items exhibiting higher intersubjectivity can be adjusted, preventing the need for recording schemes. Annotator demographic questions can be improved to allow more granular responses (e.g., allowing more options for gender identity). Additional rounds of annotation can include more emphasis on annotator explanations for their choices. This would further facilitate data perspectivist analysis of the corpus, and allow qualitative reviews to inform future iterations of the construct operationalization.

Lastly, the construction of a measurement scale for hate speech motivates usage of Rasch measurement theory in other settings relevant for machine learning. For example, tasks which are prone to lower intersubjectivity, such as assessing toxicity, disinformation, and sentiment would be served well by the development of measurement scales in the Rasch paradigm.

6. Acknowledgements

We thank our colleagues in the D-Lab for useful feedback and discussions.

7. Bibliographical References

ADL. (2016). Empowering young people in the aftermath of hate (in english and en español).

Akhtar, S., Basile, V., and Patti, V. (2019). A new measure of polarization in the annotation of hate speech. In *International Conference of the Italian Association for Artificial Intelligence*, pages 588–603. Springer.

Aroyo, L. and Welty, C. (2015). Truth is a lie: Crowd truth and the seven myths of human annotation. *AI Magazine*, 36(1):15–24.

Basile, V., Cabitza, F., Campagner, A., and Fell, M. (2021a). Toward a perspectivist turn in ground truthing for predictive computing. *arXiv preprint arXiv:2109.04270*.

Basile, V., Fell, M., Fornaciari, T., Hovy, D., Paun, S., Plank, B., Poesio, M., Uma, A., et al. (2021b). We need to consider disagreement in evaluation. In *1st Workshop on Benchmarking: Past, Present and Future*, pages 15–21. Association for Computational Linguistics.

Bender, E. M. and Friedman, B. (2018). Data statements for natural language processing: Toward mitigating system bias and enabling better science. *Transactions of the Association for Computational Linguistics*, 6:587–604.

Cercas Curry, A., Abercrombie, G., and Rieser, V. (2021). ConvAbuse: Data, analysis, and benchmarks for nuanced abuse detection in conversational AI. In *Proceedings of the 2021 Conference on Empirical Methods in Natural Language Processing*, pages 7388–7403, Online and Punta Cana, Dominican Republic, November. Association for Computational Linguistics.

Davani, A. M., Díaz, M., and Prabhakaran, V. (2022). Dealing with disagreements: Looking beyond the majority vote in subjective annotations. *Transactions of the Association for Computational Linguistics*, 10:92–110.

Engelhard, G. and Wind, S. A. (2017). *Invariant measurement with raters and rating scales: Rasch models for rater-mediated assessments*. Routledge.

Geva, M., Goldberg, Y., and Berant, J. (2019). Are we modeling the task or the annotator? an investigation of annotator bias in natural language understanding datasets. In *Proceedings of the 2019 Conference on Empirical Methods in Natural Language Processing and the 9th International Joint Conference on Natural Language Processing (EMNLP-IJCNLP)*, pages 1161–1166, Hong Kong, China, November. Association for Computational Linguistics.

Hambleton, R. K., Swaminathan, H., and Rogers, H. J. (1991). *Fundamentals of item response theory*, volume 2. Sage.

Ide, N. and Pustejovsky, J. (2017). *Handbook of linguistic annotation*, volume 1. Springer.

Kennedy, C. J., Bacon, G., Sahn, A., and von Vacano, C. (2020). Constructing interval variables via faceted rasch measurement and multitask deep learning: a hate speech application. *arXiv preprint arXiv:2009.10277.*

Kennedy, B., Atari, M., Davani, A. M., Yeh, L., Omrani, A., Kim, Y., Coombs, K., Havaldar, S., Portillo-Wightman, G., Gonzalez, E., et al. (2022). Introducing the gab hate corpus: defining and applying hate-based rhetoric to social media posts at scale. *Language Resources and Evaluation*, pages 1–30.

Krippendorff, K. (2018). *Content analysis: An introduction to its methodology*. Sage publications.

Larimore, S., Kennedy, I., Haskett, B., and Arseniev-Koehler, A. (2021). Reconsidering annotator disagreement about racist language: Noise or signal? In *Proceedings of the Ninth International Workshop on Natural Language Processing for Social Media*, pages 81–90.

Linacre, J. M. (1994). *Many-Facet Rasch Measurement*. MESA press.

Plank, B., Hovy, D., and Søgaard, A. (2014). Linguistically debatable or just plain wrong? In *Proceedings of the 52nd Annual Meeting of the Association for Computational Linguistics (Volume 2: Short Papers)*, pages 507–511.

Poletto, F., Basile, V., Sanguinetti, M., Bosco, C., and Patti, V. (2021). Resources and benchmark corpora for hate speech detection: a systematic review. *Language Resources and Evaluation*, 55(2):477–523.

Rasch, G. (1968). A mathematical theory of objectivity and its consequences for model construction. In *Report from European Meeting on Statistics, Econometrics and Management Sciences, Amsterdam.*

Röttger, P., Vidgen, B., Nguyen, D., Waseem, Z., Margetts, H., and Pierrehumbert, J. (2021). HateCheck: Functional tests for hate speech detection models. In *Proceedings of the 59th Annual Meeting of the Association for Computational Linguistics and the 11th International Joint Conference on Natural Language Processing (Volume 1: Long Papers)*, pages 41–58, Online, August. Association for Computational Linguistics.

Sachdeva, P. S., Barreto, R., von Vacano, C., and Kennedy, C. J. (2022). Assessing annotator sensitivity via item response theory: A case study in a hate speech corpus. In *Proceedings of the 2022 ACM Conference on Fairness, Accountability, and Transparency*. ACM.

Sang, Y. and Stanton, J. (2022). The origin and value of disagreement among data labelers: A case study of individual differences in hate speech annotation. In Malte Smits, editor, *Information for a Better World: Shaping the Global Future*, pages 425–444, Cham. Springer International Publishing.

Sap, M., Swayamdipta, S., Vianna, L., Zhou, X., Choi, Y., and Smith, N. A. (2021). Annotators with attitudes: How annotator beliefs and identities bias toxic language detection. *arXiv preprint arXiv:2111.07997.*

Sellars, A. (2016). Defining hate speech. *Berkman Klein Center Research Publication*, 2016(20):16–48.

Stanton, G. (2013). The ten stages of genocide. *Genocide Watch.*

Waseem, Z. and Hovy, D. (2016). Hateful symbols or hateful people? predictive features for hate speech detection on twitter. In *Proceedings of the NAACL student research workshop*, pages 88–93.

Wilson, M. (2004). *Constructing measures: An item response modeling approach.* Routledge.

Zampieri, M., Malmasi, S., Nakov, P., Rosenthal, S., Farra, N., and Kumar, R. (2019). Predicting the type and target of offensive posts in social media. In *Proceedings of the 2019 Conference of the North American Chapter of the Association for Computational Linguistics: Human Language Technologies, Volume 1 (Long and Short Papers)*, pages 1415–1420, Minneapolis, Minnesota, June. Association for Computational Linguistics.

A. Hate Speech Survey Items

We show the hate speech survey items in Table 1.

Item name	Prompt	Response options
Sentiment	How would you describe the sentiment of this comment?	Strongly negative, somewhat negative, neutral, somewhat positive, strongly positive
Respect	Is this comment respectful towards the group(s) you previously identified?	Strongly disrespectful, disrespectful, neutral, respectful, strongly respectful
Insult	Do you agree or disagree with the following statement: This comment is insulting towards the group(s) you previously identified.	Strongly disagree, disagree, neither disagree nor agree, agree, strongly agree
Humiliate	Do you agree or disagree with the following statement: This comment is humiliating towards the group(s) you previously identified.	Strongly disagree, disagree, neither disagree nor agree, agree, strongly agree
Status	This comment states that the group(s) you previously identified is:	Strongly inferior, inferior, neither superior nor inferior, superior, strongly superior
Dehumanize	Do you agree or disagree with the following statement: This comment dehumanizes the group(s) you previously identified (e.g., by comparing them to an animal).	Strongly disagree, disagree, neither disagree nor agree, agree, strongly agree
Violence	Do you agree or disagree with the following statement: This comment calls for using violence against the group(s) you previously identified.	Strongly disagree, disagree, neither disagree nor agree, agree, strongly agree
Genocide	Do you agree or disagree with the following statement: This comment calls for the deliberate killing of a large group of people from the group(s) you previously identified.	Strongly disagree, disagree, neither disagree nor agree, agree, strongly agree
Attack-Defend	Is the comment attacking or defending the group(s) you previously identified?	Strongly defending, defending, neither defending nor attacking, attacking, strongly attacking
Hate speech	Does this comment contain hate speech, defined as "bias-motivated, hostile and malicious language targeted at a person/group because of their actual or perceived innate characteristics, especially when the group is unnecessarily labeled?	Yes, no, unclear

Table 1: Survey items and ordinal responses given to annotators for each comment.

B. Annotator Identity Sub-Groups

We show the annotator identity sub-groups in Table 2.

Identity Group	**Identity Subgroups**
Race or ethnicity	Black or African American, Latino or non-white Hispanic, Asian, Middle Eastern, Native American or Alaska Native, Pacific Islander, Non-hispanic white
Religion	Jews, Christians, Buddhists, Hindus, Mormons, Atheists, Muslims
National origin or citizenship status	A specific country, immigrant, migrant worker, undocumented person
Gender identity	Women, men, non-binary or third gender, transgender women, transgender men, transgender (unspecified)
Sexual orientation	Bisexual, gay, lesbian, heterosexual
Age	Children (0 - 12 years old), adolescents / teenagers (13 - 17), young adults / adults (18 - 39), middle-aged (40 - 64), seniors (65 or older)
Disability status	People with physical disabilities (e.g., use of wheelchair), people with cognitive disorders (e.g., autism) or learning disabilities (e.g., Down syndrome), people with mental health problems (e.g., depression, addiction), visually impaired people, hearing impaired people, no specific disability

Table 2: Identity group and corresponding subgroups annotators were asked to identify as targets of comments.

Proceedings of the 1st Workshop on Perspectivist Approaches to NLP @LREC2022, pages 95–99
Marseille, 20 June 2022

Improving Label Quality by Joint Probabilistic Modeling of Items and Annotators

Tharindu Cyril Weerasooriya, Alexander G. Ororbia, Christopher M. Homan
Department of Computer Science
Rochester Institute of Technology, USA
cyriltcw@gmail.com,{ago, cmh}@cs.rit.edu

Abstract

We propose a fully Bayesian framework for learning ground truth labels from noisy annotators. Our framework ensures scalability by factoring a generative, Bayesian soft clustering model over label distributions into the classic David and Skene joint annotator-data model. Earlier research along these lines has neither fully incorporated label distributions nor explored clustering by annotators only or data only. Our framework incorporates all of these properties within a graphical model designed to provide better ground truth estimates of annotator responses as input to *any* black box supervised learning algorithm. We conduct supervised learning experiments with variations of our models and compare them to the performance of several baseline models.

Keywords: modeling annotators, graphical models

1. Introduction

The recent interest in few- and zero-shot learning as well as the re-emergence of weakly supervised learning speaks to the reality that ground truth labels are a limited resource and that, in many common situations, obtaining them remains a major challenge. Multiple sources estimate the global costs of human annotators (only one of many sources of labels) to be approaching \$1–3 billion by 2026 and growing (Metz, 2019; Research, 2020). Among the key cost-driving challenges is the noise that is associated with many of the most common processes for obtaining labels.

In this paper, we explore a novel graphical model that ties together two rather successful approaches, item-annotators tableaus (Dawid and Skene, 1979) and label distribution learning (LDL) (Geng, 2016), based on converging studies in later research (Venanzi et al., 2014; Liu et al., 2019a) on the use of clustering to boost the signal of noisy data. We adopt a theoretical framework motivated by the anthropologist Malinowski (Malinowski, 1967) and first used by Aroyo and Welty (Aroyo and Welty, 2014) in the context of machine learning to characterize meaning as a function of three components: 1) an act (represented by the learning task), 2) the symbols (the labels), and, 3) the referent (the annotators). Human labeling is a special challenge not only due to its great expense but also due to the fact that humans often disagree over the labels that they provide. In fact, it is precisely the problems where disagreement is most common that human input is hardest to replace through automation or sensing.

This paper specifically addresses the following question: *do predictive graphical models for LDL that cluster on both item AND annotator distributions outperform those that do not?* To help us answer this question, we contribute a generative graphical model that boosts conventional label distribution learning by clustering label distributions jointly in item and annotator label distribution spaces. Previous approaches have studied clustering in one space or the other. This is, to our knowledge, the first time that clustering has been applied simultaneously to both.

We evaluate the improved labels produced by our model with a downstream CNN-based classification [1]. We view this work as a universally applicable framework for any learning task where annotators are involved (Gordon et al., 2022).

2. Problem Statement

Let $\boldsymbol{X}$ be an M-element collection of (unlabeled) *data items* and $\boldsymbol{Y} \in \mathbb{N}^{M\times N}$ be a matrix of *annotator labels* for some N, where each row of $\boldsymbol{Y}$ corresponds to a data item and each column to an *annotator*. Ideally, we would regard each entry $\boldsymbol{Y}_{m,n}$ as a probability distribution over a set of labels $\{1,\ldots,P\}$ for some fixed P, where the distribution represents uncertainty about what label annotator n would provide to item m. Here, however, we simplify the model under the assumption that each annotator either provides a single label or none at all.

For our purposes, $\boldsymbol{Y}$ is a sparse matrix, where $\boldsymbol{Y}_{m,n} \in \{0,\ldots,P\}$ and $\boldsymbol{Y}_{m,n} = 0$ indicates that annotator n did not label item m. Crucially, we assume that each annotator *could* label the item if asked; however, we have no information about that particular annotator. Since this is a sparse matrix, it is convenient to simply let $A = \{(m,n) \mid \boldsymbol{Y}_{m,n} \neq 0\}$ and $A_p = \{(m,n) \mid \boldsymbol{Y}_{m,n} = p\}$.

We consider two gold standards: f_{dist} and $f_{\max}$, defined for data item $\boldsymbol{X}_m$ as $f_{\text{dist}}(\boldsymbol{X}_m) =_{\text{def}} \mathrm{P}(p = Y_{m,n} \mid m, Y_{m,n} > 0)$, for m,n chosen uniformly

[1] The experimental code available through https://github.com/Homan-Lab/ldl-pgm

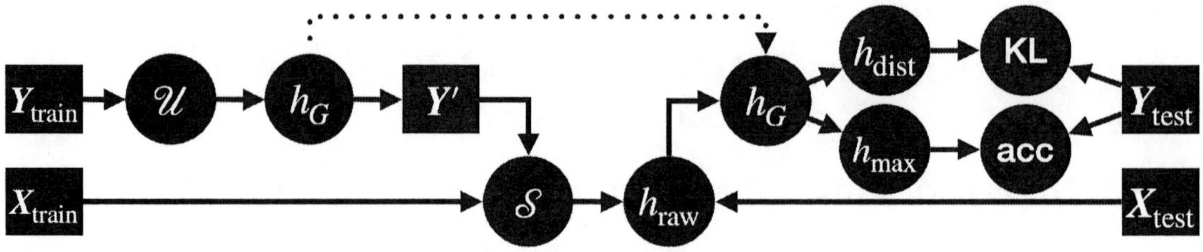

Figure 1: This workflow diagram shows the dual roles of the graphical model h_G, as the output of a supervised learning process $\mathcal{U}$ on the training labels. This model is used to improve the ground truth estimations $\boldsymbol{Y}'$ of the gold standard training label distributions $\boldsymbol{Y}_{\text{train}}$ for supervised learning $\mathcal{S}$ and, once h_{raw} is learned, as a post-processing step after prediction to generate final hypotheses h_{dist} and h_{max}. Evaluation metrics include the accuracy on the most likely label for single label prediction h_{max} and the KL divergence for label distribution learning h_{dist}.

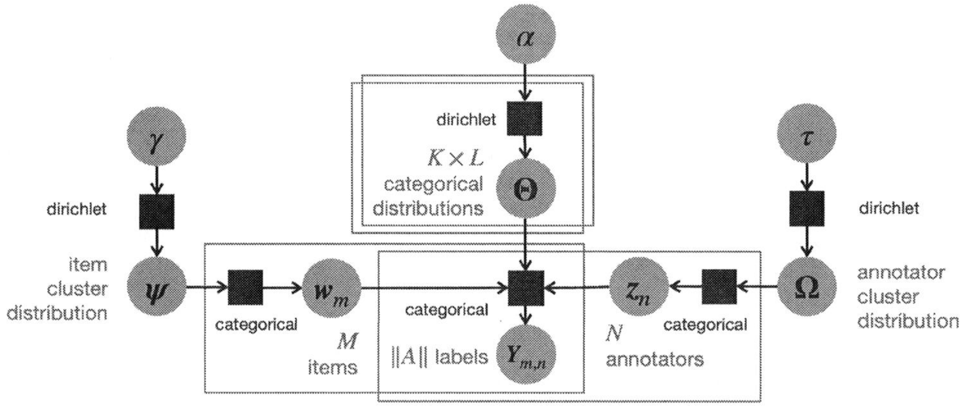

Figure 2: Plate diagram for the proposed probabilistic generative graphical model.

at random and $f_{\max}(\boldsymbol{X}_m) =_{\text{def}} \arg\max_p \mathrm{P}(p = Y_{m,n} \mid m, Y_{m,n} > 0)$. In other words, $f_{\text{dist}}(\boldsymbol{X}_m)$ represents the gold standard *label distribution* associated with each data item and $f_{\max}$ is the gold standard single label that is most likely according to f_{dist}. Note that $f_{\max}$ is more commonly used than f_{dist}.

Our learning goals, then, are to produce hypotheses h_{dist} and $h_{\max}$ that approximate f_{dist} and $f_{\max}$, respectively, given $\boldsymbol{X}$ and $\boldsymbol{Y}$. Most learning settings tacitly assume that annotator disagreement is a sign of *noise* or *error* and ignore d_{dist} entirely. *Label distribution learning* does the opposite: it assumes that annotator disagreement is *meaningful* and specifically seeks to minimize the loss between h_{dist} and f_{dist}. Obviously, both approaches rely on extreme assumptions that, in practice, are never entirely true. However, research has shown that even when $f_{\max}$ is the goal, learning h_{dist} and then taking $h_{\max}(\boldsymbol{X}_m) =_{\text{def}} \arg\max_p \mathrm{P}(h_{\text{dist}}(\boldsymbol{X}_m) = p)$ often provides better results than learning $h_{\max}$ directly (Venanzi et al., 2014; Liu et al., 2019a; Weerasooriya et al., 2020), and this is what we do here.

3. The Probabilistic Graphical Model

We call f_{dist} and $f_{\max}$ gold standards, not ground truths, because of the sparseness of $\boldsymbol{Y}$. Although several researchers have shown that, for the purpose of estimating $f_{\max}$, three to ten annotators is sufficient (Callison-Burch, 2009; Denkowski and Lavie, 2010), those numbers are far too small to provide reliable samples of the true distributions of annotator opinions. In this section, we introduce a new graphical model that estimates the ground truth label distribution, i.e., the distribution of labels from the entire population of annotators, of each item (which we normally do not have). This model is based on the assumptions that: (1) all data items (respectively, annotators) are drawn from one of K (respectively, L) latent classes[2] or *clusters*, (2) the label distribution for each item is strictly a function of the cluster to which it belongs, (3) the sample of labels given for each item is strictly a function of the distribution of the cluster to which each annotator belongs, and (4) the items and annotators are identically and independently sampled (i.i.d.) and matched uniformly at random.

We then use the graphical model h_G to guide supervised learning as a means of data regularization (see

[2]Hereafter, to reduce confusion, we reserve "class" to refer only to the different label choices, as they typically represent an observable class to which the data item belongs, even though the idea of labels as indivisible classes runs contrary to the spirit of LDL.

Algorithm 1 The generative process for h_G.

1: **Input:** Integers K, L, M, N, and P; Dirichlet hyperparameters $\alpha \in \mathbb{R}^P$, $\gamma \in \mathbb{R}^K$, and $\tau \in \mathbb{R}^L$, assignments $A \subseteq \{1, \ldots M\} \times \{1, \ldots N\}$

2: **function** GENGRAPH(K, L, M, N, P, α, γ, τ)

3: Choose $\boldsymbol{\Theta} \sim \mathrm{Dir}_P(\alpha)^{K \times L}$, ▷ One distribution for each item/annotator cluster pair (k, l)

4: Choose $\boldsymbol{\psi} \sim \mathrm{Dir}_K(\gamma)$, ▷ Distribution of item clusters

5: Choose $\boldsymbol{\Omega} \sim \mathrm{Dir}_L(\tau)$, ▷ Distribution of annotator clusters

6: Choose $\boldsymbol{w} \sim \mathrm{Cat}_K(\boldsymbol{\psi})^M$, ▷ Assign one latent cluster to each item

7: Choose $\boldsymbol{z} \sim \mathrm{Cat}_L(\boldsymbol{\Omega})^N$, ▷ Assign one latent cluster to each annotator

8: Choose $\boldsymbol{Y} \sim \times_{(m,n) \in \boldsymbol{A}} \mathrm{Cat}_P(\boldsymbol{\Theta}_{\boldsymbol{w}_m, \boldsymbol{z}_n})$. ▷ Assign labels according to each annotator, item assignment

Figure 1). We first use it as a preprocessing step to supervised learning on our label matrix Y, by reassigning to each input m the generating distribution of the most likely item cluster. Note that any supervised learning method can work as the target so long as it can use a distribution of labels and the supervising signal. For instance, in our experiments (see Section 4) we use a combination of deep language models and simple dense networks. Next, after the predictive model h_{dist} is learned, we post-process each prediction by snapping each output $h_{\text{dist}}(\boldsymbol{X}_m)$ to the most likely item cluster.

Algorithm 1 describes the model from a generative perspective (see also Figure 2). In addition to the numbers of item and annotator clusters K and L, the model takes three hyperparameters, $\alpha \in \mathbb{R}^P$ (recall that P is the number of label classes), $\gamma \in \mathbb{R}^K$, and $\tau \in \mathbb{R}^L$, each of which represents a Dirichlet prior on a categorical distribution. It produces $\boldsymbol{\Theta}_{k,l}$ (the label distribution for each item cluster k and annotator cluster l), $\boldsymbol{\psi}$ (the marginal class distribution of items), and $\boldsymbol{\Omega}$ (the marginal class distribution of annotators). $\boldsymbol{w}_n$ is the hidden/latent variable representing the class of item m and $\boldsymbol{z}_n$ is the hidden variable representing the class of annotator n. Each of these objects is a categorical distribution, and so, for convenience, we use subscripts to indicate individual categorical probabilities, e.g., $\boldsymbol{\Theta}_{k,l,p} = \mathrm{P}(\text{The category is } p)$ and $\boldsymbol{\Omega}_l = \mathrm{P}(\text{The category is } l)$.

Note that our distributions are conditioned on $\boldsymbol{A}$, i.e., we always know beforehand which annotators are assigned to which items. Unfortunately, the coupling between items and annotators makes exact inference hard and even resistant to variational approximation. It is, however, relatively easy to perform simulated annealing over the parameters $\boldsymbol{\Theta}$, $\boldsymbol{\psi}$, $\boldsymbol{\Omega}$ and latent variables $\boldsymbol{w}$, as well as $\boldsymbol{z}$. In addition, we may also employ expectation-maximization (EM), specifically using belief propagation to estimate the probability distributions of $\boldsymbol{w}$ and $\boldsymbol{z}$ during the expectation phase. We explore both learning algorithms here.

dataset	# annotators per item	# label classes	mean entropy	# of annotators
JQ1	10	5	0.746	1185
JQ2	10	5	0.586	1185
JQ3	10	12	0.993	1185

Table 1: Summary of datasets on which we conduct our experiments. Each of these contain 2000 items.

We now describe, in more detail, how we use the model. We partition our data into training $(\boldsymbol{X}_{\text{train}}, \boldsymbol{Y}_{\text{train}})$, development $(\boldsymbol{X}_{\text{dev}}, \boldsymbol{Y}_{\text{dev}})$, and test $(\boldsymbol{X}_{\text{test}}, \boldsymbol{Y}_{\text{test}})$ splits. During training, we first apply one of our two unsupervised learning algorithms $h_G = \mathcal{U}(\boldsymbol{Y}_{\text{train}})$ to learn a graphical model $h_G = (\boldsymbol{\Theta}, \boldsymbol{\psi}, \boldsymbol{\Omega}, \boldsymbol{w}, \boldsymbol{z})$ from $\boldsymbol{Y}_{\text{train}}$. Note that this provides estimates $\boldsymbol{w}$ of the latent item cluster to which each item belongs (simulated annealing provides a hard clustering while EM provides a soft clustering, but with EM we consider only the most likely cluster). Then, before supervised learning, we replace row $\boldsymbol{Y}_{\text{test},m}$ with the marginal label distribution associated with item cluster $\boldsymbol{w}_m$,

$$\boldsymbol{Y}'_m = \sum_l \boldsymbol{\Omega}_l \boldsymbol{\Theta}_{\boldsymbol{w}_m l}, \tag{1}$$

and perform supervised learning $h_{\text{raw}} = \mathcal{S}(\boldsymbol{X}_{\text{train}}, \boldsymbol{Y}')$, yielding a raw label distribution learning predictor. Note that $\boldsymbol{Y}'$ is not a matrix of annotator labels, as $\boldsymbol{Y}_{\text{train}}$ is, but a vector of probability distributions over labels.

For inference *after* training (i.e., we do not perform this step during training), for any input $\boldsymbol{x}$ we project the output of $h_{\text{raw}}(\boldsymbol{x})$ onto our graphical model h_G to predict the item cluster membership of item x, i.e., let $\mathrm{w}(\boldsymbol{x})$ denote a random variable for the item cluster assignment of $\boldsymbol{x}$. Then, we do the following:

$$\mathrm{P}(\mathrm{w}(\boldsymbol{x}) = k) \sim \sum_l \boldsymbol{\psi}_k \boldsymbol{\Omega}_l \mathrm{P}\left(h_{\text{raw}}(\boldsymbol{x}) \sim \mathrm{Cat}_P(\boldsymbol{\Theta}_{k,l})\right) \tag{2}$$

We then assign to x the item cluster $\arg\max_k \mathrm{P}(\mathrm{w}(\boldsymbol{x}) = k)$, using Equation (1) to compute $h_{\text{dist}}(\boldsymbol{x})$ and define $h_{\max}(\boldsymbol{x}) =_{\text{def}} \arg\max_p \mathrm{P}(h_{\text{dist}}(\boldsymbol{x}) = p)$.

4. Experiments

4.1. Data

We conducted our experiments on publicly available human-annotated datasets. Each dataset consists of 2000 social media posts and employs a 50/25/25 percent for the train/dev/test split.

Liu et al. (Liu et al., 2016)[3] asked five annotators each from MTurk and FigureEight to label work-related

[3] https://github.com/Homan-Lab/pldl_data

Dataset	CNN	MM + CNN	DS + CNN	CL	PGM (Annealing)	PGM (BP)
			KL-Divergence ↓			
JQ1	1.092±0.004	**0.460±0.001**	1.042 ± 0.005	2.077 ± 0.003	0.652±0.005	0.538±0.010
JQ2	1.088±0.003	**0.514±0.002**	1.035 ± 0.003	1.695 ± 0.003	0.884±0.004	0.624±0.017
JQ3	1.462±0.004	**0.888±0.001**	3.197 ± 0.034	3.862 ± 0.001	1.201±0.005	0.951±0.016
			Accuracy ↑			
JQ1	0.494±0.001	**0.842 ± 0.001**	0.684 ± 0.004	0.813 ± 0.005	0.730±0.000	0.727±0.007
JQ2	0.475±0.001	0.810 ± 0.002	0.658 ± 0.003	**0.873 ± 0.003**	0.579±0.041	0.663±0.013
JQ3	0.284±0.020	0.456 ± 0.010	0.061 ± 0.031	**0.458 ± 0.005**	0.290±0.002	0.250±0.007

Table 2: Experimental results for classification. New methods (PGM) using the development set for each dataset. CNN is a baseline where only a CNN classifier is run.Predictions are compared against the empirical ground truth.

tweets according to three questions and associated multiple choice responses: point of view of the tweet (**JQ1**: *1st person*, *2nd person*, *3rd person*, *unclear*, or *not job related*), subject's employment status (with 17 response options).
We train and test on the following models:

CNN is a 1D convolutional neural network (Kim, 2014) with no unsupervised graphical model. It contains three convolution/max pool layers followed by a dropout and softmax layer, implemented via TensorFlow (Abadi et al., 2015). We used sentence embeddings from the pretrained `paraphrase-MiniLM-L6-v2` BERT model (Reimers and Gurevych, 2019).

MM + CNN is the baseline model with the best-performing graph-based model from (Weerasooriya et al., 2020) used as a guiding model, in a manner analogous to the use of our graph model introduced earlier in this paper. The main difference between their model and ours is that it only performs item label distribution clustering; there are no annotator clusters.

DS + CNN uses the label aggregation methods introduced in DS (Dawid and Skene, 1979) and this is ultimately paired with a CNN classifier.

CL (Rodrigues and Pereira, 2018) is a neural joint modeling approach for modeling annotators and data features. Crowd layer (CL) attaches to the output of any network with a Q-dimensional output, i.e., a *crowd-layer*, which has multiple, parallel, Q-dimensional, new output layers, one for each annotator, and takes as input the old output layer. This extended model trains as a single, monolithic neural network. It then learns to predict the labels of each annotator simultaneously.

PGM is our proposed Bayesian probabilistic model, with the graph model introduced here for guidance. We set all of the Dirichlet parameters, i.e., α, γ, and τ, to 2. We consider two different learning algorithms: simulated annealing (with temperature schedule $T(t) = 1/(t+1)$) and expectation maximization (EM) with belief propagation.

For each of the the graphical models we performed (meta-)parameter search on the number of item and annotator clusters $K, L \in \{3, \ldots, 20\}$ and report the results of the best performing model (validated on development data). We evaluate these models using two different metrics. To evaluate the label distribution prediction, we report, over the test set, the mean KL divergence between each gold standard label distribution and the predicted label distribution $\mathrm{KL}(h_{\mathrm{dist}}(x)\|y)$. To evaluate single label prediction, we report the accuracy measured over the test set.

4.2. Results and Discussion

Table 2 shows the main results. We note that, with respect to KL divergence, our PGM models perform second-best, yielding better divergence than even the powerful CL model (MM+CNN only outperforming our BP/EM model by a bit). In terms of accuracy, our PGMs, while outperforming the CNN lower-bound baseline, do not unfortunately, according to this set of experiments, outperform the other baseline approaches. We suspect that our lower performance in terms of accuracy might be related to some degree of overfitting that we have, thus far, not been to control for.
Note that, in the case of all models (baselines and our proposed PGM variants), the final supervised learning classification phase was repeated 100 times (trained and evaluated) to calculate the reported error bars.

Limitations. Although we directly compared our models performance to those of (Weerasooriya et al., 2020), which represented clustering in item label space only, we did not perform head-to-head comparisons to the model of (Venanzi et al., 2014), which represents clustering in annotator label space only. This is due, in part, to the fact that the data from their studies is no longer being available. Nonetheless, we intend to run their models on the data that we do have in our next follow-up study.

5. Conclusion

In this work, we introduced a new graphical model for improving the quality of annotator labels, both from the perspective of the conventional problem of predicting the most common label as well as the emerging problem of predicting the distribution of labels that have been acquired/provided. Our methods combine label distribution learning with clustering jointly in the item and annotator label distribution spaces.

6. Bibliographical References

Abadi, M., Agarwal, A., Barham, P., Brevdo, E., Chen, Z., Citro, C., Corrado, G. S., Davis, A., Dean, J., Devin, M., Ghemawat, S., Goodfellow, I., Harp, A., Irving, G., Isard, M., Jia, Y., Jozefowicz, R., Kaiser, L., Kudlur, M., Levenberg, J., Mané, D., Monga, R., Moore, S., Murray, D., Olah, C., Schuster, M., Shlens, J., Steiner, B., Sutskever, I., Talwar, K., Tucker, P., Vanhoucke, V., Vasudevan, V., Viégas, F., Vinyals, O., Warden, P., Wattenberg, M., Wicke, M., Yu, Y., and Zheng, X. (2015). TensorFlow: Large-scale machine learning on heterogeneous systems. Software available from tensorflow.org.

Aroyo, L. and Welty, C. (2014). The Three Sides of CrowdTruth. In *Journal of Human Computation*, volume 1, pages 31–34.

Callison-Burch, C. (2009). Fast, cheap, and creative: Evaluating translation quality using amazon's mechanical turk. In *Proceedings of the 2009 Conference on Empirical Methods in Natural Language Processing: Volume 1 - Volume 1*, EMNLP '09, pages 286–295, Stroudsburg, PA, USA. Association for Computational Linguistics.

Dawid, A. P. and Skene, A. M. (1979). Maximum likelihood estimation of observer error-rates using the em algorithm. 28(1):20–28.

Denkowski, M. and Lavie, A. (2010). Exploring normalization techniques for human judgments of machine translation adequacy collected using amazon mechanical turk. In *Proceedings of the NAACL HLT 2010 Workshop on Creating Speech and Language Data with Amazon's Mechanical Turk*, CSLDAMT '10, pages 57–61, Stroudsburg, PA, USA. Association for Computational Linguistics.

Geng, X. (2016). Label Distribution Learning. In *IEEE Transactions on Knowledge and Data Engineering*, volume 28, pages 1734–1748.

Gordon, M. L., Lam, M. S., Park, J. S., Patel, K., Hancock, J. T., Hashimoto, T., and Bernstein, M. S. (2022). Jury Learning: Integrating Dissenting Voices into Machine Learning Models. *arXiv:2202.02950 [cs]*, February.

Kim, Y. (2014). Convolutional neural networks for sentence classification. In *Proceedings of the 2014 Conference on Empirical Methods in Natural Language Processing (EMNLP)*, pages 1746–1751, Doha, Qatar, October. Association for Computational Linguistics.

Liu, T., Homan, C., Ovesdotter Alm, C., Lytle, M., Marie White, A., and Kautz, H. (2016). Understanding discourse on work and job-related well-being in public social media. In *Proceedings of the 54th Annual Meeting of the ACL.*

Liu, T., Venkatachalam, A., Bongale, P. S., and Homan, C. M. (2019a). Learning to Predict Population-Level Label Distributions. In *Seventh AAAI Conference on Human Computation and Crowdsourcing*, volume 7, pages 68–76. A preliminary version appears in (Liu et al., 2019b).

Liu, T., Venkatachalam, A., Sanjay Bongale, P., and Homan, C. (2019b). Learning to predict population-level label distributions. In *Companion Proceedings of The 2019 World Wide Web Conference*, WWW '19, pages 1111–1120. ACM.

Malinowski, B. (1967). The problem of meaning in primitive languages. *Meaning in Meaning*.

Metz, C. (2019). A.i. is learning from humans. many humans. *New York Times*, August 16. https://www.nytimes.com/2019/08/16/technology/ai-humans.html, retrieved 5/21/2021.

Reimers, N. and Gurevych, I. (2019). Sentence-bert: Sentence embeddings using siamese bert-networks. In *Proceedings of the 2019 Conference on Empirical Methods in Natural Language Processing*. Association for Computational Linguistics, 11.

Research, K. (2020). *Global Data Collection and Labeling Market By Data type By End User By Region, Industry Analysis and Forecast, 2020 - 2026.*

Rodrigues, F. and Pereira, F. C. (2018). Deep learning from crowds. *32nd AAAI Conference on Artificial Intelligence, AAAI 2018*, pages 1611–1618.

Venanzi, M., Guiver, J., Kazai, G., Kohli, P., and Shokouhi, M. (2014). Community-based bayesian aggregation models for crowdsourcing. In *Proceedings of the 23rd international conference on World wide web*, pages 155–164.

Weerasooriya, T. C., Liu, T., and Homan, C. M. (2020). Neighborhood-based Pooling for Population-level Label Distribution Learning. In *Twenty Fourth European Conference on Artificial Intelligence.*

Proceedings of the 1st Workshop on Perspectivist Approaches to NLP @LREC2022, pages 100–107
Marseille, 20 June 2022

Lutma: a Frame-Making Tool for Collaborative FrameNet Development

Tiago Timponi Torrent[1,2], Arthur Lorenzi[1], Ely Edison da Silva Matos[1], Frederico Belcavello[1], Marcelo Viridiano[1], Maucha Andrade Gamonal[3]
[1] FrameNet Brasil Lab, Graduate Program in Linguistics, Federal University of Juiz de Fora
[2] Brazilian National Council for Scientific and Technological Development – CNPq
[3] LETra, Graduate Program in Linguistic Studies, Federal University of Minas Gerais
{tiago.torrent, ely.matos, fred.belcavello}@ufjf.br, {arthur.lorenzi, barros.marcelo }@estudante.ufjf.br, mgamonal@ufmg.br

Abstract

This paper presents Lutma, a collaborative, semi-constrained, tutorial-based tool for contributing frames and lexical units to the Global FrameNet initiative. The tool parameterizes the process of frame creation, avoiding consistency violations and promoting the integration of frames contributed by the community with existing frames. Lutma is structured in a wizard-like fashion so as to provide users with text and video tutorials relevant for each step in the frame creation process. We argue that this tool will allow for a sensible expansion of FrameNet coverage in terms of both languages and cultural perspectives encoded by them, positioning frames as a viable alternative for representing perspective in language models.

Keywords: FrameNet, Collaborative Frame Creation, Perspective, Multilinguality

1. Introduction

As we have claimed elsewhere, "language can be vague, messy and variable because humans cooperate while using it" (Torrent, 2021), and communicative cooperation critically involves sharing culture, and perspectives on it and inviting our interlocutors to reconstrue them as needed. We claim that computational models of language should embrace the characteristics of human language and not try to overcome them by the mathematical manipulation of linguistic form patterns extracted from large datasets alone (Bender and Koller, 2020). Moreover, we claim that the FrameNet model (Fillmore and Baker, 2010; Torrent et al., 2018b) is a good candidate for representing those characteristics, provided that it is extended to cover more languages and dialects.

Doing so is not trivial if one considers how FrameNets have been built so far – see, among others, Fillmore et al. (2003),Ohara et al. (2004), Torrent and Ellsworth (2013) and Dannélls et al. (2021). All of them relied on a relatively small team of intensively trained linguists, who invested a considerable amount of time building machine-readable frames and associating linguistic material with them based on corpus evidence representing a small number of languages and an even smaller number of variants within one same language. Due to this *modus operandi*, FrameNets usually present limited coverage, which is frequently pointed out by NLP practitioners as a reason for not using them in their applications. Nonetheless, the knowledge accumulated in the past three decades of FrameNet development allows for a methodological turn, presented in this paper in the form of a software tool: Lutma [1].

Lutma is semi-constrained, tutorial-based tool for fostering a community of distributed frame builders who will be able to enrich FrameNet with more diverse perspectives grounded on their own languages and language variants, enhancing its coverage and representativeness. In the remainder of the paper we start, in section 2, by making the case in favor of a larger, multilingual and multidialectal FrameNet, by contrasting FrameNet with Large Language Models (LLMs). Next, we present Lutma in section 3. Section 4 presents an example of culturally grounded frame creation. Finally, section 5 closes the paper by presenting the current limitations and future developments planed for collaborative FrameNet building.

[1] `https://lutma.frame.net.br`

2. The Case for a Collaborative Frame Building Tool

In recent years, discussions about perspectives have flourished in NLP, motivated by a variety of reasons, among which the problems of reducing multiple labels into a single ground-truth label, the ambiguous nature of many NLP tasks and bias encoded on large language models (Aroyo and Welty, 2015; Artstein and Poesio, 2008; Bender et al., 2021). Integrating multiple perspectives into models, however, is far from trivial, as specific model characteristics must be taken into consideration.

In white-box systems, one can take many different approaches to prevent bias and guarantee representation of multiple perspectives, namely through pre- and post-processing, but also by altering the models' internals (Ntoutsi et al., 2020). For that reason, one can argue that they are particularly useful in cases where curators and developers want to make sure that the model – or the dataset – are not encoding bias (Criado and Such, 2019).

In the case of black-box models, the strategies used in supervised and unsupervised models to introduce multiple perspectives are very distinct. For the former –

represented by Machine Translation (MT), Question Answering (QA), Named Entity Recognition (NER) and many other models – Basile et al. (2021) defend the adoption of *data perspectivism*, moving away from gold standard datasets and instead adopting different points of view for each object in the data. In practical terms, this variation is obtained by assigning the annotation task of a single data record to multiple human subjects. The way those different perspectives are integrated into a model determines whether the implementation follows a *weak* or a *strong perspectivist* approach. Any system that aggregates – using majority, average, etc. – those different perspectives into a single label is considered to follow the *weak perspectivist* method. When, instead, the model is adapted to handle the outputs from multiple annotators, it is classified as a *strong prespectivist* one. This added complexity, and consequently the amount of work, is outweighed by the ethical principles being followed, and in many cases, also leads to better performance (Basile et al., 2021).

Unsupervised methods, on the other hand, pose different types of challenges. We turn to them next.

2.1. Perspective in LLMs

Unsupervised methods are primarily represented by LLMs, such as BERT (Devlin et al., 2019), GPT-3 (Raffel et al., 2020) and T5 (Brown et al., 2020), which cannot integrate multiple perspectives into their training by expanding the number of gold standard labels per object. Rather, pre-existing bias in the data needs to be addressed during corpus curation and preprocessing.

Bender et al. (2021) state that models trained on large and uncurated text datasets encode biases that lead to unethical technology, also calling for investment to curate those datasets as a means to avoid such biases. Rogers (2021) claims that curation already takes place in the datasets feeding language models, and poses the question of what type of curation would be most effective to avoid harmful biases and improve models' abilities to understand language.

One key aspect of LLMs is that, regardless of whether data curation takes place or not, perspective understanding is treated as a byproduct of the mathematical manipulation of linguistic form. In other words, the machine's role is to "figure out" different perspectives solely from variations in form, while the researcher is responsible for making sure that the training data is representative of those perspectives. Within this framework, whether or not multiple points of view are being considered by the model depends on the dataset size and the quality of the data sample, much like the overall model performance.

We, in turn, claim that, instead of manipulating only input data, NLP systems should integrate a cognitively and culturally-oriented model that represents alternative perspectives on the meaning of linguistic forms. We also claim FrameNet to be the most suitable model for doing that.

2.2. Perspective in FrameNet

Perspective is a core aspect of Frame Semantics (Fillmore, 1982; Fillmore, 1985). Directly related to the classic Fillmorean proposition that *meanings are relativized to scenes* is the idea that different perspectives may be taken on that scene (Fillmore, 1977). The classic example revolves around the perspectives on the commercial transaction event. Fillmore (1977) demonstrates that different English verbs – namely *buy, sell, cost* and *charge* – adopt the perspectives of the different participants in the scene – Buyer, Seller, Goods and Money. Each perspective structures the scene in a particular fashion, so that some of the participants that are core to one perspective – e.g. Buyer and Goods in the perspective lexicalized in *buy.v* – may not be central to others – e.g. in the perspective lexicalized in *charge.v*, to which the Seller and the Money are central.

As the implementation of Frame Semantics, FrameNet models frames in terms of the elements in them, the coreness status of those element and the relations established between frames. The model also includes the lexical items evoking the frames. In this context, there are three aspects of FrameNet that may contribute to enrich and diversify language models:

Cognitively-based: FrameNet was initially proposed as lexical database inspired in Frame Semantics (Ruppenhofer et al., 2016). Lexical units are linked to frames, which in turn are linked to other frames. According to Frame Semantics, in order to understand a single frame, one needs to understand the structure in which it fits (Petruck, 1996). Frames are schematic representations of concepts based on recurring experiences against which the meanings of lexical units are relativized (Fillmore, 1977). This means that, instead of representing words with a single vector, or a list of senses, they can be associated with multiple activation patterns in the network. It also means, as demonstrated by Torrent et al. (2022), that FrameNet structure captures contextual information, namely commonsense knowledge.

Socially contextualized: Since frames are schematic representations of concepts, they are also used to represent socially construed entities and events, for example. The existence of specific types of frame relations also facilitates the creation of frames that may represent particular views on the same event. For example, research on Japanese noun-modification constructions by Matsumoto (2010) demonstrates that the societal grounding of the interaction and the purpose of the discourse influence on the grammar of noun-modification, claiming that interactional frames play a central role in the comprehension of those constructions.

Multilingual: Research on Frame Semantics adopting a contrastive multilingual approach has demonstrated that different languages may lexicalize different perspectives on a given scene, one of the parade examples being the study of verbs of emotion in Spanish vs. English (Subirats-Rüggeberg and Petruck, 2003). Because there are framenets under development for a number of languages, those differences are also captured via either the Global FrameNet Shared Annotation task (Torrent et al., 2018a) or the Multilingual FrameNet database alignment (Gilardi and Baker, 2018; Baker and Lorenzi, 2020). Such efforts allow for the construction of a single database supporting lexical units from any language, but at the same time not restricted to universally applicable frames. Even if some culturally specific frames are created, they can still be linked to the global network of frames. One of the challenges in this undertaking is to merge resources that were built independently for years. Nonetheless, for those working with low-resource languages (LRLs), Global FrameNet and Multilingual FrameNet are of great help, since they allow users to focus on frame-evoking units in their language, instead of modeling frames and their relations. This possibility of focusing on the language itself rather than on the underlying frame structure can be an important tool to reduce the gap of LRLs in NLP (Magueresse et al., 2020; Cruz and Cheng, 2020; Lakew et al., 2020).

Despite the three features described above, FrameNet still lacks coverage in terms of both number of languages and cognitive domains included in the model. Therefore, a fourth feature must be pursued if FrameNet is to be presented as an alternative to representing perspective in language models:

Community-based: Expanding contributions to FrameNet language resources is the main solution to increase the speed at which those resources evolve. And although some challenges come with a community-based approach, it brings an overall positive balance to research pursuits. Having a global community increases the possibility that contributors from varied backgrounds work together. This directly impacts the quality of the resource, as more languages will be supported and also new frames from specific cultural backgrounds will be created.

Implementing this feature is the purpose of Lutma, which is presented next.

3. Lutma: a Frame-Maker Tool

Lutma is one of the steps towards building an extended FrameNet resource in which language is not isolated from human cognition and social backgrounds. The project is part of the Global FrameNet effort, a collaboration between labs and affiliate researchers of twelve different countries, with the goal of facilitating the sharing of findings and research data, as well as building partnerships for the development of novel research. The way Lutma differentiates itself from the various tools used by the FrameNets around the world is that it has two design goals not shared by the others: first, that frames and LUs must have a clear indication of the languages/cultures in which they belong; second, that the user experience must be aimed towards people interested in FrameNet, but with little or no training on frame creation. These goals are both aligned with the idea of building a cognitively-based and collaborative language resource.

The main challenge of extending FrameNet lies on the fact that, until recent, it has been mostly reliant on specialists. To address this challenge, frame creation in Lutma follows a linear approach, much like a wizard, where to advance, users are asked a certain amount of information about the records. The idea of having separate steps for different pieces of data during the process also allows the system to run consistency and redundancy checks, making sure that users who are not experienced with the concepts can create frames with adequate quality.

Frame creation is separated into two execution flows, one for lexical and the other for non-lexical frames. Both are presented in the flow diagram in Figure 1. The first one starts with a lemma search: the user inputs the system with the part-of-speech and language of a lemma that will evoke the frame they want to create. The system checks if this lemma already exists in the database and, if not, searches for synonyms using Open Multilingual WordNet (OMWN) (Bond and Foster, 2013). If any of the synonyms is an LU in the database, the evoked frames are displayed and the user can decide whether a new frame needs to be created or if a new LU will be created for an existing frame. A second check is executed, but instead of looking for synonyms, Lutma searches for words in other languages with similar spelling in the same OMWN synset. This is a last measure to prevent redundancy, taking advantage of the existing data in other languages, although the multilingual synsets are limited to a small subset of languages.

When a new frame needs to be created, the user is guided to the next screen where they select its root type. They can choose from event, entity, relation, attribute, state or undefined (when it doesn't fit any of the previous). The selected type is used by the system to make suggestions of possible frame elements during the process, e. g., "Direction" or "Material" for relation and entity frames, respectively. In the next step, the user needs to fill out frame names and definitions and once again the system checks for duplicate names and if the name follows certain standards, such as scenario frame names ending with "_scenario" or state frames having names following the "Being_x" or "x_state" patterns.

In the following screen, users can create relations between their new frame and existing frames in Lutma's database. When creating those relations, the system allows users to choose whether they want to map FEs from the other frame into the frame (in the case of an inheritance relation, this is required). After storing those relations, the next step consists of creating FEs. At this point, the user's frame may already have some FEs be-

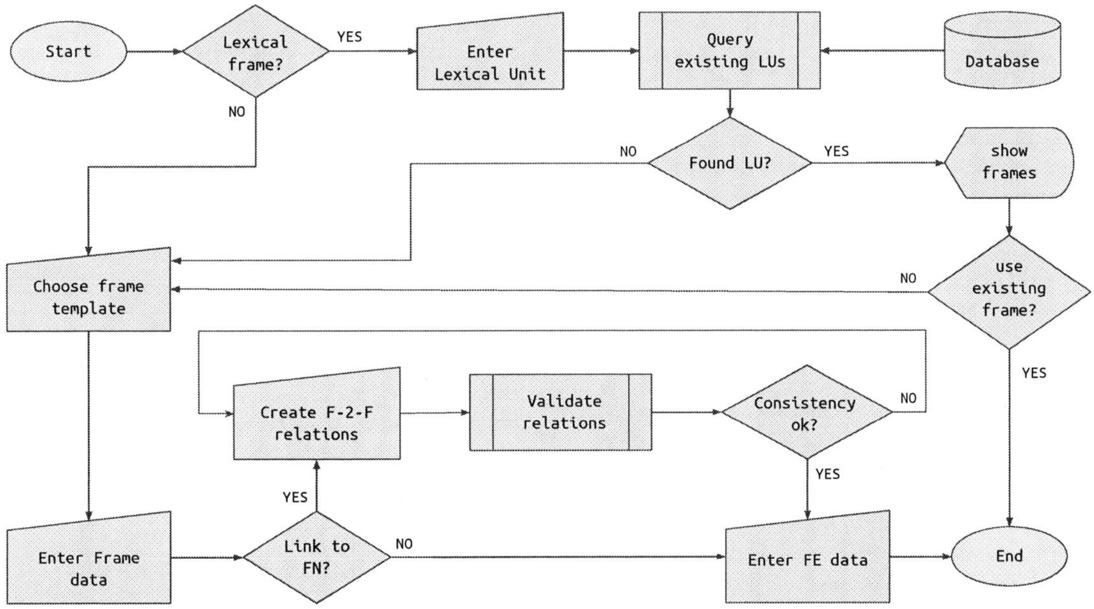

Figure 1: Lutma's frame creation flow. The diagram encompasses the creation of lexical and non-lexical frames.

cause of the frame relations, but Lutma still suggests more FEs based on the frame type. The rest of the FEs can be manually created and at least one is required to proceed. In the final step, before a summary is shown, the system asks for FE relation information. The creation summary displays all of the information related to the frame and to finish creation users must provide an example sentence for the lemma that was informed at the beginning of the process, as well as inform if it incorporates one of the FEs. After that, the frame is registered in the database.

The flow for non-lexical frames shares most of the steps with the lexical one. The first difference is the absence of a lemma search (because the frame will not be evoked by lexical material). The second is the need to inform the frame language in frame type selection step. We opted for this solution to guarantee that those frames would not be treated as universal, despite the fact that they can be associated to multiple languages.

These two execution flows separated into steps, along with the automatic quality checks run by the system, improve user experience by reducing the chances that a mistake will be made. However, when trying to build a community around this type of resource, we expect users with varying knowledge about FrameNets. For that reason, Lutma also integrates tutorials into its interface. Those tutorials can be categorized into two types, those about the system's interface, that explain how users can achieve certain goals, and those about Frame Semantics and FrameNet. The former are automatically displayed at the first time an user logs in to Lutma, while the latter can be accessed using the interface elements at any step.

These theoretical and practical tutorials found in all system screens can be further divided into two types. The simpler ones are displayed in the form of dialog boxes that are rendered every time a user clicks on one of the UI elements. For example, when searching for a lexical unit in the database, a user can click on the "Enter lemma" label of the search field to open a dialog card explaining what is the definition of lemma used in Lutma. Those small texts are useful for users that want to remember how certain concepts are defined in FrameNet. They can also be useful to users with different backgrounds in Linguistics, facilitating the comprehension of how those same concepts are represented in Lutma.

When users need more information than provided in the dialog boxes, the system presents a link to a video tutorial on the specific subject. These videos are always paired with one of the previously mentioned dialog boxes as a way of presenting a longer discussion for the concept. They are also tailored to a broader audience and explain essential concepts in a simple manner, using various examples. In total, six videos were produced, ranging from three to nine minutes in duration. Most videos address more than one topic relevant to the process of frame creation and, because of that, are linked to different parts of the systems, but effectively covering all of the dialog boxes. For future work, these tutorials could be expanded even further, including more topics and references to relevant publications.

Last but not least, to make sure that the data created by collaborators will benefit other contributors or projects, we opted for a copyleft license, namely GPLv3 [2]. With this licensing scheme, not only the data is made acces-

[2] `www.gnu.org/licenses/gpl-3.0.html`

sible for any interested party, but improvements made outside of its ecosystem can be potentially reintegrated into the database.

Since the project is quite new, there are still limitations that need to be addressed before a full release for the community. The final section discusses those and summarizes our contributions. Before turning to them, though, we present an example demonstrating how culturally specific frames can be created in Lutma and integrated to the existing FrameNet frames.

4. The Brazilian Way Frame

To provide an example of how Lutma may aid in the expansion of FrameNet to include culturally grounded frames, while linking them to the existing database, we present the creation of the `Brazilian_way` frame, evoked by LUs such as *jeitinho.n*, *malandragem.n* and *gingado.n* in Brazilian Portuguese (br-pt). Those LUs can be literally translated into English (en) as *'little way'*, *'trickery'* and *'waddle'*, respectively. Their culturally grounded meaning is quite different though.

According to DaMatta (1986), *jeitinho* is characterized as the space Brazilians find between what one can do and what one cannot do within a normative system. Such a system can be institutionalized in the Judiciary, or may correspond to implicit social norms that should be followed by everyone. When the concept of *jeitinho* is brought into play, one seeks to solve some private problem by adopting some behavior that makes the solution easier and/or faster. Such a behavior is inadequate under the strict observation of the norm regulating the problem-solving task. Nonetheless, by bringing *jeitinho* into play, such inadequacy is relativized.

The fact that the main lexical unit in this frame is in the diminutive form is not coincidental. The br-pt expression *dar um jeito* corresponds roughly to the en verb *fix* in sentences like *Alguém deu um jeito no problema do visto*, meaning that someone fixed the visa problem. On the other hand, the expression *dar um jeitinho*, by using the diminutive form of *jeito.n*, introduces a sense of empathy and proximity. Hence, in sentences like *Alguém deu um jeitinho no problema do visto*, what is being said is that someone found a non-standard, possibily illegal way of solving the visa problem. This way of solving the problem may involve a favor being granted by some authority on that matter or even the corruption of such an authority. Moreover, Schroder and Silva (2020) demonstrate that the conceptualization of *jeitinho.n* involves the idea of making rules flexible via an exchange of favors.

Given this scenario, if we want to create a frame for *jeitinho.n*, we would start by searching the Global FrameNet Database for this LU. Since there is no frame for this LU in br-pt or for any translation of it in another language, we proceed to the frame creation process. First, we select the *event* root type, since, as the example sentence in the previous paragraph shows, this LU tends to occur with support verbs and indicates an action taken by someone towards solving a problem. Next, we name the frame as `Brazilian_way` and connect it to the `Attempting_and_resolving_scenario` frame in FrameNet. We will then map FE in the latter to the ones we are in the process of creating. Hence, the AGENT FE is mapped to the INTERESTED_PARTY and the GOAL, MANNER and other non-core FEs in the mother frame are repeated in the newly created frame. Because *jeitinho.n* requires the conceptualization of an AUTHORITY being convinced – or corrupted – and of some NORM being violated, we add those two core FEs by clicking the *Create New FE* button. Next, additional non-core FEs typycally occuring in eventive frame may be added. Finally, we edit the frame definition, and the description and coreness status of some FEs. Appendix A shows how this process is performed in Lutma step by step.

5. Limitations and Outlook

Despite already being deployed, Lutma is not yet a finished project. As with most software, there is room for improvement in regards to user experience and interface. Those issues will be dealt with after we receive more user feedback. There are also important functionalities that still need to be designed and developed, and because of that, in its current state, the system has some limitations.

One of them has to do with the fact that there are no tools that could aid users in assessing the quality of newly created frames. This process is not objective either, since previous research has shown how frame annotation can be ambiguous (Burchardt et al., 2006). Interestingly, this also means that the subsystems implemented to reduce redundancy during the frame creation process could benefit from multiple perspectives. When those subsystems fail and thus, a user creates a redundant frame, or one with overall less quality, a reasonable solution is the adoption of a wiki-like approach, where users can see edits and open discussions to determine the best course of action.

One final point worth considering is that Lutma's metalanguage is English, meaning that only users proficient in this language will be able to contribute. Naturally, this can be circumvented by allowing users to translate attributes of frames, LUs, FEs and any other entities. However, this would also mean that users would spend less time actually creating those entities. For now, we have decided to leave English as the metalanguage, taking into consideration that other factors can also restrict potential users, even though we have no control over them (*e.g.* Lutma's contributors are most likely people interested in fields such as Frame Semantics or NLP).

Even given its limitations, Lutma is a step in an effort of scaling up FrameNet, without sacrificing the model's advantages, especially in regards to perspective in NLP, to the extent that it facilitates contributions from any language and from non-specialist users.

6. Acknowledgements

The development of Lutma was funded by an Anneliese Maier Research Award provided to Mark Turner by the Alexander von Humboldt Foundation. Torrent's research is funded by CNPq grant 315749/2021-0.

7. Bibliographical References

Aroyo, L. and Welty, C. (2015). Truth is a lie: Crowd truth and the seven myths of human annotation. *AI Magazine*, 36(1):15–24.

Artstein, R. and Poesio, M. (2008). Inter-coder agreement for computational linguistics. *Computational linguistics*, 34(4):555–596.

Baker, C. F. and Lorenzi, A. (2020). Exploring Crosslinguistic Frame Alignment. In *Proceedings of the International FrameNet Workshop 2020: Towards a Global, Multilingual FrameNet*, pages 77–84, Marseille, France, May. European Language Resources Association.

Basile, V., Cabitza, F., Campagner, A., and Fell, M. (2021). Toward a Perspectivist Turn in Ground Truthing for Predictive Computing. *arXiv preprint arXiv:2109.04270.*

Bender, E. M. and Koller, A. (2020). Climbing towards NLU: On Meaning, Form, and Understanding in the Age of Data. In *Proceedings of the 58th Annual Meeting of the Association for Computational Linguistics*, pages 5185–5198, Online, July. Association for Computational Linguistics.

Bender, E. M., Gebru, T., McMillan-Major, A., and Shmitchell, S. (2021). On the Dangers of Stochastic Parrots: Can Language Models Be Too Big? In *Proceedings of the 2021 ACM Conference on Fairness, Accountability, and Transparency*, pages 610–623.

Bond, F. and Foster, R. (2013). Linking and Extending an Open Multilingual Wordnet. In *Proceedings of the 51st Annual Meeting of the Association for Computational Linguistics (Volume 1: Long Papers)*, pages 1352–1362.

Brown, T., Mann, B., Ryder, N., Subbiah, M., Kaplan, J. D., Dhariwal, P., Neelakantan, A., Shyam, P., Sastry, G., Askell, A., et al. (2020). Language models are few-shot learners. *Advances in neural information processing systems*, 33:1877–1901.

Burchardt, A., Erk, K., Frank, A., Kowalski, A., Padó, S., and Pinkal, M. (2006). The SALSA Corpus: a German Corpus Resource for Lexical Semantics. In *Proceedings of the Fifth International Conference on Language Resources and Evaluation (LREC'06)*, Genoa, Italy, May. European Language Resources Association (ELRA).

Criado, N. and Such, J. M. (2019). Digital discrimination. *Algorithmic Regulation*, pages 82–97.

Cruz, J. C. B. and Cheng, C. (2020). Establishing Baselines for Text Classification in Low-resource Languages. *arXiv preprint arXiv:2005.02068.*

DaMatta, R. (1986). *O que faz o brasil, Brasil? [What makes brazil, Brazil?].* Rocco, Rio de Janeiro, Brazil.

Dannélls, D., Borin, L., and Heppin, K. F. (2021). *The Swedish FrameNet++: Harmonization, integration, method development and practical language technology applications*, volume 14. John Benjamins Publishing Company, Amsterdam.

Devlin, J., Chang, M.-W., Lee, K., and Toutanova, K. (2019). BERT: Pre-training of Deep Bidirectional Transformers for Language Understanding. In *Proceedings of the 2019 Conference of the North American Chapter of the Association for Computational Linguistics: Human Language Technologies, Volume 1 (Long and Short Papers)*, pages 4171–4186, Minneapolis, Minnesota, June. Association for Computational Linguistics.

Fillmore, C. J. and Baker, C. (2010). A frames approach to semantic analysis. In *The Oxford handbook of linguistic analysis.*

Fillmore, C. J., Petruck, M. R., Ruppenhofer, J., and Wright, A. (2003). Framenet in action: The case of attaching. *International journal of lexicography*, 16(3):297–332.

Fillmore, C. J. (1977). The Case for Case Reopened. In P. Cole et al., editors, *Syntax and Semantics Volume 8: Grammatical Relations*, pages 59–81. Academic Press.

Fillmore, C. J. (1982). Frame Semantics. In Linguistics Society of Korea, editor, *Linguitics in the morning calm.* Hanshin Publishing Co., Seoul, South Korea. pages: 111 – 138.

Fillmore, C. J. (1985). Frames and the semantics of understanding. *Quaderni di Semantica*, 6(2):222–254.

Gilardi, L. and Baker, C. (2018). Learning to Align across Languages: Toward Multilingual FrameNet. In Tiago Timponi Torrent, et al., editors, *Proceedings of the Eleventh International Conference on Language Resources and Evaluation (LREC 2018)*, Paris, France, may. European Language Resources Association (ELRA).

Lakew, S. M., Negri, M., and Turchi, M. (2020). Low resource neural machine translation: A benchmark for five african languages. *arXiv preprint arXiv:2003.14402.*

Magueresse, A., Carles, V., and Heetderks, E. (2020). Low-resource languages: A review of past work and future challenges. *arXiv preprint arXiv:2006.07264.*

Matsumoto, Y. (2010). Interactional frames and grammatical descriptions: The case of japanese noun-modifying constructions. *Constructions and Frames*, 2(2):135–157.

Ntoutsi, E., Fafalios, P., Gadiraju, U., Iosifidis, V., Nejdl, W., Vidal, M.-E., Ruggieri, S., Turini, F., Papadopoulos, S., Krasanakis, E., et al. (2020). Bias in data-driven artificial intelligence systems—An introductory survey. *Wiley Interdisciplinary Re-*

views: Data Mining and Knowledge Discovery, 10(3):e1356.

Ohara, K. H., Fujii, S., Ohori, T., Suzuki, R., Saito, H., and Ishizaki, S. (2004). The japanese FrameNet project: An introduction. In *Proceedings of LREC-04 Satellite Workshop "Building Lexical Resources from Semantically Annotated Corpora"(LREC 2004)*, pages 9–11.

Petruck, M. R. L. (1996). Frame Semantics. In Jef Verschueren, et al., editors, *Handbook of pragmatics*, pages 1–8. John Benjamins, Philadelphia.

Raffel, C., Shazeer, N., Roberts, A., Lee, K., Narang, S., Matena, M., Zhou, Y., Li, W., and Liu, P. J. (2020). Exploring the Limits of Transfer Learning with a Unified Text-to-Text Transformer. *Journal of Machine Learning Research*, 21(140):1–67.

Rogers, A. (2021). Changing the World by Changing the Data. In *Proceedings of the 59th Annual Meeting of the Association for Computational Linguistics and the 11th International Joint Conference on Natural Language Processing (Volume 1: Long Papers)*, pages 2182–2194, Online, August. Association for Computational Linguistics.

Ruppenhofer, J., Ellsworth, M., Schwarzer-Petruck, M., Johnson, C. R., and Scheffczyk, J. (2016). Framenet ii: Extended theory and practice. Technical report, International Computer Science Institute.

Schroder, U. A. and Silva, R. d. C. (2020). O 'jeitinho brasileiro' a partir de uma perspectiva cognitivo-interacional [The 'Brazilian jeitinho' from a cognitive-interactional perspective]. *Estudos da Língua(gem)*, 18(2):117–134.

Subirats-Rüggeberg, C. and Petruck, M. R. (2003). Surprise: Spanish FrameNet! In Eva Hajičová and Anna Kotéšovcová and Jiří Mirovský, editor, *Proceedings of the Workshop on Frame Semantics, XVII International Congress of Linguists (CIL)*, Prague. Matfyzpress, Matfyzpress.

Torrent, T. T. and Ellsworth, M. (2013). Behind the labels: Criteria for defining analytical categories in Framenet Brasil. *Veredas-Revista de Estudos Linguisticos*, 17(1):44–66.

Torrent, T. T., Ellsworth, M., Baker, C., and Matos, E. E. d. S. (2018a). The Multilingual FrameNet Shared Annotation Task: a Preliminary Report. In Tiago Timponi Torrent, et al., editors, *Proceedings of the Eleventh International Conference on Language Resources and Evaluation (LREC 2018)*, pages 62–68, Paris, France, may. European Language Resources Association (ELRA).

Torrent, T. T., Matos, E., Lage, L., Laviola, A., Tavares, T., Almeida, V., and Sigiliano, N. (2018b). Towards continuity between the lexicon and the constructicon in Framenet Brasil. *Constructicography: Constructicon development across languages*, 22:107.

Torrent, T. T., Matos, E. E. d. S., Belcavello, F., Viridiano, M., Gamonal, M. A., Costa, A. D. d., and Marim, M. C. (2022). Representing Context in FrameNet: A Multidimensional, Multimodal Approach. *Frontiers in Psychology*, 13.

Torrent, T. T. (2021). What a Cognitive Linguist Means by Meaning and Why It Could Impact Research in Natural Language Processing. CogSci Blog. Cognitive Science Society.

Appendix A - User Interface Screenshots

This section presents screenshots of Lutma's UI as presented to the user during the creation of the `Brazilian_way` frame as described in section 4. Since it is a mobile-first UI, we present how it is rendered in smartphones. The focus on mobile experience was a decision made by the team to make sure that users that do not have access to a desktop computer could also contribute. This decision also influenced the design of most screens. Some processes were split into multiple screens, which in the end, also makes it easier for unfamiliar users to work with some complex FrameNet concepts.

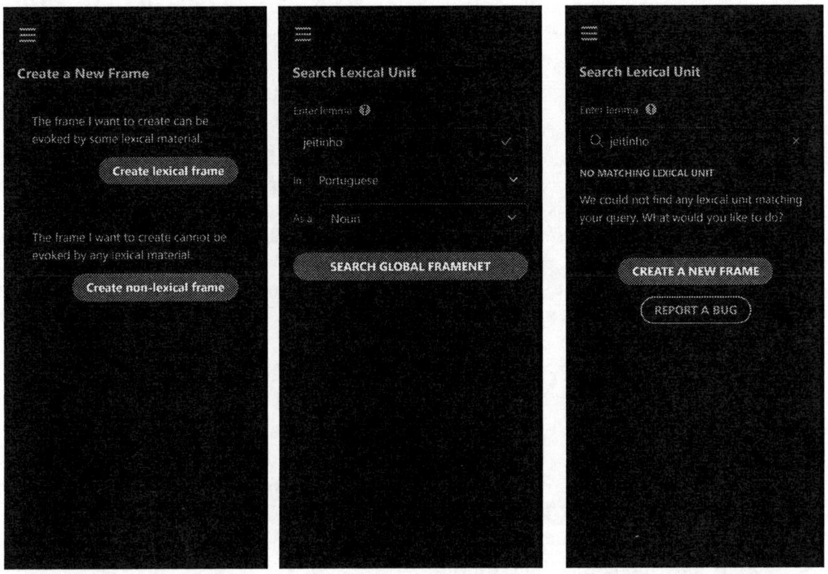

(a) Frame creation screen. (b) Lexical unit search screen. (c) Search result screen after no existing frame is found.

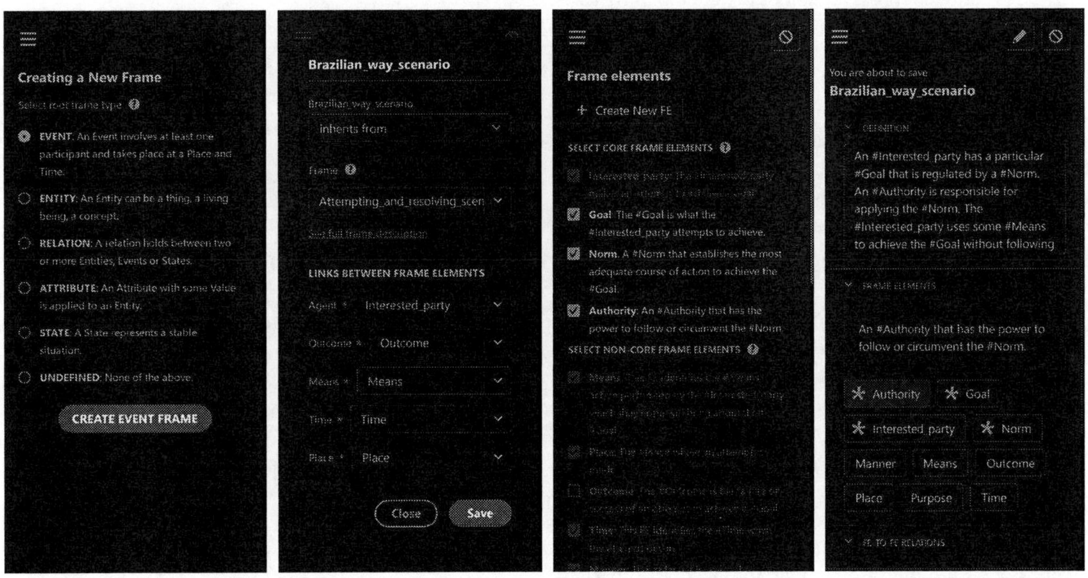

(a) Frame type selection screen. (b) Frame relation creation dialog. (c) Frame element list screen, including non-core FEs suggested by Lutma. (d) Summary screen displayed at the end of the execution flow.

Proceedings of the 1st Workshop on Perspectivist Approaches to NLP @LREC2022, pages 108–116
Marseille, 20 June 2022

The Case for Perspective in Multimodal Datasets

Marcelo Viridiano[1], Tiago Timponi Torrent[1,2], Oliver Czulo[3], Arthur Lorenzi Almeida[1], Ely Edison da Silva Matos[1], Frederico Belcavello[1]
[1] FrameNet Brasil Lab, Graduate Program in Linguistics, Federal University of Juiz de Fora
[2] Brazilian National Council for Scientific and Technological Development – CNPq
[3] Institute for Applied Linguistics and Translatology, Universität Leipzig
{barros.marcelo, arthur.lorenzi}@estudante.ufjf.br, {tiago.torrent, ely.matos, fred.belcavello}@ufjf.br, oliver.czulo@uni-leipzig.de

Abstract

This paper argues in favor of the adoption of annotation practices for multimodal datasets that recognize and represent the inherently perspectivized nature of multimodal communication. To support our claim, we present a set of annotation experiments in which FrameNet annotation is applied to the Multi30k and the Flickr 30k Entities datasets. We assess the cosine similarity between the semantic representations derived from the annotation of both pictures and captions for frames. Our findings indicate that: (i) frame semantic similarity between captions of the same picture produced in different languages is sensitive to whether the caption is a translation of another caption or not, and (ii) picture annotation for semantic frames is sensitive to whether the image is annotated in presence of a caption or not.

Keywords: multimodal datasets, annotation setup, multilingual annotation, multimodal annotation, perspective, frame semantic analysis

1. Introduction

Multimodal datasets that combine textual and visual information are gaining popularity in Natural Language Processing tasks such as multimodal machine translation (Specia et al., 2016; Elliott et al., 2017; Elliott, 2018), multimodal lexical translation (Lala and Specia, 2018), visual sense disambiguation (Gella et al., 2016), grounded representation of lexical meaning (Silberer and Lapata, 2014), and lexical entailment detection (Kiela et al., 2015). For all of those tasks – and especially for tasks of multimodal translation – the general claim is that using textual data in combination with the "ground truth" information provided by a visual mode would improve the performance of multimodal models, allowing them to surpass baselines and equivalent monomodal models.

In this paper, we describe the first steps into exploring what frame semantic analyses can tell us about multiperspectivity in multimodal datasets annotated in different languages and in different annotation settings. Based on the Flickr 30k dataset (Young et al., 2014) and its variants – Multi30k (Elliott et al., 2016) and Flickr 30k Entities (Plummer et al., 2015) – we conduct a set of experiments in which automatic frame semantic annotation for image captions and manual frame annotation for images are assessed for their semantic similarity. Image captioning and translation of captions were done by humans. Comparisons adopt both (1) a multilingual perspective with English and Portuguese originals and English-Portuguese translations of image descriptions and (2) multisetup perspective with English image annotations with or without image captions visible to annotators.

The contributions of this paper are two-fold:

- the multilingual setting is a first probing into how similar or different perspectives may be in different languages without digging deeper into how systematic differences might be.
- the multisetup perspective tests the assumption that visual information holds some sort of unbiased "ground truth".

In the remainder of this paper, we discuss, in section 2, how Frame Semantics and its computational implementation – FrameNet – incorporate perspective to the core of semantic representations. Next, in section 3, we explain compilation, translation and annotation of the corpus used for the experiments devised in section 4. Results and discussion are presented in sections 5 and 6, respectively, while section 7 finalizes the paper.

2. Frame Semantics and Perspective

The main idea behind Fillmore's frame semantics (Fillmore, 1982) is that human beings understand the meaning of a linguistic expression against the cognitive backdrop of a schematized scene, i.e. a *frame*. A frame is defined as "any system of concepts related in such a way that to understand any one of them you have to understand the whole structure in which it fits" (Petruck, 1996, 1).

A central notion in frame semantics is perspective. One of Fillmore's (1985) classic examples refers to the semantic distinction between *coast.n* and *shore.n* in English: Both refer to the `Relational_natural_features` frame, describing the stretch where land mass and sea water meet. While the former lexeme describes the view from the land, the latter is perspectivized from the point of view of the sea.

#0 A street performer on stilts walks on the stone tiles and discovers the thief escaping with the suitcase.

#1 A pair of street performers one on stilts and the other with a suitcase, perform outdoors.

#2 A man on stilts walks behind a woman holding a suitcase and wearing yellow sunglasses.

#3 A man in a white suit walking on stilts.

#4 Street performers entertain on street.

Figure 1: Captions and coreference chains from the Flickr 30k Entities dataset.

Berkeley FrameNet (Fillmore et al., 2003; Johnson et al., 2016) was the first lexicographic incarnation of Frame Semantics, building a frame-based lexicon to cover the general vocabulary of English. For each recorded frame that is lexically realizable, the database lists:

1. **Frame Elements (FE)**: represent the corresponding participants and objects of a frame. Based on the type of supporting information they contribute, frame elements can be categorized as core and non-core. For the frame `Commerce_buy`, for instance, BUYER and GOODS are core FEs while PLACE is non-core.

2. A list of **Lexical Units**: The list of known lexical units (single or multiple words) that can evoke the frame. For the frame `Commerce_buy`, this includes *buyer.n*, *client.n* and *purchase.n.*

3. **Frame Relations**: Each frame is connected to related frames with edges denoting the kind of relation (eg. *precedence*, *inheritance*, etc.) that exists between the interconnected frames. `Commerce_buy` *inherits* from `Getting` and is a *perspective on* `Commerce_goods-transfer`

Currently, there are FrameNet projects for several languages including German, Japanese and Brazilian Portuguese. A part of these groups forms an initiative for multilingual research in frame semantics, Global FrameNet[1].

Lately, full-text annotation, translation analysis (Czulo, 2017; Torrent et al., 2018, i.a.) and multimodal annotation (Belcavello et al., 2020) have seen increasing interest in frame semantics, shifting the annotation focus. In lexicographic annotation, annotation practice usually is aimed at making clear decisions on categories. Annotation accuracy is often measured in relation to a gold standard or by inter-annotator agreement. A lesson from frame-semantic annotation, however, is that not all annotation cases can be decided and multiple interpretations are possible. This issue has seen more attention in the above-mentioned more recent trends. In a phrase such as *Kinder, die dieses Jahr in die Schule gehen* 'children who start going to school this year', the annotation of *Schule* 'school' in this context could either be argued to be a LOCALE_BY_USE (a place with a certain purpose) or to refer to EDUCATION_TEACHING (a domain). In the end, one can wonder whether a decision for either of the two has an added benefit, or whether this actually represents the range of possible interpretations. Indeed, already in the early design of his theory, Fillmore points out that frames (in the terminology at that time 'scenes') are associated with and activate each other (Fillmore, 1975, 124). Considering this as well as the fact that frames are, in general, prototypical categories, they mostly cannot be understood as sharply distinct, necessarily discrete categories.

3. The Framed Multi30k Dataset

In recent years, several projects have been expanding the popular dataset for sentence-based image description Flickr30k (Young et al., 2014): a multimodal dataset containing 31,783 images of everyday activities, events and scenes, each paired with five different English captions providing clear descriptions of the salient entities and events. The Multi30k dataset (Elliott et al., 2016) is a multilingual expansion of the Flickr30K with five German original conceptual descriptions (Hodosh et al., 2013) crowdsourced independently of the original English captions. The German translations of the English captions were created by professional translators. The Flickr30k Entities dataset (Plummer et al., 2015) adds image-to-text relations by manually annotating bounding boxes that assign region-to-phrase correspondences, linking mentions to the same entities in images with lexical items in the five captions describing that image (Figure 1).

For the experiments reported in this paper, we rely on yet another extension of Flickr 30k: the Framed Multi30k dataset (Torrent et al., 2022), which augments both Flickr30k Entities and Multi30k datasets with (a) semantic annotation based on the network of

[1]https://www.globalframenet.org/

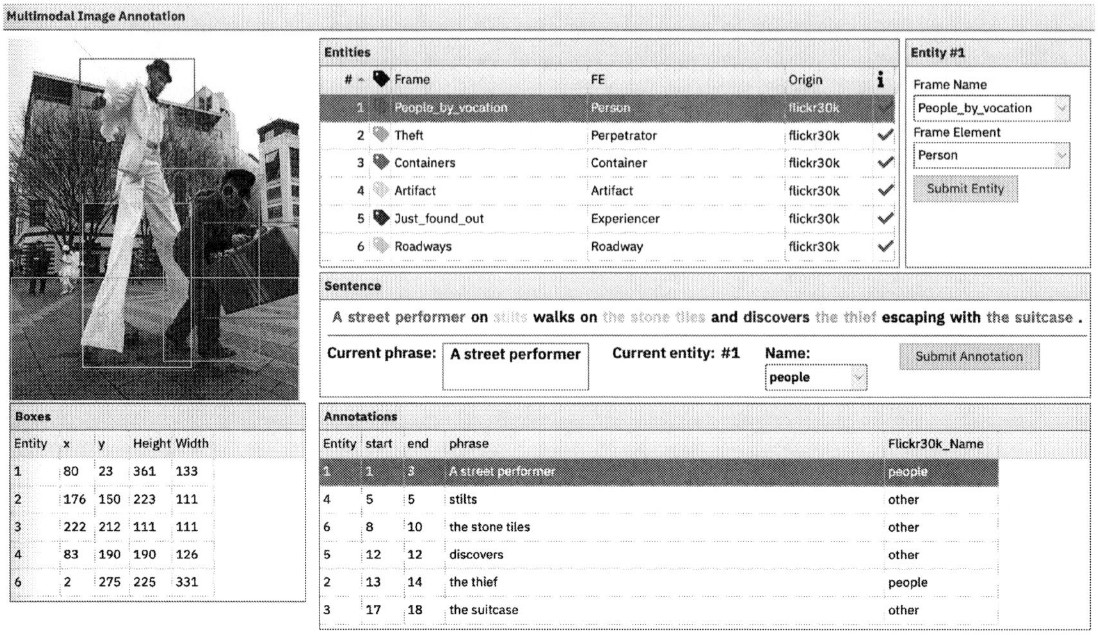

Figure 2: User interface for the multimodal annotation tool used for building the Framed Multi30k dataset.

frames and relations from FrameNet Brasil and (b) Brazilian Portuguese captions to the images. Framed Multi30k includes both English-Portuguese Translation (PTT) of the English Original captions (ENO) and Brazilian Portuguese Original descriptions (PTO) for each image in Flickr 30k. For the translation task, grad students majoring in translation studies were presented with one of the original English captions and instructed to translate the descriptions sticking as closely as possible to the English source sentence. For the task of creating original descriptions, native speakers of Brazilian Portuguese majoring in Language and Linguistics were presented with an image and instructed to write an original conceptual description (Hodosh et al., 2013). The instruction said to describe only what is depicted in the scene – its entities, their attributes, and relations – as opposed to providing additional background information that cannot be obtained from the image alone, such as about the situation, time, or location in which the image was taken.

As for the annotation of images, Framed Multi30k associates, via manual annotation, the bounding boxes in Flickr 30k Entities with frames and frame elements, using the annotation interface shown in Figure 2. Note that, based on the original Flickr 30k Entities dataset organization, the bounding boxes presented for annotation are only the ones grounded in the referential noun phrases found in the caption. This is to say that different captions of one same picture usually have different sets of bounding boxes.

Because Framed Multi30k is still under construction, for this paper, we selected a random sample of 2,000 images for which there already are both the PTT and the PTO captions, in addition to the ENO captions. Those images and their corresponding captions comprise the dataset used in the experiments.

Portuguese original captions are usually shorter than the original English captions, both in terms of the number of tokens (27,421 PTO x 38,881 ENO), types (3,747 PTO x 3,809 ENO), and characters (128,659 PTO x 152,837 ENO). When comparing the original descriptions with their translations to Brazilian Portuguese, we observe that, despite having fewer tokens (35,074 PTT x 38,881 ENO), translated sentences are more varied in terms of types (4,712 PTT x 3,809 ENO) and have a higher character count (165,724 PTT x 152,837 ENO). The properties of PTO and PTT captions are similar to the ones found for German original and translated captions when the Multi30k dataset was built (Elliott et al., 2016). Inflectional properties of German, in comparison to English, may in part be responsible for the differences; they may also reflect the oft-made observation that translations have a tendency to be longer than originals.

4. Experiments

Experiments were set up so as to assess frame semantic similarity across languages and across communicative modes. In both cases, we use the cosine similarity (CS) between the frame semantic representations generated either automatically by a semantic parser or manually, via annotation.

The CS algorithm used to measure frame semantic similarity between two annotations comprises three stages:

1. building an associate table using frames from FrameNet;

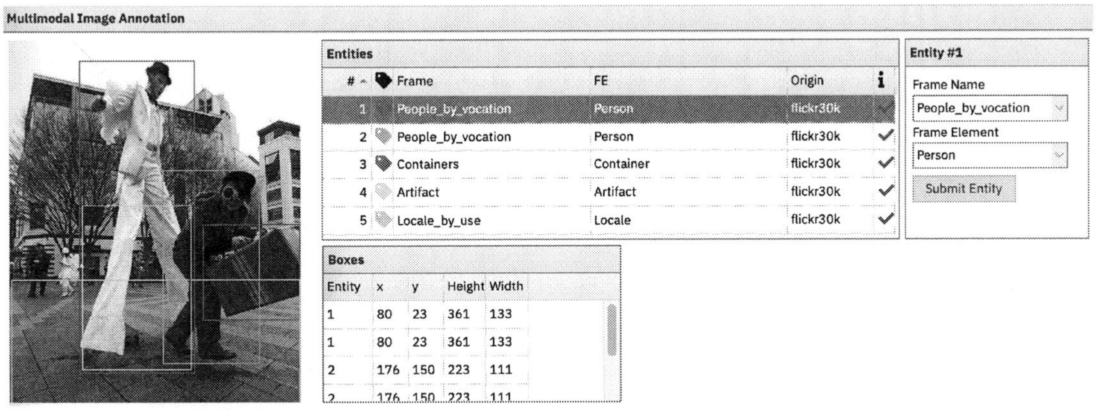

Figure 3: User interface of the multimodal annotation tool adapted for the second task.

2. building associative arrays associating each annotation – automatic or manual – with the directly evoked and related frames in the FrameNet database;

3. measuring cosine similarity between associative arrays.

In this application, the FrameNet network is represented as an Acyclic Directed Graph – the FN graph – where each node (frame) is associated with another node (frame) higher in the same hierarchy. The FN graph is used to build the associative table for each frame. This table indicates a relatedness metric and is calculated using Spread Activation (SA) (Gouws et al., 2010). The SA algorithm models an iterative energy propagation process from one or more nodes to other nodes in a graph in three stages: (i) pre-adjustment, (ii) spreading, and (iii) post-adjustment (Crestani, 1997).
Before the spreading stage, the energy value for each node was calculated during the pre-adjustment stage. Energy decay was calculated for the value of the node so that this value is within the [0,1] interval. The calculated value was then output to the neighboring nodes. Post-adjustment was not used, since the FN graph is acyclic and the FN hierarchies do not comprise many levels.
From the associative table of each frame present in an annotation, the associative arrays were built. Each index in the array corresponds to an associated frame and the value of the index indicates the activation level of that frame. When comparing two annotations, for example a1 and a2, the array for a1 is completed with the frames evoked by a2 but not evoked by a1, and vice versa. A zero value is computed for each of those "completion frames". Finally, the relatedness between the two annotations is measured using the standard CS between two associative arrays.
CS of associative arrays were used as a metric for assessing semantic similarity of both captions in a crosslinguistic perspective, and communicative modes in a crossmodal perspective. We describe the experimental designs used for each perspective next.

4.1. Semantic similarity across languages

To evaluate semantic similarity of image captions across languages, we compare the semantic frame representation of the original English captions (ENO) provided by the Flickr 30K dataset with the Brazilian Portuguese translations of those captions (PTT) and the original Portuguese captions produced for the same pictures (PTO). Comparisons are pairwise and are assessed using the cosine similarity between associative arrays generated for each caption. Therefore, three measures are extracted from this experiment, namely, cosine similarities for the ENO x PTT, ENO x PTO and PPT x PTO pairs.
Frame-evoking lemmas from all captions in each language were automatically retrieved using DAISY (Torrent et al., 2022), a disambiguation algorithm that uses the network of semantic frames, Frame Elements (FEs) and Lexical Units (LUs) from the FrameNet database to assign the correct frames to each lexical item based on the context provided by each sentence. By treating word forms, lexemes, LUs and frames as nodes in a graph, and attributing values to each node and also to each candidate lemma, the disambiguation algorithm uses a spread activation search method (Diederich, 1990; Tsatsaronis et al., 2007) to calculate the energy decay of each lemma as it propagates through the nodes in the network. This method takes into account not only how far a specific node is from the beginning nodes – meaning, how much energy is lost as connections need to be traversed in order to reach that specific node – but also how it is activated by liked neighboring nodes, receiving more energy, which helps determine its relative importance in the network.
Table 1 presents the differences among the multilingual corpora. Brazilian Portuguese translations have a lower average number of lemmas than the original English captions (19.44 ENO x 17.54 PTT) and also fewer frame-evoking lemmas (17.78 ENO x 12.38

PTT). Original descriptions in Portuguese also have a lower average number of lemmas than the English captions (19.44 ENO vs. 13.71 PTO lemmas) and also evoked fewer frames (17.78 ENO vs. 9.98 PTO frames). Considering the normalized number of frames per lemma, the original English caption ratios (M = 0.92, SD = 0.33) are significantly higher than the Portuguese translations (M = 0.71, SD = 0.28) and original descriptions (M = 0.75, SD = 0.32), with $t(3996) = 21.28, p < 0.001$ and $t(3996) = 16.35, p < 0.001$, respectively, using Welch's t-test (Welch, 1947). This difference is a consequence of the broader lexical coverage of English in relation to Portuguese. It is worth noting, however, that this difference does not impact the validity of the comparisons between cosine similarities because the vectors representing frames evoked by a sample in English are always paired with samples of the other corpora. Any variation in a comparison between a translation and a original sentence in Portuguese is caused by their own differences.

Portuguese originals also have a higher frame:lemma ratio, although this difference is lower than the others ($t(3996) = -3.83, p < 0.001$). In this case, since both corpora are on the same language, the difference can be explained by the lexical choices of the annotators: the translation corpus contains 2,755 singletons, while the original Portuguese annotations have 2,118.

		ENO	PTT	PTO
Frames	avg. #	17.78	12.38	9.98
	stdev	8.04	5.96	4.86
Lemmas	avg. #	19.44	17.54	13.71
	stdev	6.47	6.21	5.48
Frame:Lemma	avg.	0.92	0.71	0.75
	stdev	0.33	0.28	0.32

Table 1: Counts and ratios for annotated frames and for lemmas

4.2. Semantic similarity across modes in different annotation setups

For assessing similarity of semantic annotation of different communicative modes and how it may be influenced by the annotation setup, the results of two annotation tasks for tagging bounding boxes in the Flickr 30k Entities dataset for frames and frame elements were used.

The first is the one originally designed for building the Framed Multi30k dataset, where native speakers of Brazilian Portuguese, who are also fluent in English, are assigned the task of enriching the multimodal dataset with FrameNet frame and frame element tags while analyzing image-caption pairings – see Figure 2. Before being assigned this task, annotators were trained on the guidelines and the quality of their annotation work was manually checked for a first batch comprised of six hundred annotations, one hundred images from each of the six annotators involved. After validating the control quality batch, a second batch with 275 images per annotator was assigned to them. For this first task, annotators were instructed to follow the FrameNet annotation guidelines and to assign a semantic frame and a frame element to the objects in the bounding boxes.

In the example annotation (Fig. 2), the lexical items "A street performer," "stilts," "the stone tiles," "discovers," "the thief," and "the suitcase," from the original English caption created to describe this image, are correlated to bounding boxes containing the entities referred to by those lexical items. For the first bounding box – colored red and correlated with the also red sentence segment "A street performer," – the annotator assigned the frame `People_by_vocation`, which contains words for individuals as viewed in terms of their vocation, and the core frame element PERSON. For the second bounding box – colored green and correlated with the green sentence segment "the thief" – the annotator assigned the frame `Theft`, which is evoked by lexical items describing situations in which a perpetrator takes goods from a victim, and the core frame element PERPETRATOR – the person (or other agent) that takes the goods away.

The second annotation task was specifically devised for this paper. We asked a different group of five annotators to annotate a subset of 1,000 images within the original 2,000 images sample for frames and frame elements in the bounding boxes associated with each image. This time, however, annotators were not presented with the captions. In other words, they should apply FrameNet labels while having only the visual mode as reference. Given the nature of the visual corpus, annotators were instructed to only assign Entity frames and the related core frame element. The same manually created bounding boxes from Flickr 30k Entities were used to determine which objects from each image should be annotated. This time, however, all bounding boxes associated with each image were presented (Fig. 3). As in the first task, the quality of the annotations was assessed by manually checking a subset before allowing annotators to proceed to the full task.

5. Results

In the following subsections we present the results for each of the experiments described in section 4.

5.1. Similarity of semantic representations across languages

Average cosine similarity measures for each caption type pair – ENO x PTT, ENO x PTO and PTT x PTO – are presented in Table 2. The distributions of those similarities are shown in Figure 4.

Taking into consideration how the cosine similarity distributions shown in Figure 4 approximate a normal

	ENO		PTO	
	avg. cos	stdev	avg. cos	stdev
ENO	-	-	0.33	0.14
PTT	0.51	0.14	0.43	0.2
PTO	0.33	0.14	-	-

Table 2: Average cosine similarity between Associative_arrays built for the frame semantic representations of ENO, PTT and PTO captions

distribution and the almost equivalent variances, Student's and Welch's t-test were used to verify the significance of the differences, according to the variables variance. The cosine similarities between PTT and ENO (M = 0.51, SD = 0.14) were significantly higher than those between PTO and ENO (M = 0.33, SD = 0.14), $t(1998) = 41.78, p < 0.001$. Additionally, the average similarities between PTO and PTT (M = 0.43, SD = 0.2) are higher than those between PTO and ENO, with test statistic $t(1998) = 19.98, p < 0.001$. At the same time, those similarities are significantly smaller than those between PTT and ENO, with $t(1998) = -13.71, p < 0.001$.

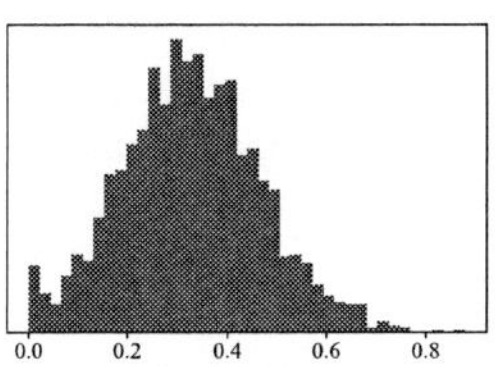

(a) ENO × PTO

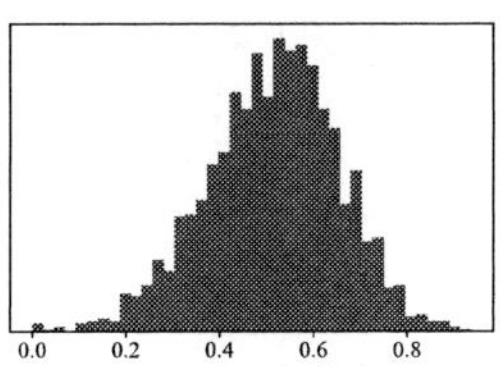

(b) ENO × PTT

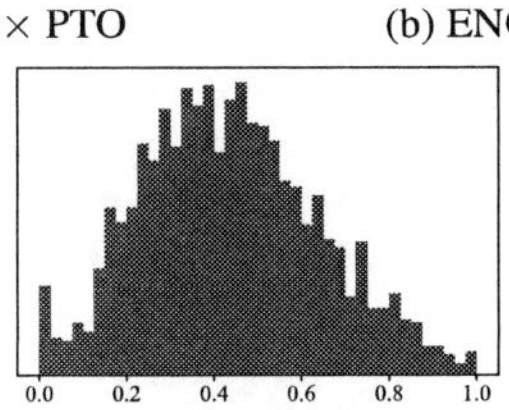

(c) PTT × PTO

Figure 4: Distribution of cosine similaritiy values between ENO, PTT and PTO.

5.2. Similarity of semantic representations across modes in different annotation setups

Average cosine similarity measures and the standard deviation for image annotations compared to the original English textual annotations are presented in Table 3. The distributions of those similarities are shown in Figure 5. The annotations made with a reference caption in English (VWC), when compared against ENO, had higher cosine similarities (M = 0.43, SD = 0.13) than the ones annotated without any reference (VWoC) (M = 0.38, SD = 0.12), with Student's t-test statistic $t(998) = 8.64, p < 0.001$.

	ENO	
	avg. cos	stdev
VWC	0.43	0.13
VWoC	0.38	0.12

Table 3: Similarity for image frame annotation setups with and without captions present.

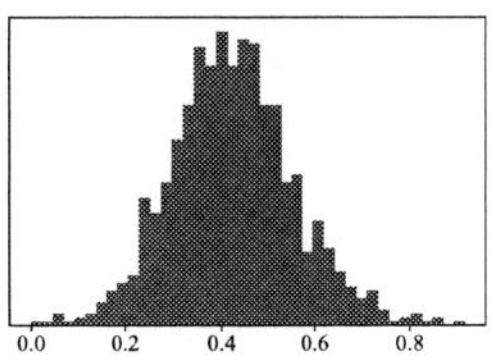

(a) ENO × VWC

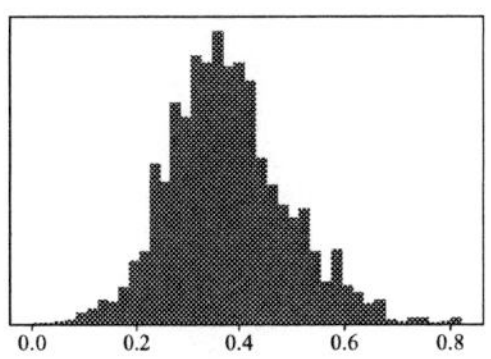

(b) ENO × VWoC

Figure 5: Distribution of cosine similaritiy values between ENO, VWC and VWoC.

6. Discussion

The similarity coefficients from the multilingual comparison indicate that in terms of perspective of annotation, PTT seems to be somewhere between ENO and PTO, with a comparable distance to either. In some way, this was to be expected, given that the translation brief required translators to make a close rendition of the English original. With the cumulative analysis performed here, we cannot make the claim that this a clear case of *shining through* (Teich, 2003), i.e. a case of source text features being over-represented in the target text. For the domain of motion events, systematic framing differences between languages are well documented (Talmy, 2000; Slobin, 2004). In the image annotation, however, we will find a vastly broader annotation including people and artifacts, and we do not yet know whether any of the involved languages has a preference for a certain framing or interpretation of these categories in image descriptions. Also, the variation we see between ENO and PTO might be due to randomness, with PTT being an intented close rendition of ENO.

Besides a better understanding of potential framing preferences in a language, we also need to cross-check against variation that can happen within one language, or in other words: If we had two sets of annotations for English by different annotators, might they be as similar/distant as ENO/PTO or rather as ENO/PTT? While the numbers presented here may be first indicators, clearly more elaborate setups and evaluations are needed to dig deeper into the questions of framing preferences between languages and translation effects.

As to the latter, it is not a given that influence from the source language is the only factor to be taken into account: As shown, e.g., in (Vandevoorde, 2020), *normalization* (Baker, 1995), i.e. the (over-)adherence to target language conventions is another semantic effect that can be witnessed in translation, or re-framings due to an open list of factors such as those described, i.a., in (Slobin, 2005; Rojo and Valenzuela, 2013; Czulo, 2017; Ohara, 2020).

As for the image annotation setups, the experiments indicate that, under a model that takes perspective into account, labels assigned to images are not to be taken as some sort of "ground truth" representation. Annotators taking part in the experiment tended to frame the image according to the caption, which is shown by a significant higher cosine similarity between ENO and VWC. The very examples in Figures 2 and 3 give an indication of that: while the person holding the suitcase was annotated as a thief when in presence of the caption, they were tagged as a person in the absence of the caption clue.

This is an indication that the role of images as proxies for "ground truth" in multimodal datasets is, at the very least, limited, if one considers that meanings are relativized to perspectivized scenes, as pointed out by Fillmore (1977). The main issue at stake here is that, in general, image annotation in multimodal datasets involve the assignment of labels from a categorization system that does not encode perspective.

In cases where the annotation is carried out by humans, which is the case for the Flickr 30k Entities dataset, the categories available for annotation of the bounding boxes are very coarse-grained and include only: people, clothing, body parts, animals, vehicles, instruments, scene, not visual and other. In this scenario, the distinction between thief and person, for instance, would be subsumed under the "people" tag. The scenario is even more concerning when we consider that, among the 559,767 bounding boxes in the Flickr 30k Entities dataset, 182,136 (32.53%) received the "people" tag and 138,658 (24.77%) received the "other" tag.

In the cases where image annotation is conducted automatically, using computer vision algorithms such as YOLOv3 (Redmon and Farhadi, 2018), for example, the core problem remains unchanged. Such systems are trained on datasets such as MS-COCO (Lin et al., 2014) or Open Images (Kuznetsova et al., 2020). In both cases, the categories used for tagging bounding boxes are organized in ontologies that do not encode perspective either. Last but not least, even in the case of Open Images, where, on top of the categories assigned to each image, attributes and relations can also be assigned as triplets, it is not made clear whether the different perspectives on them are encoded.

Because the way humans interpret the entities in an image may be influenced by the text accompanying it – as the results in Table 3 suggest –, the current configuration of image annotation systems may limit the role of images in downstream tasks such as multimodal machine translation. Even in Flickr 30k, where captions are conceptual descriptions of images, the relation between image and text is not equivalent to that of an absolute fact and one possible description of it. Images may too accommodate different perspectives and accounting for those differences is key for assuring that the relation between the image and the text is preserved, for instance, in a translated sentence.

7. Conclusion(s) and further work

The experiments and analyses described in this contribution have produced two results:

1. Frame semantic similarity for image captions in different languages are sensitive to whether a description is a translation or not.

2. Semantic similarity was also influenced by the annotation setup in that presenting captions with images to be annotated produced higher semantic similarity across modes, indicating that image description data cannot be assumed to be an "independent source" or "ground truth" of semantic information.

The former result needs further investigation in order to test for its generalizability. This would include extending the experiment to different language pairs as well as comparing such results with variation within a language, e.g., with multiple captions per image in one language. Also, the question of whether there are language-specific framing preferences at play can only be answered by means of deeper analyses of the frame semantic annotation of the original captions.

The latter result in a sense is analogous to the observation that the translation of image captions seems to carry, in parts, influence from an "anterior" - for the case of translation, this the description to be translated, with regard annotation setup, shown to annotators. If priming is to be assumed as a relevant factor in both cases, then the observation does not come as a surprise, but at the same time commands caution for future annotation setups. Priming as a factor could be tested for in order to corroborate this assumption.

8. Acknowledgements

Authors acknowledge the support of the Graduate Program in Linguistics at the Federal University of Juiz de Fora. Research presented in this paper is funded by CAPES PROBRAL grant 88887.144043/2017-00 and CNPq grants 408269/2021-9 and 315749/2021-0. Viridiano's research was funded by CAPES PROBRAL PhD exchange grant 88887.628830/2021-00.

9. Bibliographical References

Baker, M. (1995). Corpora in translation studies: an overview and some suggestions for future research. *Target*, 7(2):223–243. Hier werden die verschiedenen Typen von Korpora diskutiert.

Belcavello, F., Viridiano, M., Diniz da Costa, A., Matos, E. E. d. S., and Torrent, T. T. (2020). Frame-based annotation of multimodal corpora: Tracking (a)synchronies in meaning construction. In *Proceedings of the International FrameNet Workshop 2020: Towards a Global, Multilingual FrameNet*, pages 23–30, Marseille, France, May. European Language Resources Association.

Crestani, F. (1997). Application of spreading activation techniques in information retrieval. *Artificial Intelligence Review*, 11(6):453–482.

Czulo, O. (2017). Aspects of a primacy of frame model of translation. In S. Hansen-Schirra, et al., editors, *Empirical modelling of translation and interpreting*, number 6 in Translation and Multilingual Natural Language Processing, pages 465–490. Language Science Press, Berlin.

Diederich, J. (1990). Spreading activation and connectionist models for natural language processing. 16(1):25–64.

Elliott, D., Frank, S., Sima'an, K., and Specia, L. (2016). Multi30K: Multilingual English-German image descriptions. In *Proceedings of the 5th Workshop on Vision and Language*, pages 70–74, Berlin, Germany, August. Association for Computational Linguistics.

Elliott, D., Frank, S., Barrault, L., Bougares, F., and Specia, L. (2017). Findings of the second shared task on multimodal machine translation and multilingual image description. *arXiv preprint arXiv:1710.07177*.

Elliott, D. (2018). Adversarial evaluation of multimodal machine translation. In *Proceedings of the 2018 Conference on Empirical Methods in Natural Language Processing*, pages 2974–2978, Brussels, Belgium, October-November. Association for Computational Linguistics.

Fillmore, C. J., Johnson, C. R., and Petruck, M. R. (2003). Background to framenet. *International journal of lexicography*, 16(3):235–250.

Fillmore, C. J. (1975). An alternative to checklist theories of meaning. In *Annual Meeting of the Berkeley Linguistics Society*, volume 1, pages 123–131.

Fillmore, C. J. (1977). The case for case reopened. In P. Cole et al., editors, *Syntax and Semantics Volume 8: Grammatical Relations*, pages 59–81. Academic Press.

Fillmore, C. J. (1982). Frame Semantics. In Linguistics Society of Korea, editor, *Linguitics in the morning calm*. Hanshin Publishing Co., Seoul, South Korea. pages: 111 – 138.

Fillmore, C. J. (1985). Frames and the semantics of understanding. *Quaderni di Semantica*, 6(2):222–254.

Gella, S., Lapata, M., and Keller, F. (2016). Unsupervised visual sense disambiguation for verbs using multimodal embeddings. In *Proceedings of the 2016 Conference of the North American Chapter of the Association for Computational Linguistics: Human Language Technologies*, pages 182–192, San Diego, California, June. Association for Computational Linguistics.

Gouws, S., van Rooyen, G.-J., and Engelbrecht, H. A. (2010). Measuring conceptual similarity by spreading activation over Wikipedia's hyperlink structure. In *Proceedings of the 2nd Workshop on The People's Web Meets NLP: Collaboratively Constructed Semantic Resources*, pages 46–54, Beijing, China, August. Coling 2010 Organizing Committee.

Hodosh, M., Young, P., and Hockenmaier, J. (2013). Framing image description as a ranking task: Data, models and evaluation metrics. *Journal of Artificial Intelligence Research*, 47:853–899.

Johnson, C. R., Schwarzer-Petruck, M., Baker, C. F., Ellsworth, M., Ruppenhofer, J., and Fillmore, C. J. (2016). Framenet: Theory and practice. Technical report, International Computer Science Institute.

Kiela, D., Rimell, L., Vulić, I., and Clark, S. (2015). Exploiting image generality for lexical entailment detection. In *Proceedings of the 53rd Annual Meeting of the Association for Computational Linguistics and the 7th International Joint Conference on Natural Language Processing (Volume 2: Short Papers)*, pages 119–124, Beijing, China, July. Association for Computational Linguistics.

Kuznetsova, A., Rom, H., Alldrin, N., Uijlings, J., Krasin, I., Pont-Tuset, J., Kamali, S., Popov, S., Malloci, M., Kolesnikov, A., Duerig, T., and Ferrari, V. (2020). The open images dataset v4: Unified image classification, object detection, and visual relationship detection at scale. *IJCV*.

Lala, C. and Specia, L. (2018). Multimodal lexical translation. In *Proceedings of the Eleventh International Conference on Language Resources and Evaluation (LREC 2018)*, Miyazaki, Japan, May. European Language Resources Association (ELRA).

Lin, T.-Y., Maire, M., Belongie, S., Hays, J., Perona, P., Ramanan, D., Dollár, P., and Zitnick, C. L. (2014). Microsoft coco: Common objects in context. In David Fleet, et al., editors, *Computer Vision – ECCV 2014*, pages 740–755, Cham. Springer International Publishing.

Ohara, K. (2020). Finding corresponding constructions in English and Japanese in a TED talk parallel corpus using frames-and-constructions analysis. In *Proceedings of the International FrameNet Workshop 2020: Towards a Global, Multilingual FrameNet*, pages 8–12, Marseille, France, May. European Language Resources Association.

Petruck, M. R. L. (1996). Frame Semantics. In Jef Verschueren, et al., editors, *Handbook of pragmatics*, pages 1–8. John Benjamins, Philadelphia.

Plummer, B. A., Wang, L., Cervantes, C. M., Caicedo, J. C., Hockenmaier, J., and Lazebnik, S. (2015). Flickr30k entities: Collecting region-to-phrase correspondences for richer image-to-sentence models.

In *2015 IEEE International Conference on Computer Vision (ICCV)*, pages 2641–2649.

Redmon, J. and Farhadi, A. (2018). Yolov3: An incremental improvement. *arXiv preprint arXiv:1804.02767*.

Rojo, A. and Valenzuela, J. (2013). Constructing meanings in translation: The role of constructions in translation. In Ana Rojo et al., editors, *Cognitive linguistics and translation: advances in some theoretical models and applications*, number 23 in Applications of Cognitive Linguistics, pages 283–310. De Gruyter Mouton, Berlin.

Silberer, C. and Lapata, M. (2014). Learning grounded meaning representations with autoencoders. In *Proceedings of the 52nd Annual Meeting of the Association for Computational Linguistics (Volume 1: Long Papers)*, pages 721–732, Baltimore, Maryland, June. Association for Computational Linguistics.

Slobin, D. I. (2004). The many ways to search for a frog: linguistic typology and the expression of motion events. In S. Strömqvist et al., editors, *Relating Events in Narrative: Typological Perspectives*, pages 219–257. Lawrence Erlbaum Associates, Mahwah, N.J.

Slobin, D. (2005). Relating Narrative Events in Translation. In Dorit Diskin Ravit et al., editors, *Perspectives on Language and Language Development: Essays in Honor of Ruth A. Berman*, pages 115–129.

Specia, L., Frank, S., Sima'an, K., and Elliott, D. (2016). A shared task on multimodal machine translation and crosslingual image description. In *Proceedings of the First Conference on Machine Translation: Volume 2, Shared Task Papers*, pages 543–553, Berlin, Germany, August. Association for Computational Linguistics.

Talmy, L. (2000). *Toward a cognitive semantics: Vol. II: Typology and process in concept structuring*. MIT Press, Cambridge, MA.

Teich, E. (2003). *Cross-linguistic variation in system and text. A methodology for the investigation of translations and comparable texts*, volume 5 of *Text, Translation, Computational Processing*. Mouton de Gruyter, Berlin/New York.

Torrent, T. T., Ellsworth, M., Baker, C., and Matos, E. E. d. S. (2018). The Multilingual FrameNet Shared Annotation Task: a Preliminary Report. In Tiago Timponi Torrent, et al., editors, *Proceedings of the Eleventh International Conference on Language Resources and Evaluation (LREC 2018)*, pages 62–68, Paris, France, may. European Language Resources Association (ELRA).

Torrent, T. T., Matos, E. E. d. S., Belcavello, F., Viridiano, M., Gamonal, M. A., Costa, A. D. d., and Marim, M. C. (2022). Representing context in framenet: A multidimensional, multimodal approach. *Frontiers in Psychology*, 13.

Tsatsaronis, G., Vazirgiannis, M., and Androutsopoulos, I. (2007). Word sense disambiguation with spreading activation networks generated from thesauri. In *IJCAI*, volume 27, pages 223–252.

Vandevoorde, L. (2020). *Semantic differences in translation: Exploring the field of inchoativity*. Language Science Press. OCLC: 1229399854.

Welch, B. L. (1947). The generalization of 'student's'problem when several different population varlances are involved. *Biometrika*, 34(1-2):28–35.

Young, P., Lai, A., Hodosh, M., and Hockenmaier, J. (2014). From image descriptions to visual denotations: New similarity metrics for semantic inference over event descriptions. *Transactions of the Association for Computational Linguistics*, 2:67–78.

Proceedings of the 1st Workshop on Perspectivist Approaches to NLP @LREC2022, pages 117–125
Marseille, 20 June 2022

Change My Mind: how Syntax-based Hate Speech Recognizer can Uncover Hidden Motivations based on Different Viewpoints

Michele Mastromattei*, **Valerio Basile**†, **Fabio Massimo Zanzotto***
* Department of Enterprise Engineering, University of Rome Tor Vergata, Italy
† Department of Computer Science, University of Turin, Italy
michele.mastromattei@uniroma2.it, valerio.basile@unito.it, fabio.massimo.zanzotto@uniroma2.it

Abstract

Hate speech recognizers may mislabel sentences by not considering the different opinions that society has on selected topics. In this paper, we show how explainable machine learning models based on syntax can help to understand the motivations that induce a sentence to be offensive to a certain demographic group. To explore this hypothesis, we use several syntax-based neural networks, which are equipped with syntax heat analysis trees used as a post-hoc explanation of the classifications and a dataset annotated by two different groups having dissimilar cultural backgrounds. Using particular *contrasting trees*, we compared the results and showed the differences. The results show how the keywords that make a sentence offensive depend on the cultural background of the annotators and how this differs in different fields. In addition, the syntactic activations show how even the sub-trees are very relevant in the classification phase.

Keywords: Hate speech recognizer, Explainable models, Perspectivism

1. Introduction

Hate speech recognizers (HSRs) (Warner and Hirschberg, 2012; Djuric et al., 2015; Gambäck and Sikdar, 2017) can be a great tool to contrast offensive terms, limit negative debates, and protect ethnic minorities. Indeed, these recognizers are excellent for spotting sentences containing offensive words as, over the years, several datasets focussing on this phenomenon have been released and used as training models (Waseem and Hovy, 2016; Davidson et al., 2017; Founta et al., 2018; Basile et al., 2019). However, these standardized datasets focus purely on offensive terms and indicate sentences as *hate speech* only because they contain words typically labeled as hate. This becomes a serious problem as hate speech recognition is done only focusing on *trigger words*. The context where sentences are written is disregarded as well as the addressees of the messages in these sentences.

Anyway, focusing on trigger words, HSRs increase the probability of tagging sentences from dialects of specific ethnic communities as hate speech. The result is that users who should be protected may risk banning (Sap et al., 2019). This is because some words are not offensive to some groups of people with particular ethnic backgrounds. On the contrary, the use of apparently inoffensive words can have a huge offensive impact on the society of other ethnic groups. So, the problem of hate speech and automatic hate speech detectors cannot be summarized in the classification of offensive elements but has a broader impact that includes who reads those sentences and how they are written.

Word-based and transformer-based models have a debias problem that is difficult to mitigate or easy to escape (Hosseini et al., 2017), and a typical solution is to use regularization techniques as in the case of transformers, by fashioning their attention mechanism (Kennedy et al., 2020). Although, attention seems to capture syntactic information (Eriguchi et al., 2016; Chen et al., 2018; Strubell et al., 2018; Clark et al., 2019), it is not clear how these regularizations reduce the use of trigger words.

In this paper, we want to find out - through syntactic models - what are the substructures that make a sentence labelable as hate speech, comparing explainable models trained on the same dataset but labeled by groups of people with different backgrounds. Our results show how the hate speech phenomenon is quite subjective and how the underlying motivations are different according to the cultural background of the annotators.

2. Background and related works

Methods to improve the interpretability of the predictions of supervised machine learning models and deep learning models are generally found in the literature around Explainable AI (XAI) (Samek et al., 2017; Samek and Müller, 2019; Vilone and Longo, 2020). For text classification tasks such as sentiment analysis or hate speech detection, methods have been proposed that work at the lexical level (Clos et al., 2017) or by highlighting subsequences of text that contribute to the final label (Perikos et al., 2021). Most modern models of neural interpretability rely on attention-based techniques (Bodria et al., 2020), using auxiliary tasks such as Aspect-Based Sentiment Analysis for Document-Level Sentiment Analysis interpretability (Silveira et al., 2019), or external knowledge (Zhao and Yu, 2021). While it has been postulated that attention-based models learn syntactic structure to a certain degree (Manning et al., 2020), the role of syntax in the interpretation of the model is still understudied, as opposed to classification (Cignarella et al., 2020).

The massive use of syntax, defined as heat parse trees and used as a post-hoc explanation of the classification, has shown that in the hate speech phenomena, syntax alone is not able to distill the prejudice because it is already intrinsic in the most common hate speech training corpora and so, syntax cannot drive the "attention" of hate speech recognizer to ethically-unbiased features (Mastromattei et al., 2022).
The potential impact of a perspectivist approach towards improving the interpretability of supervised Linear Programming (LP) models has been explored by Basile (2021). In the cited paper, the author proposed a simple method to derive a description of the different perspectives taken by the annotators of a hate speech corpus in the form of bags of words. Fell et al. (2021) further pursue this direction by proposing a method to cluster annotators, providing at the same time word clouds highlighting the terms that trigger a sensible response by different groups of people.

3. Methods and data

To explore perspectivism in explainability models we used the following steps: 1) a structured dataset having polarized labels (Sec. 3.1), 2) two or more explainable models (Sec. 3.2) and 3) an algorithm that explains how to analyze an outcome according to two different viewpoints and how these viewpoints conflicting (Sec. 3.3).

3.1. Brexit Hate Speech Dataset

To validate our method, we tested it on real-world data annotated with hate speech and several other phenomena. We selected the dataset by Akhtar et al. (2021), a corpus of 1,120 English posts from Twitter. The dataset was originally gathered for research on stance detection (Lai et al., 2019), and it has been further annotated with four binary labels: hate speech, (presence of) stereotype, aggressiveness, and offensiveness, adapting the guidelines used for the annotation of the Italian Hate Speech Corpus (Sanguinetti et al., 2018). Interestingly for our work, the Brexit dataset is annotated in its entirety by six different annotators belonging to two distinct social groups. The *target* group is composed of three Muslim immigrants in the United Kingdom, while the *control* group is composed of three Ph.D. students with western backgrounds. The inter-annotator agreement computed on the two groups separately shows that each group is fairly consistent internally (a high intra-group agreement) across all four dimensions, while they agree much less between members of different groups (low inter-group agreement). Using only the hate speech label, the inter-annotator agreement for both groups is a *Fair agreement*, employing the Fleiss' kappa measure.

3.2. Explainable Syntax-based models

Model interpretability is crucial in the study of divisive topics because it increases the trust that humans place in models and also for its fair and ethical decision-making. Especially, in the text-classification task, explainable syntax-based models return syntactic structures that are ideal for understanding sentence labeling and analyzing the substructures that influenced that target.
For this purpose, we used KERMIT (Zanzotto et al., 2020) and KERM-HATE (Mastromattei et al., 2022): two explainable syntax-based models that return heat-colored parse trees according to the values of activation of the model during the evaluation phase. Both models are based on the same components: a KERMIT component (that allows the encoding and the visualization of the activations of universal syntactic interpretations in a neural network architecture) and a transformer model. KERM-HATE differs from KERMIT only for a four-layer fully-connected neural network at the top of the model. KERMIT*viz* (Zanzotto et al., 2020), makes the KERMIT component the most relevant part of the two models. KERMIT*viz* gives the possibility to extract as output not only the classification target but especially the colored parse tree with the activation value of every single node that composes a generic sentence. Thus, KERMIT*viz* allows us to visualize how decisions are made according to activations of syntactic structures.

3.3. Contrasting trees

Using KERMIT and KERM-HATE (Sec.3.2), it is possible to study perspectivism through syntax trees. Given two equal KERMIT-like models and a sentence $\mathcal{S}$, it is possible to derive a syntactic tree (*constrasting tree*) whose activation values are the result of the difference between the activation values of the two models. The final result should be displayed using KERMIT*viz*. In this way, it is visible which are - after the two trees and their activations - the most active subparts and which are the syntactic structures that influence the classification of a sentence for a given model. This analysis is important to understand how salient are the syntactic substructures of a sentence and how they affect the final classification.
To generate a contrasting tree, we used the following method: let $\mathcal{T}_A =< \bar{T}, \bar{V}_A >$ and $\mathcal{T}_B =< \bar{T}, \bar{V}_B >$ two trees obtained from the same sentence $\mathcal{S}$ such that: $\bar{T} = \{\bar{t}_i, ..., \bar{t}_n\}$ is the ordered list of non-empty subtrees that makes up $\mathcal{T}_i$ (with $i = \{A, B\}$) and $\bar{V}_i = \{\bar{v}_{i,1}, ..., \bar{v}_{i,n}\}$ is the list of activation values where $\bar{v}_{i,j}$ is the activation value of subtree $\bar{t}_j$ (with $1 \leq j \leq n$). Thus the contrast tree $\mathcal{T}_{i-k} =< \bar{T}, \bar{V}_{i-k} >$ is obtained from $\mathcal{T}_i - \mathcal{T}_k$ and so $\bar{V}_{i-k} = \{(\bar{v}_{i,1} - \bar{v}_{k,1}), ..., (\bar{v}_{i,n} - \bar{v}_{k,n})\}$ (with $i, k = \{A, B\}$ and $i \neq k$).
In this way $\bar{V}_{i-k}$ contains only the relevant activations $\mathcal{T}_i$ because if $\bar{v}_{i,j} \approx \bar{v}_{k,j} \Rightarrow (\bar{v}_{i,j} - \bar{v}_{k,j}) \approx 0$, while if $\bar{v}_{k,j} >> \bar{v}_{i,j}$ then the result is a negative value and so a *zero activation value*.

4. Experiments

This section describes all the parameters and pretrained models used during our analysis (Sec. 4.1). Finally in

Sec 4.2 all obtained final results are shown and analyzed.

4.1. Experimental set-up

We tested our dataset using several models according to Mastromattei et al. (2022) tests: two *transformer-based* models and three *syntax-based* models. The two transformer-based model are Bert (Devlin et al., 2018) and XLNet (Yang et al., 2019) while the syntax-based are: KERM-HATE (Mastromattei et al., 2022), KERMIT (Zanzotto et al., 2020) and a modified version of KERMIT called KERMIT$_{XLNet}$ in which the original transformer sub-network has been replaced with XLNet. In this way, it is easier to visualize and compare all the models presented because for each transformer-based model, the syntax-based one was also generated. To assess statistical significance, each experiment was repeated 10 times with different seeds for initial weights. The meta-parameters utilized in training phrase are the following: for the syntax-based models (KERM-HATE, KERMIT and KERMIT$_{XLNet}$): (1) the tree encoder is on a distributed representation space R^d with $d = 4000$ and has penalizing factor $\lambda = 0.4$ (Moschitti, 2006); (2) constituency parse trees have been obtained by using Stanford's CoreNLP probabilistic context-free grammar parser (Manning et al., 2014). KERM-HATE's fully-connected four-layers network change the representation space four times: $R^n \rightarrow R^m \rightarrow R^n \rightarrow R^m$ where $m = 2,000$ and $n = 4,000$, before concluding with the final classification layer. (3) the decoder layer is a fully connected layer with the ReLU activation function (Agarap, 2018) applied to the concatenation of the KERMIT sub-network output and the final `[CLS]` token representation of the transformer model. Bert and XLNet model but also the transformer sub-networks component in the syntax-based models were implemented using Huggingface's transformers library (Wolf et al., 2019). For all models, the class weight w_i is inversely proposional to its $class_i$ (C_i) cardinality ($w_i = \frac{1}{|C_i|}$) and the optimizer used is AdamW (Loshchilov and Hutter, 2019) with the learning rate set to $2e^{-5}$. All models used a batch size of 64 and are trained for 3 epochs. The dataset described in Sec. 3.1 was divided into 80% for training and a 20% for testing. The two output datasets were used in the training and testing phase for all models used. Our hardware system consists of: 4 Cores Intel Xeon E3-1230 CPU with 62 Gb of RAM and 1 Nvidia 1070 GPU with 8Gb of onboard memory.
To generate contrasting trees, we used the algorithm described in Sec. 3.3 and - using KERMIT*viz* - showed the final results.

4.2. Result and discussion

In Table 1 we show the results in the testing phase of the five analyzed models. As it can be observed, KERM-HATE and KERMIT result to be the best models obtaining higher performances than the other models. It is important to note that the dataset is strongly unbalanced in favor of the *"no hate speech"* class. For this reason, in order to calm the results obtained and to continue the analysis, we use as visualization model KERMIT and not KERM-HATE, which has lower performances in the F1-measure *"hate speech"* class than KERMIT. In Figure 1 we graphically show the output of KERMIT, trained using both *control group* (KERMIT$_C$) and *target group* (KERMIT$_T$) labels on the same sentence: *"Time to kick Islam out of Britain"*.

Sentence: *Time to kick Islam out of Britain*

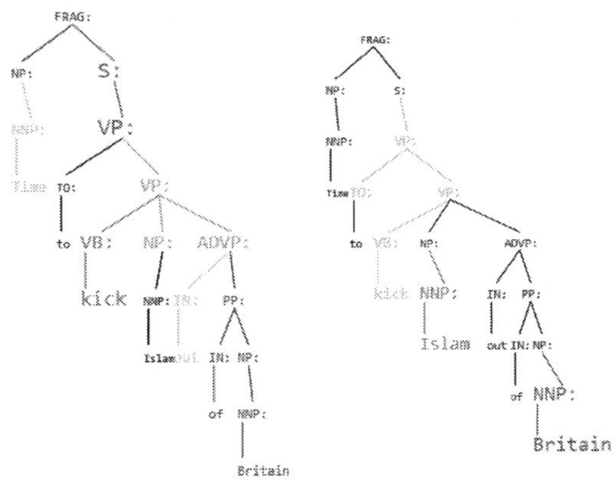

(a) Labeled as **hate speech** for the model trained using the *control group* labels (KERMIT$_C$)

(b) Labeled as **hate speech** for the model trained using the *target group* labels (KERMIT$_T$)

Figure 1: KERMIT colored parse trees output

We can observe that the output of KERMIT$_C$ is composed of subtrees that are much more active than those of KERMIT$_T$, which concentrates on its leaves. If we analyze each tree individually, we discover that the label *"hate speech"* for KERMIT$_C$ (Figure 1a) is generated by the leaf *"time"*, its parent node and by the right subtree of depth 4. KERMIT$_T$, on the other hand, although it has the same label (*"hate speech"*), concentrates more on terminals and on hate/racial keywords, such as *"kick"* and *"Islam"*, but also on *"Britain"* (Figure 1b).
Using these trees, we created their *contrasting trees* to visualize which are the sub-structures keys in KERMIT$_C$ and KERMIT$_T$ excluding the similar activations in both models (Figure 2). The result obtained confirms our analysis done previously on the individual trees (Figure 1) and adds further details. In particular, even if some sub-structures result to be unaltered, in Figure 2a we have a prevalence of active non-terminal nodes compared to Figure 2b which instead continues to concentrate on leaf nodes.
This analysis does not show an isolated case. We performed a *quantitative analysis* of the data by analyzing over 8,600 subtrees from several sentences within

Model	*Control* group			*Target* group		
	Accuracy	**F1 measure**		**Accuracy**	**F1 measure**	
		Macro	**Weighted**		**Macro**	**Weighted**
Bert	0.61 ($\pm$ 0.33)$^{\diamond}$	0.38 ($\pm$ 0.15)$^{\diamond}$	0.62 ($\pm$ 0.31)$^{\diamond}$	0.45 ($\pm$ 0.16)$^{\diamond}$	0.39 ($\pm$ 0.19)$^{\diamond}$	0.27 ($\pm$ 0.36)$^{\diamond}$
XLNet	0.70 ($\pm$ 0.29)$^{\dagger,\bullet}$	0.42 ($\pm$ 0.14)$^{\dagger,\bullet}$	0.70 ($\pm$ 0.28)$^{\dagger,\bullet}$	0.53 ($\pm$ 0.22)	0.37 ($\pm$ 0.12)	0.45 ($\pm$ 0.25)
KERM-HATE	**0.92 ($\pm$ 0.01)**$^{\diamond,\dagger,*}$	**0.49 ($\pm$ 0.04)**$^{\diamond,\dagger}$	**0.88 ($\pm$ 0.08)**$^{\diamond,\dagger,*}$	**0.64 ($\pm$ 0.11)**$^{\diamond,\triangleleft}$	**0.48 ($\pm$ 0.05)**$^{\diamond,*}$	**0.61 ($\pm$ 0.08)**$^{\diamond,*}$
KERMIT	0.81 ($\pm$ 0.13)$^{\bullet}$	**0.49 ($\pm$ 0.04)**$^{\bullet}$	0.82 ($\pm$ 0.08)$^{\bullet}$	0.55 ($\pm$ 0.12)$^{\triangleleft}$	0.47 ($\pm$ 0.05)	0.55 ($\pm$ 0.10)
KERMIT$_{XLNet}$	0.31 ($\pm$ 0.33)*	0.21 ($\pm$ 0.19)	0.27 ($\pm$ 0.36)*	0.56 ($\pm$ 0.12)	0.46 ($\pm$ 0.05)*	0.56 ($\pm$ 0.09)*

Table 1: Performance of all model tested. Mean and standard deviation results are obtained from 10 runs. The symbols $\diamond$, $\dagger$, $*$, $\bullet$ and $\triangleleft$ indicate a statistically significant difference between two results with a 95% of confidence level with the sign test.

Sentence: *Time to kick Islam out of Britain*

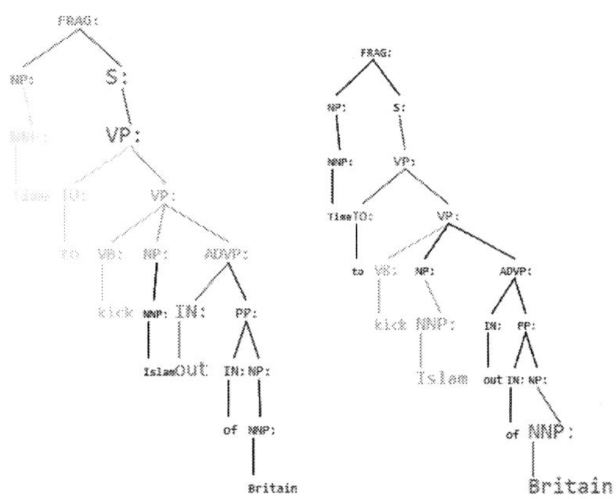

(a) Tree obtained subtracting from KERMIT$_C$ activation values those of KERMIT$_T$

(b) Tree obtained subtracting from KERMIT$_T$ activation values those of KERMIT$_C$

Figure 2: Contrasting trees

the dataset. If the prediction was *"hate speech"* for both KERMIT$_C$ and KERMIT$_T$, then KERMIT$_T$ focuses predominantly on tree leaves (the depth of activated subtrees is approximately 1) while the activation of KERMIT$_C$ is more distributed along with the syntax trees, with the average depth of activated subtrees equal to 1.7.

For a more accurate view of other sentences and their activations, in Appendix A we show more examples where both KERMIT$_C$ and KERMIT$_T$ predict the same sentence as *"hate speech"* but also cases where the label between the two models differs (*"no hate speech"* - *"hate speech"*).

5. Conclusion

Hate speech recognizers (HSRs) typically label a sentence as offensive by counting only the number of trigger words. In this paper, we have shown how, using syntax-based explainable models and a dataset labeled by two groups with different backgrounds, it is possible to view the motivations that lead HSRs to classify a sentence in a certain way and how those motivations change. Using contrast trees, we show the salient points that make a sentence offensive for each group. In this way, we can understand the motivations that each group used, giving us a wider and less critical view of their thinking (*"Change my mind"*).

Performing a quantitative analysis of the dataset - we confirmed our hypothesis that sentence labeling depends on the cultural background of each annotator. This implies that the use of syntax is useful in the hate speech phenomena and that the use of common *hate speech corpora* as training datasets, does not include the different aspects of society on a theme so subjective as hate speech.

Acknowledgments

This work is partially funded by the 2019 BRIC INAIL ID32 SfidaNow project.

6. Bibliographical References

Agarap, A. F. (2018). Deep Learning using Rectified Linear Units (ReLU). *CoRR*, abs/1803.0.

Akhtar, S., Basile, V., and Patti, V. (2021). Whose opinions matter? perspective-aware models to identify opinions of hate speech victims in abusive language detection. *CoRR*, abs/2106.15896.

Basile, V., Bosco, C., Fersini, E., Nozza, D., Patti, V., Rangel Pardo, F. M., Rosso, P., and Sanguinetti, M. (2019). SemEval-2019 task 5: Multilingual detection of hate speech against immigrants and women in Twitter. In *Proceedings of the 13th International Workshop on Semantic Evaluation*, pages 54–63, Minneapolis, Minnesota, USA, June. Association for Computational Linguistics.

Basile, V. (2021). It's the end of the gold standard as we know it. In Matteo Baldoni et al., editors, *AIxIA 2020 – Advances in Artificial Intelligence*, pages 441–453, Cham. Springer International Publishing.

Bodria, F., Panisson, A., Perotti, A., and Piaggesi, S. (2020). Explainability methods for natural language processing: Applications to sentiment analysis. In Maristella Agosti, et al., editors, *Proceedings of the 28th Italian Symposium on Advanced Database Systems, Villasimius, Sud Sardegna, Italy (virtual due to Covid-19 pandemic), June 21-24, 2020*, volume 2646 of *CEUR Workshop Proceedings*, pages 100–107. CEUR-WS.org.

Chen, K., Wang, R., Utiyama, M., Sumita, E., and Zhao, T. (2018). Syntax-directed attention for neural machine translation. In *Proceedings of the AAAI Conference on Artificial Intelligence*, volume 32.

Cignarella, A. T., Basile, V., Sanguinetti, M., Bosco, C., Rosso, P., and Benamara, F. (2020). Multilingual irony detection with dependency syntax and neural models. In *Proceedings of the 28th International Conference on Computational Linguistics*, pages 1346–1358, Barcelona, Spain (Online), December. International Committee on Computational Linguistics.

Clark, K., Khandelwal, U., Levy, O., and Manning, C. D. (2019). What does bert look at? an analysis of bert's attention. *arXiv preprint arXiv:1906.04341*.

Clos, J., Wiratunga, N., and Massie, S. (2017). Towards explainable text classification by jointly learning lexicon and modifier terms. In *IJCAI-17 Workshop on Explainable AI (XAI)*, page 19.

Davidson, T., Warmsley, D., Macy, M., and Weber, I. (2017). Automated hate speech detection and the problem of offensive language. In *Proceedings of the International AAAI Conference on Web and Social Media*, volume 11, pages 512–515.

Devlin, J., Chang, M.-W., Lee, K., and Toutanova, K. (2018). Bert: Pre-training of deep bidirectional transformers for language understanding. *arXiv preprint arXiv:1810.04805*.

Djuric, N., Zhou, J., Morris, R., Grbovic, M., Radosavljevic, V., and Bhamidipati, N. (2015). Hate speech detection with comment embeddings. In *Proceedings of the 24th international conference on world wide web*, pages 29–30.

Eriguchi, A., Hashimoto, K., and Tsuruoka, Y. (2016). Tree-to-sequence attentional neural machine translation. *arXiv preprint arXiv:1603.06075*.

Fell, M., Akhtar, S., and Basile, V. (2021). Mining annotator perspectives from hate speech corpora. In Elena Cabrio, et al., editors, *Proceedings of the Fifth Workshop on Natural Language for Artificial Intelligence (NL4AI 2021) co-located with 20th International Conference of the Italian Association for Artificial Intelligence (AI*IA 2021), Online event, November 29, 2021*, volume 3015 of *CEUR Workshop Proceedings*. CEUR-WS.org.

Founta, A. M., Djouvas, C., Chatzakou, D., Leontiadis, I., Blackburn, J., Stringhini, G., Vakali, A., Sirivianos, M., and Kourtellis, N. (2018). Large scale crowdsourcing and characterization of twitter abusive behavior. In *Twelfth International AAAI Conference on Web and Social Media*.

Gambäck, B. and Sikdar, U. K. (2017). Using convolutional neural networks to classify hate-speech. In *Proceedings of the first workshop on abusive language online*, pages 85–90.

Hosseini, H., Kannan, S., Zhang, B., and Poovendran, R. (2017). Deceiving google's perspective api built for detecting toxic comments. *arXiv preprint arXiv:1702.08138*.

Kennedy, B., Jin, X., Mostafazadeh Davani, A., Dehghani, M., and Ren, X. (2020). Contextualizing hate speech classifiers with post-hoc explanation. In *Proceedings of the 58th Annual Meeting of the Association for Computational Linguistics*, pages 5435–5442, Online, July. Association for Computational Linguistics.

Lai, M., Tambuscio, M., Patti, V., Ruffo, G., and Rosso, P. (2019). Stance polarity in political debates: A diachronic perspective of network homophily and conversations on twitter. *Data Knowledge Engineering*, 124:101738.

Loshchilov, I. and Hutter, F. (2019). Decoupled weight decay regularization. *7th International Conference on Learning Representations, ICLR 2019*.

Manning, C. D., Surdeanu, M., Bauer, J., Finkel, J., Bethard, S. J., and McClosky, D. (2014). The {Stanford} {CoreNLP} Natural Language Processing Toolkit. In *Association for Computational Linguistics (ACL) System Demonstrations*, pages 55–60.

Manning, C. D., Clark, K., Hewitt, J., Khandelwal, U., and Levy, O. (2020). Emergent linguistic structure in artificial neural networks trained by self-supervision. *Proceedings of the National Academy of Sciences*, 117(48):30046–30054.

Mastromattei, M., Ranaldi, L., Fallucchi, F., and Zanzotto, F. M. (2022). Syntax and prejudice: ethically-charged biases of a syntax-based hate speech recognizer unveiled. *PeerJ Computer Science*, 8:e859.

Moschitti, A. (2006). Making tree kernels practical for natural language learning. In *11th conference of the European Chapter of the Association for Computational Linguistics*.

Perikos, I., Kardakis, S., and Hatzilygeroudis, I. (2021). Sentiment analysis using novel and interpretable architectures of Hidden Markov Models. *Knowledge-Based Systems*, 229:107332.

Samek, W. and Müller, K.-R. (2019). Towards explainable artificial intelligence. In *Explainable AI: interpreting, explaining and visualizing deep learning*, pages 5–22. Springer.

Samek, W., Wiegand, T., and Müller, K. (2017). Explainable artificial intelligence: Understanding, visualizing and interpreting deep learning models. *CoRR*, abs/1708.08296.

Sanguinetti, M., Poletto, F., Bosco, C., Patti, V., and Stranisci, M. (2018). An Italian Twitter corpus of hate speech against immigrants. In *Proceedings of the Eleventh International Conference on Language Resources and Evaluation (LREC 2018)*, Miyazaki, Japan, May. European Language Resources Association (ELRA).

Sap, M., Card, D., Gabriel, S., Choi, Y., and Smith, A. N. (2019). The risk of racial bias in hate speech detection. In *ACL*.

Silveira, T. D. S., Uszkoreit, H., and Ai, R. (2019). Using aspect-based analysis for explainable sentiment predictions. In *CCF International Conference on Natural Language Processing and Chinese Computing*, pages 617–627. Springer.

Strubell, E., Verga, P., Andor, D., Weiss, D., and McCallum, A. (2018). Linguistically-informed self-attention for semantic role labeling. *arXiv preprint arXiv:1804.08199*.

Vilone, G. and Longo, L. (2020). Explainable artificial intelligence: a systematic review. *CoRR*, abs/2006.00093.

Warner, W. and Hirschberg, J. (2012). Detecting hate speech on the world wide web. In *Proceedings of the second workshop on language in social media*, pages 19–26.

Waseem, Z. and Hovy, D. (2016). Hateful symbols or hateful people? predictive features for hate speech detection on twitter. In *Proceedings of the NAACL student research workshop*, pages 88–93.

Wolf, T., Debut, L., Sanh, V., Chaumond, J., Delangue, C., Moi, A., Cistac, P., Rault, T., Louf, R., Funtowicz, M., and Brew, J. (2019). HuggingFace's Transformers: State-of-the-art Natural Language Processing. *ArXiv*, abs/1910.0.

Yang, Z., Dai, Z., Yang, Y., Carbonell, J., Salakhutdinov, R. R., and Le, Q. V. (2019). Xlnet: Generalized autoregressive pretraining for language understanding. *Advances in neural information processing systems*, 32.

Zanzotto, F. M., Santilli, A., Ranaldi, L., Onorati, D., Tommasino, P., and Fallucchi, F. (2020). Kermit: Complementing transformer architectures with encoders of explicit syntactic interpretations. In *Proceedings of the 2020 Conference on Empirical Methods in Natural Language Processing (EMNLP)*, pages 256–267.

Zhao, A. and Yu, Y. (2021). Knowledge-enabled bert for aspect-based sentiment analysis. *Knowledge-Based Systems*, 227:107220.

A. Qualitative analysis: extra examples

In this appendix, we show extra qualitative examples using KERMIT$_C$ and KERMIT$_T$ but also *contrasting trees*. We use the same schema used for Fig. 1 and Fig. 2.

Sentence: *Fuck Obama and nobody listen to anymore fuck that Muslim*

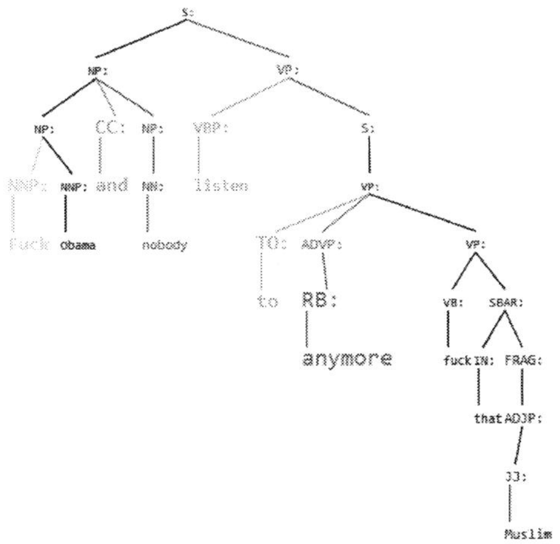

Labeled as **hate speech** for KERMIT$_C$

Contrasting trees

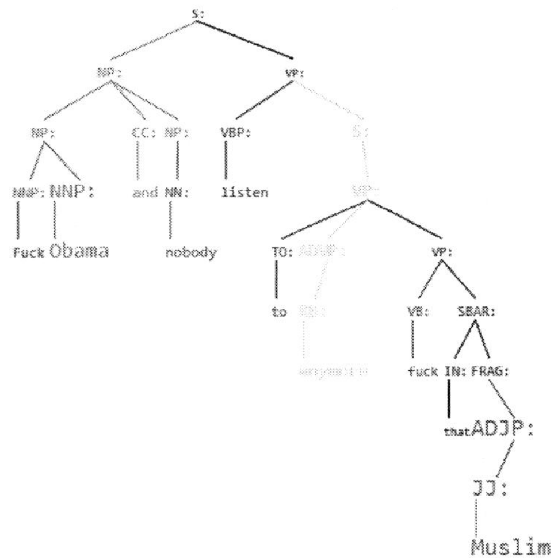

KERMIT$_C$ - KERMIT$_T$

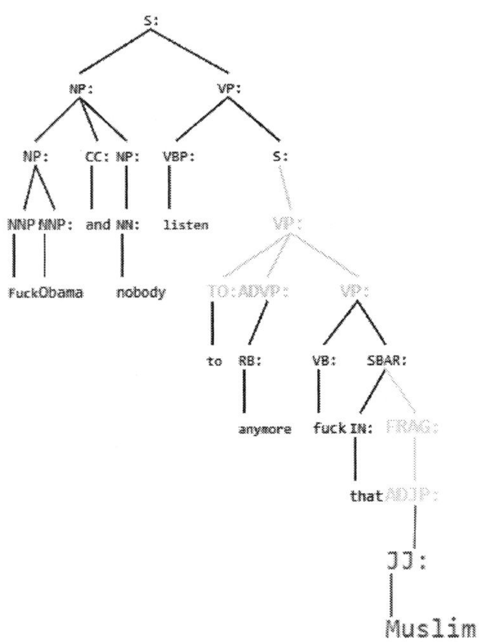

Labeled as **hate speech** for KERMIT$_T$

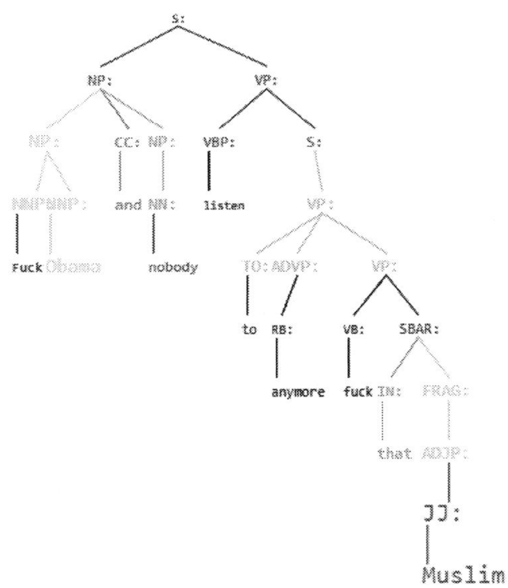

KERMIT$_T$ - KERMIT$_C$

Sentence: *It's your fault Muslim and African immigrants! Stay the fuck away*

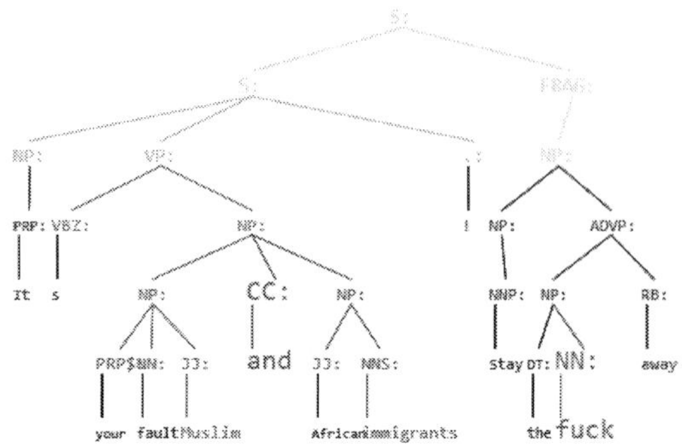

Labeled as **hate speech** for KERMIT_C

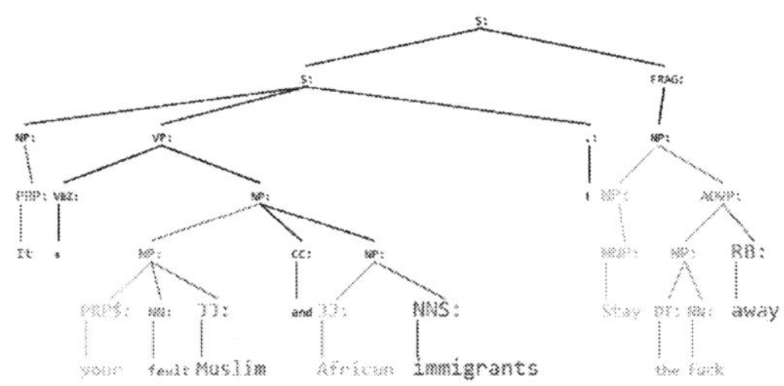

Labeled as **hate speech** for KERMIT_T

Contrasting trees

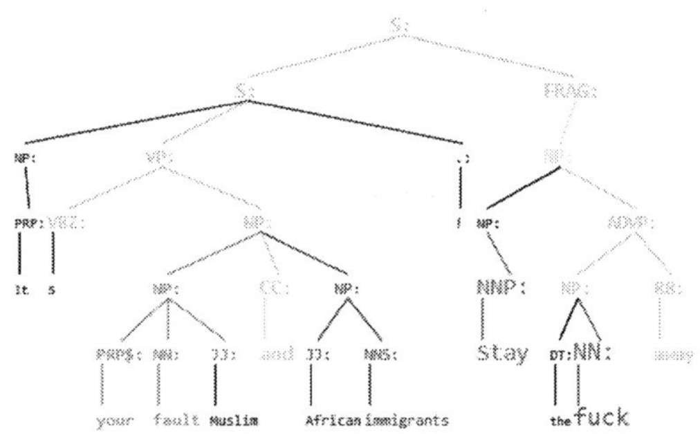

KERMIT_C - KERMIT_T

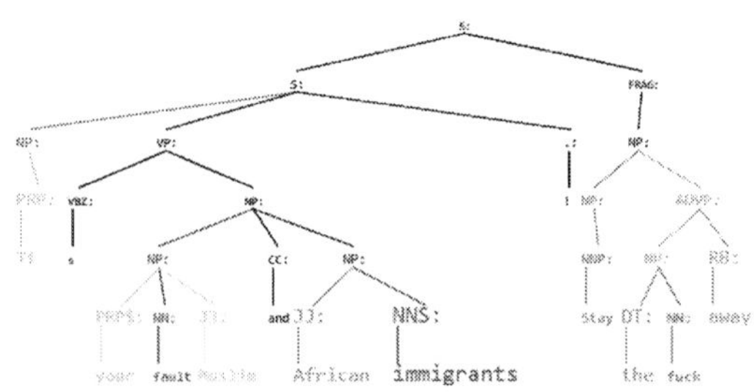

KERMIT_T - KERMIT_C

Sentence: *Bloody foreigners causing a spike in racist hate crimes*

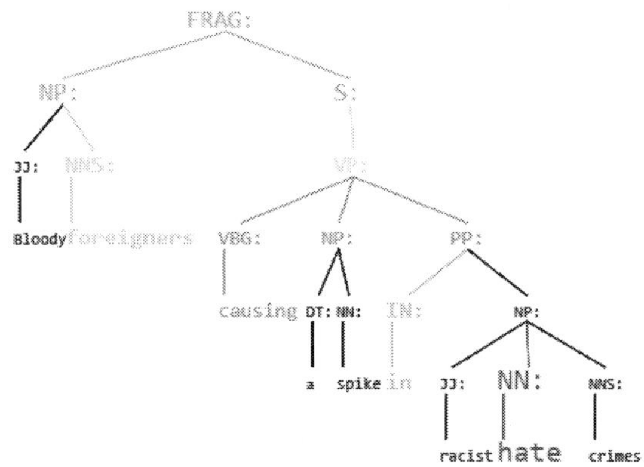

Labeled as **no hate speech** for KERMIT_C

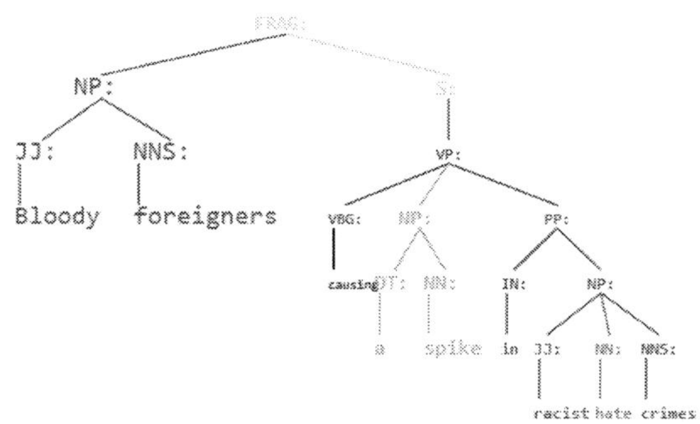

Labeled as **hate speech** for KERMIT_T

Contrasting trees

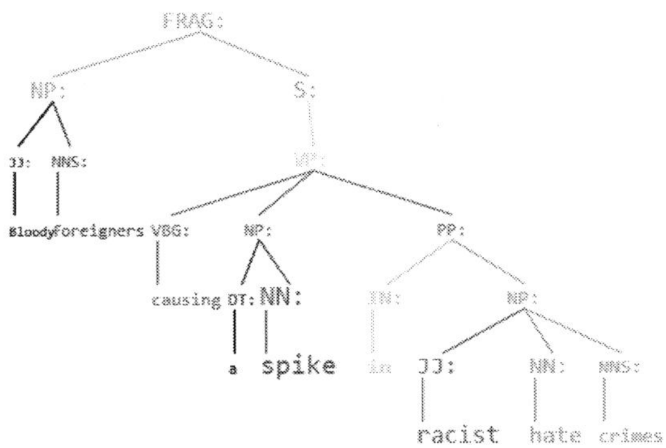

KERMIT$_C$ - KERMIT$_T$

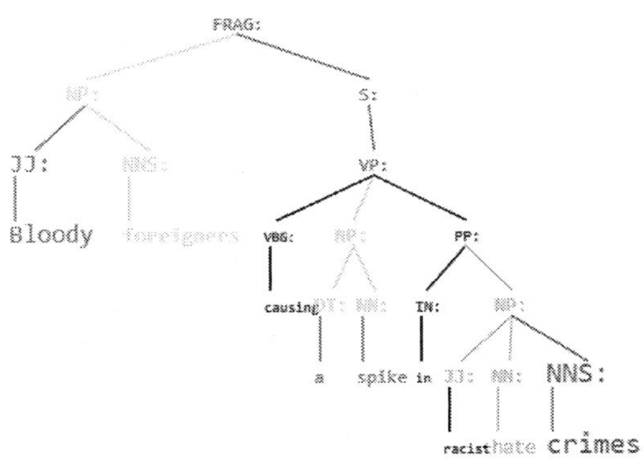

KERMIT$_T$ - KERMIT$_C$

Sentence: *blame Muslim for brexit hypocrisy*

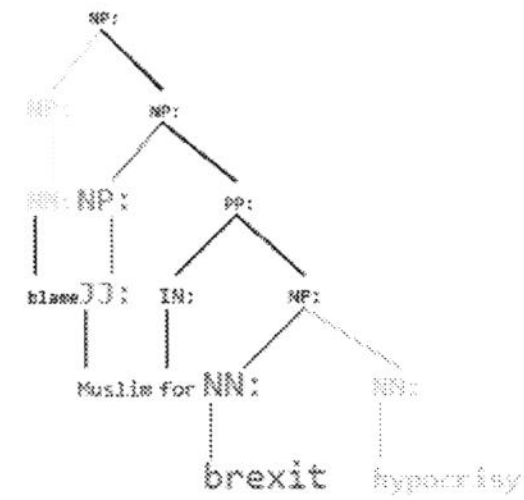

Labeled as **no hate speech** for KERMIT$_C$

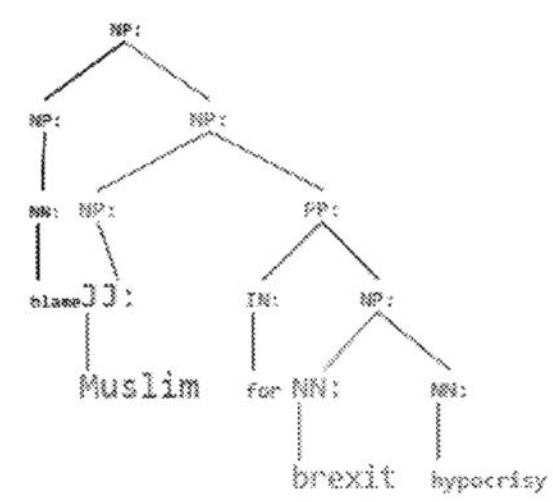

Labeled as **hate speech** for KERMIT$_T$

Contrasting trees

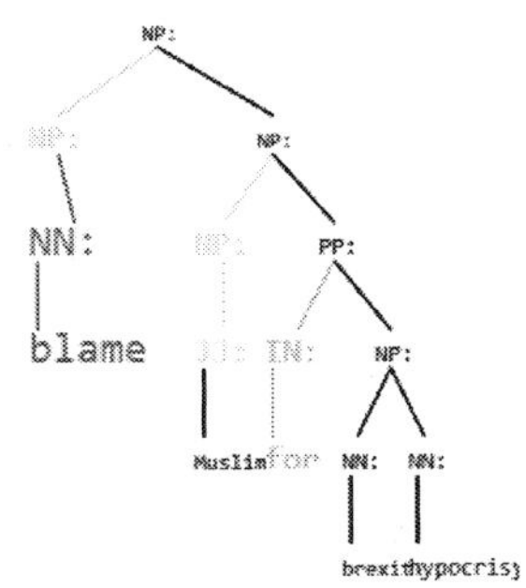

KERMIT$_C$ - KERMIT$_T$

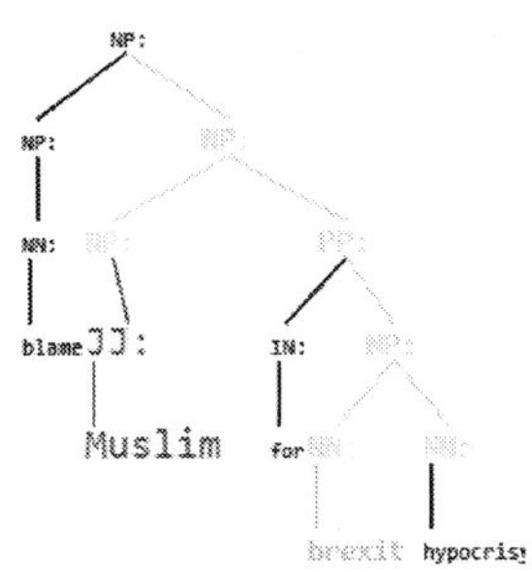

KERMIT$_T$ - KERMIT$_C$

Author Index

Association for Computational Linguistics
209 N. Eighth Street
Stroudsburg, Pennsylvania 18360

ISBN 978-1-7138-6130-0

CURRAN ASSOCIATES INC.
proceedings.com